Thomas Crump taught Anthropology at Amsterdam University. He is author of many books, including *A Brief History of Science* and *A Brief History of the Age of Steam*.

A BRIEF HISTORY OF

HOW THE INDUSTRIAL REVOLUTION CHANGED THE WORLD

THOMAS CRUMP

ROBINSON

Constable & Robinson Ltd
3 The Lanchesters
162 Fulham Palace Road
London W6 9ER
www.constablerobinson.com

First published in the UK by Robinson,
an imprint of Constable & Robinson, 2010

A copy of the British Library Cataloguing in Publication
Data is available from the British Library

UK ISBN 978-1-84529-897-5

3 5 7 9 10 8 6 4 2

Typeset by TW Typesetting, Plymouth, Devon

Printed and bound by CPI Group (UK) Ltd, Croydon, CR0 4YY

CONTENTS

PREFACE

The Industrial Revolution is a unique challenge to historians. A few, but not many, even refuse to recognize it as a subject in its own right. My book takes the majority view, that the world as we have come to know it in the twenty-first century is impossible to understand without looking at the foundations laid – mainly in the English-speaking world of the eighteenth century – in the course of what is known now, but not then, as the 'Industrial Revolution'.

Whatever the Industrial Revolution may be, it is certainly well documented. It would take more than a lifetime to work through the Archives and Heritage Department of the Birmingham Central Library, to say nothing of the material to be found in other places, not only in Britain but in the world at large such as London's Science Museum or Washington's Smithsonian. As a professional anthropologist I have observed, time and again, how even the most remote communities had experienced, by the mid-twentieth century, the impact of the Industrial Revolution. Having written this book as a historian however, I have relied mainly on secondary published sources, such as those to be found in the bibliography. The problem is that too many authors are more interested in arguing with others of the same kind than in enlightening the world outside academe – which incidentally, is where I am myself most at home. In particular I have made a point of reading and, where appropriate, quoting from, the works of well known nineteenth-century novelists – Charlotte Brontë, Charles Dickens, Benjamin Disraeli, George Eliot, Elizabeth Gaskell, to name only a few – which together evoke the world as it was being created and transformed by the Industrial Revolution. For purely descriptive writing relating to this world, readers should turn to a book first published in German in 1846, Friedrich Engels' *The Condition of the Working Class in England*; the fact that it has long been a part of the Marxist canon does not detract from its value as a unique primary source. As for seeing what the world of the Industrial Revolution looked like, both on land and at sea, there is little that rivals the work of the great English artist, J.M.W. Turner. London's National Gallery, where his *Rain, Steam and Speed – The Great Western Railway*, and *The Fighting 'Téméraire', tugged to her last Berth to be broken up* are both powerful evocations of the new industrial world as it emerged during his lifetime. This is a good place to start, before looking at other more extensive collections, such as that in Tate Britain.

Beyond working with written material, I have visited, often quite recently, places whose historical importance derives from their contribution to the Industrial

Revolution. In particular I made a point of looking at sites outside Britain – where, incidentally, I have not lived for nearly forty years. In addition therefore, to such important British locations as Birmingham, Walsall, Kidderminster and Stoke on Trent in the West Midlands, Coalbrookdale (with Abraham Darby III's remarkable iron bridge) in the upper Severn valley, Cromford (the site of Richard Arkwright's pioneering cotton mill) on the River Derwent in Derbyshire, woollen mills in the West Riding of Yorkshire, Cornwall with its numerous abandoned tin mines, the north-east of England (where the railway revolution started long before the day of its greatest hero, George Stephenson), and Clydeside in Scotland, I visited the heartland of the American industrial revolution both in the Connecticut valley of New England, and in the mid-Atlantic states of Pennsylvania, Maryland and Virginia – where I became acquainted with sites such as that of the Cornwall Ironworks (in continuous operation from colonial times until the end of the nineteenth century) in Pennsylvania and Cumberland, in Maryland; the final terminal of the Chesapeake and Ohio Canal (which never reached its planned destination). Sad to say, during my extensive travels across the Mississippi river system, I only once – on a short voyage downstream from Memphis, Tennessee, in October 2007 – was able to travel on an authentic paddle-wheeled steamboat. Of the few – out of thousands – remaining from the river world notably described by Mark Twain, most are now casinos at anchor in places such as Natchez and Vicksburg, both in the state of Mississippi.

On the continent of Europe I have at one time or another visited the coal and iron works of Germany's

Ruhr valley, the Belgian industrial centres of Mons, Charleroi and Verviers, together with the adjacent parts of France (where in quite another part of the country I have visited the long-standing industrial complex extending from Lyons to St Etienne), to say nothing of Venice which, with its vast Arsenale, was some 500 years ago, the most important industrial city in Europe (with other Italian cities such as Genoa and Milan as its main rivals). Finally, in South Africa, I once knew well the mining centres of Kimberley (diamonds) and Johannesburg (gold) where the industrial revolution exploded in the last quarter of the nineteenth century.

Needless to say, all these visits would have been next to impossible without the help, over a period of more than fifty years, of any number of friends and colleagues. In 1956, with Pat Whitworth, my Cambridge contemporary and now one of my oldest friends, I spent a week taking photographs of textile mills in the West Riding, starting with the mill, in Halifax, of his own family business, Joseph Whitworth and Sons – which seemed hardly to have changed (except for the installation of electric lighting in place of gas) since the early nineteenth century.

In 1958, John Rudd, helped by a kind word from his grandfather in Kimberley (who, at the turn of the twentieth century, had been one of Cecil Rhodes' fellow directors at De Beers Consolidated Mines), arranged for me to stay in the grandest suite of the Kimberley Club, from which base, in the course of a week, a chauffeur-driven car took me around one of the world's most remarkable mining and industrial sites – with every door opened to me.

In 1967, as a visiting scholar of the Predigerseminar in Dortmund, a city in the heartland of the Germany's industrial revolution, I was able to visit the giant local steel works, and enjoy a weekend as the guest of the Lutheran minister of the coal mining centre of Recklinghausen.

In the years since 1972 (when I moved house to Amsterdam after having been appointed a lecturer at the university), I have become involved in the history of my wife's Prakke family whose factories in the textile town of Eibergen, in the east of Holland, enjoyed a world market for the leather driving belts and other accessories for textile machinery which they manufactured. The local museum, which has a whole floor devoted to the Prakke family business, is a treasure house of the Dutch industrial revolution. Now, like the Whitworths in Halifax (or, for that matter, the Rudds in Kimberley), there are no longer any Prakkes in business in Eibergen, although one or two members of the family still live there.

Living in the Netherlands also allowed me to get to know the Haarlemmermeer; one of the greatest public works projects of the industrial revolution. This considerable area of land, just outside Amsterdam, was until the middle of the nineteenth century a vast shallow lake; which the Dutch had for centuries planned to reclaim as new land fit for agriculture. In the late 1840s, three great steam-powered pumps were opened along the edge of the lake, and within three years of operation the Haarlemmermeer was pumped dry. One of the three pumps, named Cruquius after a seventeenth century Dutch engineer, was operated by the most powerful

steam engine ever built. This has now been restored as a
museum: within seventy years of the reclamation project
being completed it proved to have a bonus for the city of
Amsterdam that no one could have foreseen in the
nineteenth century. The entire land area of Schiphol, one
of the world's great international airports, belongs to the
Haarlemmermeer.

In 1997, as part of a visit to Kidderminster (where my
own family made carpets in the nineteenth century), I
was able to visit Brintons Carpets, the leading manufacturer, on the invitation of Michael Brinton, the present
chairman. Unlike so many other manufactures established in the early days of the Industrial Revolution,
Brintons is a flourishing business, with worldwide sales,
still run by the same family. I was able to visit the
original premises in the centre of Kidderminster, where
some processes such as wool dying were still carried out,
and the modern, fully automated factory on a hill
overlooking the town – where the early nineteenth
century French Jacquard loom is still state-of-the-art.

In the first decade of the twenty-first century – with
my steadily increasing interest in the history of science
and technology and the additional advantage of retire-
ment from the University of Amsterdam – I devoted
more time than ever to exploring the world of the
industrial revolution on both sides of the Atlantic. From
their homes in Loudoun County, Virginia, John and
Taylor Chamberlin, second cousins who are among my
oldest friends, guided me around the mid-Atlantic
heartland of the American industrial revolution, allowing me to see a wealth of abandoned watermills and iron
foundries, to say nothing of the country's oldest railroad,

the Baltimore and Ohio, which unlike the Chesapeake and Ohio Canal, the waterway that it was built to rival, eventually reached the Ohio River. In New England, Barbara Edwards – another Chamberlin second cousin – with the welcome mat always put out in her home in Essex, Connecticut, brought me to such local sites as the Connecticut River Museum (also in Essex) and the factory of the Winchester Repeating Arms Company in New Haven. During my extensive travels in 2007 criss-crossing the Mississippi basin, there was, much to my regret, less to see of the American industrial revolution; for not only is the riverboat era no more, but the same is largely true of that of the railroads – so that the train station in St Louis, once the largest in the United States, is now a shopping mall. The traditional long freight trains, with their unmistakable sad whistles, still run with diesel rather than steam locomotives, but the romance is gone. Here, as in many other parts of the country, the rust-belt is the legacy of the industrial revolution.

Finally, in the United Kingdom, the year 2009 provided the opportunity to visit, for the first time, some of the best known sites of the Industrial Revolution. Another old friend, Peter Stefanini, enabled me to visit, from his home outside York, Benjamin Gott's woollen mill in Armley, Leeds, and Richard Arkwright's re-nowned cotton mill at Cromford on Derbyshire's River Derwent. A few days later, John Nightingale, from his home in Birmingham, not only accompanied me to the great industrial sites of the Severn Valley, such as Ironbridge and Coalbrookdale, but also gave me the benefit of a vast knowledge of the Industrial Revolution gained from years of service in the Anglican ministry in Manchester, Coventry and Birmingham. Being his guest in Birmingham also enabled me to attend the international conference, held mainly at the University, commemorating the 200th anniversary of the death, in 1809, of Matthew Boulton; one of the greatest figures in British industrial history. As to the conference itself, I am most grateful both to Professor Peter Jones, of the University's History Faculty and Dr Malcolm Dick, of its Centre for Birmingham and Midlands History, for a very warm welcome. Finally, within my own family I would like to thank by cousin, Adam Sedgwick, for his invaluable advice about Britain's coal industry, in which he himself played a role in the final third of the twentieth century.

In writing this book age has proved to be a great practical advantage. My youth goes back to the true age of steam, and indeed far enough to include a brief sight of the Crystal Palace, as it was rebuilt at Sydenham in south London after the Great Exhibition of 1851, and before it burnt down to the ground in 1936, shortly after my seventh birthday. Going much further back, different branches of my father's family had their homes in the West Midlands, and while some members manufactured carpets – with little long term success – most were involved, as I have always been, in religious dissent, teaching and the learned professions – to say nothing of writing books. Such then, is the background from which I have been able to write this one.

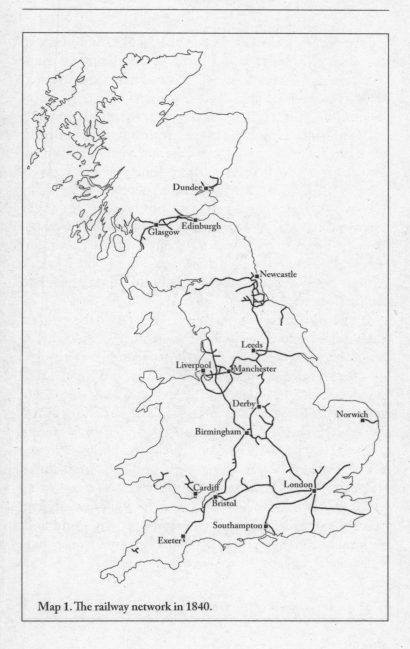

Map 1. The railway network in 1840.

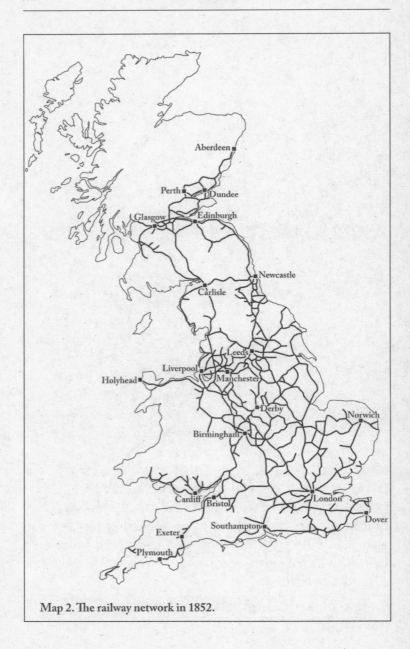

Map 2. The railway network in 1852.

I

THE GREAT EXHIBITION, BRITISH ASCENDANCY AND THE INDUSTRIAL REVOLUTION

1851

The Great Exhibition, which opened in London on 1 May 1851, was – in spite of its welcome to *all* nations – an exercise in British triumphalism. The exhibition defined a race in which Britain was the winner, as was made quite explicit by a *Punch* cartoon entitled *The Great Derby Race For Eighteen Hundred and Fifty-One*.[1] Indeed, those responsible for the exhibition, led by Queen Victoria's consort, Prince Albert, knew only too well that, with industry as its theme, they had chosen a field in which Britain had been pre-eminent for at least a hundred years.

To prove this, over half the exhibition space in the Crystal Palace; an entirely new glass and iron building erected in Hyde Park, was devoted to works originating in Britain, while the invitation to some thirty-three other countries to display what their own industries had achieved was a recognition that industrialization, halfway through the nineteenth century, extended far beyond the shores of the United Kingdom. What is more, almost any visitor to the exhibition could hardly have failed to realize that it put an entirely new world on display.

The Crystal Palace itself was a monument to industry; the materials out of which it was constructed, and above all the range of the objects displayed, including such oddities as a stuffed weasel; reflected the cutting edge of technology. To many, this defined a new and very different world to that in which they had spent their childhood – and in which many of them were still living. To all but local visitors this was clear even before arriving at Hyde Park; the great majority of those from outside London had come by train, a form of transport which for foreign visitors was supplemented by the steamboats that had brought them to British shores. In the event, railway companies greatly underestimated the extent to which cheap fare offers increased the number of passengers, which by the end of the exhibition was not far short of one million.[2] This was the largest movement of population ever to take place in Britain.

In 1851, recent history – particularly in continental Europe – had given revolution a bad name, but what Britain presented to the world in Hyde Park were the fruits of a revolution, even if other words such as 'achievement' and 'progress' came more readily to the lips of the thousands of British citizens who visited

London for the Great Exhibition. If, at this point of time, a somewhat obscure French diplomat, Louis Otto, had written of a 'revolution industrielle'[3] and a now much better known German, Friedrich Engels, of an 'industrielle Revolution',[4] it would be another generation before Arnold Toynbee, a young Oxford scholar, wrote in English about an 'industrial revolution'. By his time this had become a statement of the obvious: the major achievements of the Industrial Revolution – and, above all, those of Britain – were already there to be shown to the world in London in 1851.

What led Prince Albert, and those who joined in supporting his cause in the face of considerable opposition, to devote so much time and trouble to so grandiose a venture? By temperament the Prince was a man who wanted to see the world become a better place; as consort to Queen Victoria he found the opportunity to achieve this result, not only within her own realm but in the wider world where she was related to the ruling houses – a position which in the course of time would be strengthened by the marriages of her own children.

In the early years of his wife's reign, there was opportunity enough to start this process within the United Kingdom; the Prince became president of the Society for Improving the Conditions of the Labouring Classes, a patron of the Servants' Providential and Benevolent Society, and so on, with any number of other institutions whose names evoke the character of early Victorian philanthropy. Above all, he was most keenly involved in the realm of art, and as early as 1841 he became head of the Royal Commission on Rebuilding the Houses of Parliament.[5] The greatest scope for furthering his good causes was offered by the Society for the Encouragement of Arts, Manufactures and Commerce, founded in the mid-eighteenth century. Invited to become its President in 1845, he procured a royal charter from the Queen, much enhancing the status of what then became known simply as the Royal Society of Arts (RSA).

The Prince was not a man to let the grass grow under his feet, and the same was true of an ambitious civil servant, Henry Cole, whose remarkable record of achievements included the first systematic catalogue of the Public Record Office, the introduction (in collaboration with Rowland Hill) of the Penny Post in 1840, editing the *Historical Register*, the *Journal of Design* and the *Railway Chronicle*, writing several books for both children and adults, and publishing the first Christmas Card.[6] The Prince knew Cole as a fellow member of the Council of the Royal Society of Arts. Their first joint achievement was a show designed to display works of art, broadly defined, executed in metals, woods, ceramics and glass, which took place in the rooms of the Society in 1847. This, contrary to the expectation of any number of influential doomsayers, was resoundingly successful.

Furthermore, the exhibition proved that the British were equal in their interest in the arts to the French, who in 1849 organized the eleventh Quinquennial Exhibition of French Industry. This was attended by Henry Cole who, once in Paris, learnt that some months earlier, M. Buffet, the Minister for Agriculture and Commerce, had proposed that the twelfth Quinquennial – scheduled for 1854 – should be planned on an international scale. At a time when France was the only great power to be a serious rival to Britain, to the likes of Henry Cole and his patron, Prince Albert, this was an unmistakable challenge.

One thing led to another, and with the Prince's approval and support granted on 29 June 1849, the project for a British exhibition took off in the face of any number of obstructions and criticisms. Organization was to be in the hands of a Royal Commission, announced by Queen Victoria on 3 January 1850, with Prince Albert as president. The fact that both the Prime Minister, Lord John Russell, and the Leader of the Opposition, Lord Stanley, were members, shows how powerful it must have been, as is also confirmed by the distinction of its other members, described by *The Times* as representing 'every shade of political opinion in the country, and every great interest in the state'.[7]

Although all-party support, at a time when the repeal of the Corn Laws in 1846 under Sir Robert Peel was still a recent memory, depended upon denying any link between the exhibition and the free trade cause,[8] in reality – at least as seen by the Peelite *Morning Chronicle* – it was 'the inaugural festival of free trade'.[9] (Indeed, Peel, although no longer Prime Minister, was regarded as a valuable supporter, and his death, after he was thrown from his horse on 29 June 1850, seen as a major loss.)

Strong support from cities, particular those such as Manchester, Bradford, Leeds and Liverpool[10] that had played a major part in the Industrial Revolution, reflects the popularity of the exhibition with industry and commerce. This, combined with its unpopularity among agricultural interests, shows how to much of Britain's rural population it represented propaganda on behalf of a particular value system rather than the embodiment of nationwide shared consensus.[11]

In the course of 1850 the Commission took two key decisions: the first was to locate the exhibition in Hyde Park, the second was to entrust the building to Joseph Paxton, who had become famous for what he had achieved for the Duke of Devonshire with the gardens at Chatsworth House. The result was the Crystal Palace, constructed almost entirely out of glass and cast iron.

The palace and the Great Exhibition were ready to open on time on 1 May 1851. If it was on a scale far greater than anything France might have achieved three years later, France, next to Britain, was still the largest contributor to the exhibition; winning also the second largest number of medals – with all other countries exhibiting far behind.[12] More significant, in the long run, were the American exhibits; which included machinery that was already making American agriculture more productive than that of any other country. One exhibit, Cyrus McCormick's reaper, was described by *The Times* as a 'contraption seemingly a cross between a wheelbarrow, a chariot, and a flying machine', but it still won a gold medal, bringing world fame to its inventor. Even with such successes, as Horace Greeley of the *New York Tribune* and America's most influential journalist noted, his country's contribution 'fell far short of what it might have been, and did not fairly exhibit the progress and present condition of the Useful Arts in this country'.[13]

What all this involved can best be seen from the list issued to the internationally constituted juries appointed to judge the exhibits and award medals to the most outstanding in every category.[14] Exhibits were divided into four categories: raw materials, machinery, manufactures and the fine arts. Each category, except for fine arts, was then divided into a number of sub-categories. Machinery was undoubtedly the category that best reflected the achievements of British industry, as can be seen by the fact that it accounted for fifty-two out of the seventy-eight medals won by British exhibitors. Visiting journalists noted how, above all other exhibits, the collection of machinery – much of it, such as the ingenious De la Rue envelope machine, actually working on site – appealed to visitors.[15]

London manufacture was the source of many of the exhibits[16] such as notably sixty motive-power machines,[17] including Nasmyth's steam-hammer, McNicholl's travelling crane and Garforth's riveting machine. Not only that, but many of the medals awarded in the category of manufactures were undoubtedly for products made with the help of British machinery, or at least machinery based on British models. A textile mill operating on an industrial scale in almost any part of the world, with no local manufacture of heavy machinery, would work with looms and spindles imported from Britain and, if powered by steam, with a British-made engine.

All this can be seen from the sort of objects exhibited by the great majority of the thirty-three countries represented in the Crystal Palace. With few restrictions as to what could be shown, it was not surprising that a very large number of exhibits, from countries as diverse as Peru and Tuscany, Portugal and Persia, Egypt and Russia, were the products of craftsmanship rather than industry, although some contributions, such as the watches from Switzerland, were extremely skilful and ingenious.[18]

The 160 years separating 1850, the critical year of organization and planning leading up to the Great Exhibition, and 2010, this book's year of publication, show first how the Industrial Revolution, which until 1850 was almost entirely a British achievement, proceeded to conquer the world, and second, how the world presented in 1851 was not going to stand still in any respect – economic, political or cultural.

The history of industrial achievement, as it was presented to the hundreds of thousands of visitors in 1851, showed how transient was the world they lived in. The world, as they saw it within the Crystal Palace, was largely the creation of the eighty-odd years that had elapsed since 1769, the year in which James Watt – by 1851 long recognized as the Industrial Revolution's greatest hero[19] – by inventing the separate condenser, opened the way for machinery of almost any kind to be powered by steam, at least so long as it was not to be used for locomotion.

By 1851, however, this restriction had been overcome by George Stephenson's locomotives; the famous *Rocket* had pulled the first train on the Liverpool and Manchester Railway in 1830. Appropriately Stephenson's son Robert, a distinguished locomotive engineer in his own right, was the chairman of the executive committee of the Great Exhibition.[20]

The World Outside London
The picture of the world beyond the shores of Britain presented by the exhibits in the Crystal Palace from

other nations was far from realistic, given that each single state naturally chose its exhibits to present itself in the most favourable possible light. For the most part, the countless objects displayed told next to nothing about the circumstances, material and human, in which they been manufactured – let alone the social unrest that had led to popular uprisings at the end of the 1840s.

The year 1848 in particular was noted for civil strife throughout Europe. In France, a violent workers' uprising on the streets of Paris on 22 February had led, at the end of the year, to the election of Louis Napoleon (nephew of the renowned emperor, finally defeated at Waterloo in 1815) to be the first president of the new Second Republic.[21] What France chose to display in London in 1851 reflected its success in overcoming the turmoil of 1848, and the same was true of other European states, such as Austria's Hapsburg Empire, where in the same year, a revolution led by the Hungarian patriot, Lajos Kossuth, had failed to detach Hungary from the empire. Even Britain could take comfort from the collapse of the much less threatening Chartist movement in 1848, following the peaceful dispersal of a crowd of its supporters on London's Kennington Common on 10 April.[22] A conspiracy of silence, to which almost every state was a party, meant therefore that there was little concern about the social unrest that was part of the price paid for industrialization.

In the rest of the world, Europe still had to come to terms with significant changes in political geography. In North America, Canada (whose long frontier with the United States had only been definitively settled by the

Oregon Treaty of 1846) was still governed, in one way or another, from London, while the United States was in the process of radical transformation as the result of acquiring vast new territories following its victory in war with Mexico (1846–8).

One immediate result, the admission of California to the Union as the thirty-first state in 1850, had repercussions worldwide. California gave to the United States not only a long Pacific coastline, with all that this would mean for trade with the Far East, but much more dramatically, the immeasurable wealth of the world's richest seams of gold, following the first discovery at Sutter's Mill in January 1848.

But for all these new gains, in Britain, Lancashire's cotton mills would still – for another ten years or so – depend on raw cotton from American plantations worked by slaves. Nonetheless the events of 1850, widely reported outside the United States, led inexorably to the Civil War (1861–5) and the final abolition of slavery.

South of the United States, the American mainland, with only minor exceptions, comprised some sixteen sovereign states. Of these, fifteen, extending from the Rio Grande (Mexico's frontier with the United States) to Tierra del Fuego, were republics of remarkable diversity with Spanish as their official language.[23] However, they were overshadowed by Brazil, much the largest nation in South America, where Portuguese was the official language, and where, unlike in Spanish America, slavery still survived.[24] For Britain in particular, Latin America was a promising field for investment; as early as 1824, Robert Stephenson and Richard Trevithick had gone to

Colombia to survey the prospects for gold and silver-mining in a continent known since the days of the Spanish *conquistadores* for its vast mineral wealth. Exploitation, in the mid-nineteenth century, meant the construction of railways, and in 1850 the first short line linking Lima, the capital of Peru, with its seaport, Callao, was opened for traffic. That it was the product of British enterprise explains why it soon became known as *El Ferrocarril Ingles*[25] – and this was only the beginning of massive railway investment throughout the continent.

Next to the vast continental land mass stretching from the Arctic wastes of Canada and Alaska to the storm-beaten islands of Tierra del Fuego, which looked south only to Antarctica, the Atlantic side of the western hemisphere contained, inside the tropics, an assortment of islands in the Caribbean sea. For centuries these had been exploited ruthlessly by five European powers: Britain, Denmark, France, the Netherlands and Spain. By the seventeenth century this meant the cultivation of tropical plantations by slave labour, bringing vast wealth to the European planters and those still in Europe who had invested in their enterprise. Plantations were also at the heart of the export economy of colonies on the Atlantic coast of the mainland, from Virginia and the Carolinas, ruled by Britain in the north to Brazil, ruled by Portugal in the south. In the whole Caribbean region only a single slave uprising, that on the island of Santo Domingo at the end of the eighteenth century, had led to the emergence of an independent Afro-American state: Haiti. The result, the loss to France of one of its richest colonies, was a major factor in the decision by Napoleon, only three years later in 1803, to sell the extensive North

American mainland territory of Louisiana to the newly constituted United States.

In 1851, much of the Caribbean was a region in economic decline. While in the eighteenth century its plantations accounted for at least part of the wealth needed for industrial investment, particularly in Britain, their economies in the nineteenth century provided little surplus for investment. The market, largely as a result of overproduction, had moved against them. One key factor here was the abolition of the slave trade by Britain and the United States in 1807, followed, in the case of Britain, by the end of slavery in the colonies in 1833. In 1851 slavery still existed in the plantations of Brazil and the Dutch colonies (where it was abolished in 1863) and, much more critically, in the United States. In this case there was one paramount reason for its survival: the demand for plantation-grown cotton by the new textile mills which, from the end of the eighteenth century had been not only at the heart of the Industrial Revolution, but had become, for many – particularly in Britain – its defining characteristic.

Africa in 1851 was still largely the 'unknown continent', offering little to outside investors. The Atlantic slave trade, which led to any number of European trading posts along the west coast, from Senegal to Angola, had ended at the beginning of the century. Within ten years, however, Britain, in the aftermath of the Napoleonic wars, had established in the far south of Africa two new colonies, Natal and the Cape Colony, which were open to British settlers. Although there had been Dutch settlements for more than 150 years, the view taken by the British in the 1820s was that there was room for all in a sparsely settled continent. As for the rest of Africa south of the Sahara desert, although occasional British explorers had by then travelled far into the interior (not for nothing known as 'the white man's grave'), their discoveries had not led to any significant British settlement or investment in the 'dark' continent.

For all these limitations, in 1851 there was still a place in the Crystal Palace not only for exhibits from Africa, but also, according to the memory of the artist Henrietta Ward, some seventy years, later, for 'broad-faced, woolly-headed . . . chiefs, wearing bright colours'.[26] The unmistakable message was that Africans, along with Russians, Native Americans and Orientals of every stamp, were exotic and different.

To the east of Africa, in the vast world of the Orient, India, which in 1851 was still governed by the East India Company, had already been reached by the Industrial Revolution – or just about. By the end of the 1830s, steamships – made in Britain but assembled in India – were plying the Ganges,[27] and there were also steadily developing coastal routes. Railways came a generation later. Following the appointment by the Governor-General, Lord Dalhousie, of a consulting engineer in 1850, the Great Indian Peninsular Railway opened its first short line in 1853, running a few miles inland from Bombay.

As to the other great European presence in the Orient, that of the island empire of the Netherlands East Indies, the colonial economy was decidedly pre-industrial. The so-called 'culture system', introduced by Governor-General Johannes van den Bosch in the early 1830s, created an agricultural export economy based upon the labour-intensive cultivation of coffee, sugar and indigo.[28] For more than thirty years these products could only be transported to Europe in sailing ships: steamships bound for the Far East had to wait for the opening of the Suez Canal in 1869. Before 1850, and for some years after, there was little question of Dutch industry exploiting the colonial market; by mid-century there had been so little growth that in the decade 1839–49 the urban population of the Netherlands actually decreased.[29]

Outside the colonial empires of Britain and the Netherlands, the Far East comprised two considerable sovereign states, China and Japan, at least seven lesser principalities in south-east Asia, the Spanish colony of the Philippines, and Siberia, a remote region of the Russian empire (to which Alaska was added in 1784). If to the rest of the world, as it was represented in London in 1851, all this added up to a vast *terra incognita*, the position was already beginning to change quite radically.

For almost the whole of the eighteenth century, imperial Russia, with a common land frontier, was the only foreign country with a regular and profitable trade with China. But then, in 1792, Britain sent a mission, led by Lord Macartney, to the Jing court in Beijing, with the remit to negotiate trade by sea. This achieved little beyond the British envoy's fascinating report of life at the centre of the 'middle kingdom', and his prediction that the days of this ancient empire were numbered. Lord Napier – sent to China in 1834 to negotiate control of the trade in opium (which was supplied by the East India Company) – was no more successful. His failure, however, led directly to the first Opium War (1840–42), which Britain – with all the resources of a modern industrial state – was bound to win, even if all the fighting was on the other side of the world. The result, in 1842, was the Treaty of Nanking; this not only provided for Hong Kong to be ceded to Britain in perpetuity, but also for the establishment of five treaty ports: Canton (which had always been the main port of entry into China), Amoy, Foochow, Ningpo and Shanghai, in which the expatriate community, exempt from regulation by the imperial bureaucracy, had privileged trading access to the Chinese interior. This was the start of a process that continued for another sixty-odd years, during which time many other great powers (including the United States and Japan) – operating through some fifty treaty ports – joined Britain in the exploitation of China in a process that would lead to the final demise of the empire in 1912. In 1851, however, there was still a long way to go.

In this same year, Japan was even more shut off from the outside world, as it had been from the beginning of the seventeenth century. A small Dutch trading post on the island of Deshima in the bay of Nagasaki – at the other end of the country from the seat of the government in Edo – was its only contact with the West. That the American Commodore Matthew Perry, in command of a squadron of steam-powered, iron clad battleships, only arrived in Tokyo Bay in 1853, meant that in 1851 the Japanese court, at the head of a traditional feudal state, still had two years before it would have to come to terms with the outside world, as it was represented in London's Great Exhibition.

South-east Asia was again another story. Although the islands of the South China Sea and beyond had a long history of colonial exploitation – by Spain, Portugal and above all, the Netherlands – by mid-century only Britain retained anything beyond a foothold on the mainland. Already in the late eighteenth century the Alaungpaya kings of Burma were set on a policy of aggression and expansion at the cost of its neighbours, from which Thailand suffered most. When, however, in the early 1820s, Burma tried to expand into India, this led to war with Britain. Inevitably this ended on British terms, which meant that a part of northern Burma was added to India in 1826, in a process that culminated in the fall of the Alaungpaya dynasty and complete annexation in 1885.

Shortly before Britain became involved with Burma, it was also concerned to come to terms with the sultanates of the Malayan peninsular, whose location between the Indian Ocean and the South China Sea made them strategically important for European trade to the Far East. Although the British presence on the west coast dated back to the foundation of the port of Penang in 1786, it was finally consolidated by Sir Stamford Raffles' organization of the Straits Settlements in the period 1818–21, together with the port of Singapore in 1819.

Finally, Australia and New Zealand, far away in the southern hemisphere, completed the world as seen from London in 1851. Although by this time both were uncompromisingly British – and also close to each other in relation to their distance from other parts of the world – socially and economically they were quite different. In late 1849, Australia, after having been, for just over sixty years, the destination of tens of thousands of convicted criminals transported from Britain to serve out long terms of imprisonment, received – in what had then become Sydney Cove – the last two shiploads of convicts.[30] By this time the Australian colonies were mainly settled by men and women who had emigrated of their own accord, and sooner or later the end to the transport of convicts was bound to come in response to local popular demand at a level that the colonial authorities could not ignore. If, at the half century, there was any doubt about when this day would come, it was put to rest, for once and always, by the discovery of gold on 12 February 1851, in the Wellington district of New South Wales. (The fact that Western Australia, on the other side of the continent, continued to receive convicts until the 1860s did not affect the situation in the other five colonies[31]). By the end of May 1851, barely three weeks after the opening of the Great Exhibition in London, thousands of diggers had crossed the Blue Mountains as part of a gold rush equal to that in California three years earlier. The two were linked, because Edward Hammond Hargraves, who made the first Australian discovery, had just returned home after failing to make his fortune in California, but was able to recognize, nonetheless, the geological formations in New South Wales, which hid gold in vast quantities. This was only the beginning: in September 1851, even richer seams of gold were discovered near Ballarat, in Victoria, only seventy-five miles away from Melbourne. Within months the mines in Victoria were shipping half a ton of gold to London every week, with one single ship, the *Dido*, carrying ten and a half tons. It was no wonder that *The Times*, in November 1852, described the flood of Australian gold as 'simply bewildering'.[32]

Although the news from Australia did not reach London until after the end of the Great Exhibition, the new market for British industry – above all in the realm of railways and shipping – which opened up as a result of the new mines, foreshadowed, for the second half of the nineteenth century, developments in many other remote corners of the world offering new opportunities for British investment. For these new markets, the Industrial Revolution, as presented by London to the world in 1851, was the essential foundation.

As for New Zealand, there is little to tell in comparison with Australia. In 1850 British colonists were just beginning to come to terms with the land, after making peace in 1840 – on terms extremely advantageous to themselves – with the native Maori population according to the Treaty of Waitangi. Before then, the Colonial Office in London saw New Zealand as essentially a Maori state, in which, somehow, a place had to be found for European settlers.[33] These in turn were concerned mainly to exploit the colony's agricultural potential: gold, in much smaller quantities than in Australia, would only be discovered in the 1860s. Together with the Australian colonies, New Zealand sent exhibits to London for the 1851 Exhibition; the official catalogue, however, gave little space to colonial handicrafts, promoting Australia as 'the most extensive wool-producing country in the world'.[34] A year later the picture would have been very different.

Finally, a number of quite general points are useful in placing the world of 1851, as it is presented above, in the broad sweep of history. To begin with, at a time when steam was already well on the way to taking over from sail in the oceans of the world, very few of its coastlines remained to be discovered. The last great circumnavigation under sail, the voyage of the *Beagle* (1831–6), with Charles Darwin as its most distinguished passenger, did not lead to the discovery of any new territories. Outside Antarctica this process was completed by the three great voyages of Captain James Cook, which, taking place in the years 1768–80,[35] coincided with the beginning of the Industrial Revolution in Britain.

By 1851, railways were already proving their capacity to transform the transport infrastructure of the interior of any continent save Antarctica. By this time there was no doubt whatsoever that the success of the Industrial Revolution would lead to the transformation of the world's economic geography. If, internationally, the same was true of its political geography was less certain; with the Industrial Revolution opening the way to overseas imperialism on an unprecedented scale, national regimes – at least in Europe – had proved surprisingly resistant to change. France, on the face of it, was the obvious exception, but from 1789 to 1815, the years, first of revolution and then of rule by Napoleon Bonaparte, had led those who ruled the European states that had combined to defeat the French emperor once and for all at Waterloo, to defend existing power structures at almost any price. Even among the working classes (still in 1851 with little prospect of any effective voice in national politics), few saw much to gain by following France along the path of revolution. What had happened in France in the years since 1815 provided little incentive for popular uprisings elsewhere in Europe, and when they did occur – mainly in 1840s – they met with little success.

By 1851, however, it was beginning to become clear that time was on the side of the working classes; even such limited reforms as Lord Grey's Reform Act of 1832, Sir Robert Peel's repeal of the Corn Laws in 1846, or J.R. Thorbecke's landmark constitution for the Netherlands in 1848 were recognizably steps on the way to universal popular representation. If, for the working class city dwellers still unrepresented in parliament, the pace was too slow, rural landowners and those who still depended upon them had – according to their own lights – every reason for seeing things differently.

Demography also carried the tide of reform; populations increased, with Britain leading the way – with the gains accruing mainly to new industrial towns, such as Manchester, Birmingham or Sheffield (which, following the Reform Act of 1832 were electing their own Members of Parliament). With young men in the cities anxious to remain in touch with their old homes, the success of the British Penny Post – first introduced in 1840,[36] with Europe and the United States soon following – reflected levels of literacy which, in the eighteenth century, only the odd country such as Sweden had managed to attain. The widespread introduction of Samuel Morse's electric telegraph in the course of the 1840s also added immeasurably to the range of the communications infrastructure.

Looking back on 1851, the year did not herald an era of peace, despite all the material progress celebrated in the Crystal Palace. The 1850s, on both sides of the Atlantic, were years of strife. In Europe the Crimean War (1854–6) pitted Britain and France against Russia, which soon learnt how steam transport – whether by land or sea – was transforming the logistics of war, while the artillery produced notably by the French Schneider ironworks and armoury at Le Creusot[37] had devastating new power.

On the other side of the Atlantic, the United States, in coming to terms with what opening up the West was going to involve in the railroad age, was discovering a fault line between north and south that in the period 1861–5, under the presidency of Abraham Lincoln, led – with hundreds of thousands of casualties on both sides – to a terrible Civil War. In the defeated southern states, this put an end to a way of life and a pre-industrial ordering of society which, taking slavery for granted, had existed for 200 years.

In Europe, the principalities of Italy, with a brilliant leader, Giuseppe Garibaldi, were, with French support, fighting successfully for independence – and eventual unity – with the tradition-bound Austrian empire as their principal enemy. In the north of Europe Prussia was also shaping up to be in the vanguard of German unification, a result finally achieved in 1870.

The following chapters show how the growth of manufacturing industry, supported by an unprecedented level of invention and innovation, created the world celebrated in London's Crystal Palace in the summer of 1851. If by this year the process reflected coordination between different economic sectors – coal and iron, textiles, ceramics, chemicals, power, transport – at the dawn of the Industrial Revolution a hundred years earlier, these sectors were developing more or less independently, with progress marked by the creation of new linkages between them. At this time also, there were great differences in the extent to which different regions, and even different towns or villages, were involved in the various components of the revolutionary process.

In some areas, the old world survived until well into the nineteenth century; in others it had long disappeared before the end of the eighteenth. By 1851 however, the new world – at least in Britain – had reached almost every corner of the land: the map on page xvi of British railways as they were in 1852 is proof enough of this. Even in agriculture, new mechanical implements eased the tasks of labourers in the field – or at least made them more productive. All this together was the secret of success of the Great Exhibition. There was no way back, not for Britain, nor – at the end of the day – for the rest of the world.

2

THE ATMOSPHERIC STEAM ENGINE

Thomas Newcomen's Invention
In 1712 at a coalmine in Staffordshire, a new engine, capable of pumping floodwater out of the underground workings more efficiently than any other machinery used for this purpose, came into operation for the first time. This simple, single-action, atmospheric steam engine was a completely new source of power. The main principle on which it operated – that is, harnessing the force of atmospheric pressure to drive machinery – was still being applied until well into the nineteenth century.

The race to design an engine of unprecedented power to pump water was already underway before the end of the seventeenth century, when London – with its brick houses designed to be heated by coal – was still being rebuilt after the great fire. In the first half of the century a young Italian scientist, Evangelista Torricelli, who had been Galileo's favourite pupil, discovered that the earth's atmosphere had weight, which meant that the whole of the earth's surface was subject to the pressure of the atmosphere upon it. What is more, Torricelli invented a practical means of measuring this atmospheric pressure. Following him, noted scientists, such as the Frenchman Blaise Pascal, the Dutchman Constantijn Huygens and the Englishman Robert Boyle[1] all became involved in the study of atmospheric pressure. These were eminent men belonging to an international community, so it was natural enough that when a young Huguenot, Denis Papin, who had worked for Huygens in Paris, fled France in 1675 to escape religious persecution; he went to London with an introduction to Boyle. There he was invited to explain a number of ingenious inventions to the Royal Society, one of which demonstrated, quite spectacularly, the force of atmospheric pressure. This was a vertical cylinder closed at both ends and containing a piston which, at its upper end, outside the cylinder, was connected by a rope and pulley to a very considerable weight. At the start of Papin's demonstration, there was a small quantity of water at the bottom of the cylinder, while the rest of it was filled with air. A fire lit under the cylinder caused the water to boil, filling the cylinder with steam, and so driving the piston head to the top end, with the air above it escaping through a one-way valve, such as is still to be found on any pneumatic tyre. Quenching the fire allowed the cylinder to cool, so that the steam condensed to water, leaving a vacuum above it. A tap was then opened, allowing air from outside to enter the top of the cylinder, to drive the piston downwards with more than sufficient force to raise the weight to which it was connected.[2]

Papin may have been on the brink of success as an inventor of useful machinery, but nevertheless he soon turned to other experiments of no practical use. At the same time, an ambitious, prosperous and conceited West Countryman, content to be known as Captain[3] Thomas Savery, took over from Papin in demonstrating steam-powered machinery to the Royal Society, to which he was elected in 1705. Unlike Papin, Savery was a serious businessman who had, on 25 July 1698, already been granted a patent for 'raising water by the impellent force of fire'. He went on to set up, in the heart of London, what was intended to be 'the world's first steam pump manufactory'.[4]

Proprietors of mines and collieries who did business with Savery were bound to be disappointed as his engines never solved their most pressing problem, which was to get rid of water from deep mines.[5] By the end of the seventeenth century the need for a solution was critical. Where historically British mining was concerned to exploit tin and copper, with the ores mainly found in Cornwall and the adjacent parts of Devon, coal was now becoming much more important. While seams were to be found in many parts of Britain, the richest were in the hills along the great rivers of north-east England, notably the Tyne and Wear. This location had the advantage of being easily accessible to London by sea, where domestic users in built-up areas constituted a rapidly growing market.

Even so, the first success of a viable steam-powered pumping engine was not in this part of the country. Thomas Newcomen (1663–1729) was born in Dartmouth into a family of merchants. True to the family business tradition, he set up as an ironmonger in the town in about 1685, with a partner, John Calley, who like him was a devout Baptist.[6] Being a provincial ironmonger in early eighteenth-century Britain did not involve running a shop with a stock in trade supplied by wholesalers and manufacturers. On the contrary, an ironmonger would only succeed if he actively sought his customers outside his home town, supplying them with parts made of iron – and to a lesser extent other metals such as copper and tin – required by their own business operations.

For a Devonshire ironmonger this meant finding clients among the proprietors of local mines, especially mines in Cornwall, which, with a long-established export market, still made a major contribution to the national economy. Although, in Newcomen's day, brick and stone for buildings, and wood for machinery, were essential production goods for mining operations in Cornwall as they were in the rest of the kingdom, iron was still essential for certain components. As machinery became more elaborate, iron was steadily gaining ground (as can also be seen from contemporary advances in the iron-founding centres of the English Midlands).

Along his business circuit, Newcomen was inevitably confronted not only by the critical need to pump water out of mines, but also by the inadequacy of the machinery used for this purpose. The problem was an acute shortage of power, which wooden machinery, driven by horses, was quite unable to alleviate. It is unlikely that Newcomen knew anything of the scientific theory of atmospheric pressure, as it is described above, but it is certain that he knew not only of Savery's attempts to build steam engines to operate pumps, but also of his patent taken out in 1698.

If the existence of the patent, combined with Savery's business reputation, were sufficient to reassure Newcomen that steam-powered water pumps, sooner or later, would become standard in British mining, he must have realized at a very early stage that Savery's own inventions were not up to the task. On the other hand, given the wide range of Savery's patent, Newcomen prudently took him on as a partner in 1698. This move was essentially pre-emptive; there is little record of any useful contribution by Savery, nor of how he was to share in any profits made from steam engines designed and installed by Newcomen. For all practical purposes, Newcomen was not only the sole inventor of the steam engine named after him, but also the dominant partner in the business of selling and installing it.

Unlike Savery, John Calley was essential to the scheme and the two worked together for some ten years, developing a fire machine, which was ready to go to market around 1710. The basic operating principle was that of the apparatus demonstrated by Papin to the Royal Society, but whereas Papin's engine had to be set up again for every stroke of the piston, Newcomen overcame this obstacle by raising the steam in a separate boiler, with the fire continuously burning in a furnace underneath it. Although this was an innovation borrowed from Savery's dysfunctional engines, it was their only contribution to Newcomen's quite different design. The steam, admitted to the cylinder through an inlet valve, drove the piston to the top of its stroke. If, then, the steam was forced to condense, atmospheric pressure would – as it had with Papin's apparatus – drive the piston down. After some ten years of trial and error, Newcomen and Calley invented a cock that would automatically send a jet of cold water directly into the cylinder, every time the piston reached the top of its stroke. Because the steam condensed almost immediately, the downstroke of the piston was almost instantaneous. This final innovation was then sufficient to create a steam engine that was sufficient for its intended purposes for more than half a century.

For Newcomen, the invention of a viable steam engine was only the first step on the way to producing and marketing it on a commercial scale. There is no way of telling when, or how, Newcomen first tried to establish a market. Intuition suggests that his first attempts would have been close to home, particularly in view of the costs of flooding encountered by the Cornish mine owners.

They were reluctant buyers, however, and for this there are three possible explanations: first, there is simply the innate conservatism of a still flourishing industry that had existed for centuries; second, the market might already have been spoilt by attempts made by Savery to sell his own dysfunctional engine; and third, the extravagant demand for fuel inherent in Newcomen's engines – which to function at all efficiently had to be built on a vast scale – was unacceptable in a part of England far from any reserves of coal.

In the event Newcomen's first 'fire machine' was installed not in the West Country, but near Dudley Castle in Staffordshire, in the West Midlands, in 1712. The opportunity arose as a result of a contact with Humphrey Potter, a leading member of the local Baptist

Church, which had long been linked by friendship to the Baptists in Dartmouth. Although the building of the engine is well recorded, its actual location and ownership are not. It was used for pumping water out of a coalmine which, needless to say, also supplied its fuel in the form of 'small' coal accumulated at the pit head and of little use for any other purposes.

It was soon recognized, however, that the Dudley Castle pump represented no more than a prototype in its own field. What is more, existing records do not make clear precisely what stage in the design of his engine Newcomen had reached in 1712. Was it, for instance, self-acting, so that the movement of the beam was linked mechanically to the various cocks and valves controlling the intake of steam into the cylinder from the boiler, the jet of water for condensing the steam and the expulsion of the condensed water from the cylinder? All that is known is that such an engine is undoubtedly the subject of an engraving entitled *The ENGINE for Raising Water (with a power made) by Fire*, dated 1717 and made by Henry Beighton, a fellow of the Royal Society and the first man ever to publish a scientific study of the steam engine.

As the engine steadily evolved in the years after 1712, a side view after every improvement would have shown a steadily more complicated mechanical system. Successive innovations increased the power, efficiency and economy, both in fuel and maintenance of the engine, and this incremental process continued unabated after Newcomen's death in 1729.

The most important early innovation was the substitution of cast iron cylinders for brass; a process that started in Richard Beach's Staffordshire coalmines in 1724.[7] The new cast iron cylinders came from the Coalbrookdale Company's foundry in the Severn Valley and were only possible as a result of the advances in iron founding made by Abraham Darby I (1678–1717) at Coalbrookdale at the beginning of the century. Iron, if heavier than brass, was much cheaper, and had the additional advantage that much larger cylinders could be made out of it. Nevertheless its use in Newcomen engines was slow to spread beyond the West Midlands, no doubt because the Coalbrookdale Company had a monopoly there.

It is uncertain how far Newcomen, after 1712, actually profited from the success of his engine, or was responsible for the series of improvements made to it up to the time of his death. The problem was that after the death of Savery (who had long been a sleeping partner) in 1715, his executors sold all his patent rights, including those relating to Newcomen's engine, to a syndicate. This in turn employed men who, having gained their experience from working under Newcomen, were ready to switch their loyalties. Confronting the syndicate, Newcomen's only hold on the engine was his know-how, together with his proven capacity to design improvements to the engine, which would undoubtedly increase its market value. Yet he undoubtedly played an important part in bringing his engines to the coalmines of the north-east, where the Tanfield Lea colliery had a working 'fire engine' no later than November 1715.

By the time the Savery patent expired in 1733, there were already fourteen engines operating in the north-east, and of these some at least were constructed under contracts made with Newcomen. By the time of his death, his engines were to be found at many British sites, from the Firth of Forth in Scotland to Mounts Bay in Cornwall, and also in Hungary, Belgium, France, Germany, Austria, Sweden and possibly Spain.

Not all were at mines, however. The French engine, at Paris, was for pumping water out of the Seine to ensure a municipal water supply. In London, the York Buildings waterworks, where Savery's engine had been a complete failure some twenty years earlier, acquired a Newcomen engine in 1726. The fact that Newcomen himself died in London in 1729, suggests that the city may have become his base of operations, although his family continued to live in Dartmouth.

As far as his reputation goes, history has not done justice to Newcomen, but there is no reason to believe that he was ever close to destitution, however reluctant the syndicate that owned Savery's patent was to recognize him as the first man ever to build a workable 'fire engine'. If the historical record suggests that Newcomen would have done better to be more streetwise, it equally allows the conclusion that – given the state of English patent law at the beginning of the eighteenth century – he could not have achieved any better results as a businessman. His work in the years before 1712 showed that he had quite exceptional perseverance in the face of adversity. All this combined well with his dedication to the cause of the Baptists, which after all had played an important part in his securing the contract for the engine at Dudley Castle. Newcomen comes across as being pre-eminently serious and hard-working, as well as creative, and without these attributes he would certainly not have made his mark in industrial history.

Inevitably, as time went on, the success of Newcomen's engine was increasingly the achievement of other men, as were the improvements that were made to it. By 1733, four years after Newcomen's death, Savery's patent expired and the atmospheric engine was effectively in the public domain. If, for another half century, it had no rivals, there was still room for improvement and an extension of the market – indeed, the two went together. As for improvement, there was hardly any established principle for determining the dimensions of the three main components – the cylinder, the boiler and the furnace – or their size in relation to each other. Any engine, to operate efficiently, had to be of a size so considerable as to dwarf any men working it, as can be seen from any number of contemporary illustrations.[8] Because only a massive brick wall could support the trunnion, which carried the whole weight of the beam at its midpoint, this also generally constituted the outside wall of the engine house. As a result, the pump operated by the engine was also outside. Given the vast quantity of bricks required, these could not for economic reasons be imported from far afield, and the same was true, if to a lesser degree, of the wood required by the engine, and more particularly for its massive beam.

Construction therefore was largely a business for local contractors and suppliers. Even with the metal components, which could not be made on site, shipping costs were a major factor in explaining why in the north-east mine-owners were reluctant to convert from locally made brass cylinders to iron cylinders transported from Coalbrookdale.

A breakthrough was bound to come sooner or later, and finally, in 1752, a forty-seven inch iron cylinder, bought from Coalbrookdale, was installed at the Tyne-side Throckley colliery by William Brown, the most celebrated and influential engine builder in the north[9]. This initiated a process by which much more powerful engines could pump out mine water on an unprece-dented scale. In the twenty years, 1756–76, Brown himself installed twenty-two in the north-east and another three in Scotland.

On a list he made in 1769, giving the specifications of ninety-nine engines, the majority had a cylinder diam-eter beyond the capacity of any brass founder: of the two engines at the Walker colliery in County Durham, both had a cylinder diameter of more than seventy inches. If this was all very well for coalmines, it still offered little prospect for tin mines in Cornwall, which even at this late stage preferred, for the most part, to use horses for powering water pumps.

On the other hand, at locations closer to Coalbrook-dale, where coal was also cheaper, Newcomen engines were installed to pump water up to reservoirs that would then, at least in time of drought, help feed the streams that powered watermills. This means of ensuring year-round operation was adopted notably by Richard Arkwright's great cotton mill at Cromford, Derbyshire, and Matthew Boulton's Soho Manufactory, just outside Birmingham.

Because continuing improvements to Newcomen en-gines were often the result of local engineers determined to improve the performance of those for which they were directly responsible, they often failed to be adopted further afield in spite of their merits. This was even the experience of John Smeaton (1724–94), better known for constructing the third Eddystone lighthouse, who, more than any contemporary engineer, recorded in exact figures the performance of engines of different dimensions and with the knowledge so acquired was responsible for any number of useful innovations. When in 1811, George Stephenson – knowing nothing of what Smeaton had achieved some forty years earlier – was confronted with a poorly performing but still new Newcomen engine at the Killingworth High Pit, he distinguished himself as an engineer by unwittingly adopting expedients first developed by Smeaton to remedy its defects. Given the character of the times, such unwitting duplication of effort was almost impossible to avoid.

By the time James Watt's inventions revolutionized the use of steam power, the Newcomen engine, in the half century that it held the field more or less alone, still attracted the interest of such leading figures as the second Abraham Darby, John Wilkinson (the Severn Valley's most successful ironmaster), Matthew Boulton, Richard Arkwright and John Smeaton. In doing so it became linked with many different strands of what is now known as the Industrial Revolution, in a way that Newcomen himself could never have foreseen. It was a hundred years or more before its potential was fully realized, and even then the accolades went to men such as James Watt and George Stephenson. Without Newcomen, they would not even have started.

James Watt's Revolution
During the last thirty years of the eighteenth century, the Newcomen fire engine was transformed into an

all-purpose steam engine, capable of providing mechanical power for almost any industrial purpose, whether in mining or manufacturing. This transformation – at the heart of the industrial revolution – was the achievement of one man, the inventor James Watt (1736–1819). Born in the Scottish town of Greenock, the son of a local man – also James Watt – known both as a merchant and a shipbuilder, he was fortunate in the circumstances of his birth.

In the course of the eighteenth century Greenock, favourably located at the furthest point upstream, where the River Clyde was still navigable by ocean-going ships, became ever more prosperous as the main British destination for tobacco imported from the Virginia plantations. James Watt senior, who built the first crane for unloading tobacco at the dockside,[10] shared in this prosperity, to become first, the treasurer of Greenock (in 1755) and then its bailie (in 1757).[11] By this time, the young James Watt had already left home, to follow the vocation of an instrument maker, for which he was so well suited as to be recognized by one of his father's workmen with the words, 'Jamie has got a fortune at his fingers' ends'[12] – a prophetic judgement.

James Watt went first to Glasgow (in 1754), where his mother's family might have helped him with useful introductions, and then (in 1755) – after making little progress in a city known more for its university[13] than for its industry – to London, a city whose instrument-makers were world renowned. Although he had little prospect of becoming either an apprentice (for being too old) or a journeyman (for never having served a master), he found employment with John Morgan, who had a shop in Cornhill in the City, where he made for his customers all kinds of brass instruments. In the making of rules, scales, quadrants and other instruments in current use, James Watt proved to be a remarkably quick learner, a skilled craftsman and, above all, a workaholic; no doubt it helped that if he went abroad in the streets of the city, he ran the risk of bring impressed for service in the Seven Years War, which had just begun.

After one year of a somewhat irregular London apprenticeship, James Watt returned home in July 1756 with £20 in materials and tools and a 1723 edition of N. Bion's *Construction and Principal Uses of Mathematical Instruments*. Before the end of the year, good fortune and family contacts brought him employment in Glasgow as 'mathematical instrument maker to University'. Although his somewhat improbable first task was to put in order a collection of mathematical instruments, which, having been bequeathed to the university by a merchant of Jamaica, had deteriorated in the sea air on the long voyage across the Atlantic, he was free to build up his own trade as an instrument maker on the university premises. There, as throughout his life, he continued to make new and above all useful friends, such as Joseph Black, recently appointed Professor of Anatomy and Chemistry, and destined to become one of the great scientists of the eighteenth century.

Ambitious to expand his business, Watt – getting around the restrictions imposed by the city's guilds – set up, with finance provided by a new partner, John Craig, as a shopkeeper in Glasgow's Saltmarket, with stock comprising 'mathematical and musical instruments, with variety of Toys and other goods'.[14] In 1764, after business success had allowed him to move to a better address, James Watt was able to marry his cousin, Margaret Miller, and move into a new home in Delftfield Lane.[15] By this time he had begun to experiment with steam.

This turning point in Watt's career was the result of his being asked to repair a model of Newcomen's atmospheric steam engine belonging to the Natural Philosophy Class (which would now be known as the science faculty) of the university. The model itself had never worked satisfactorily, and although Watt rightly concluded that this, at least in part, was because it was built on too small a scale, he also realized that the engine was inherently inefficient. The problem was the cold water jet, which – at the top of the stroke – condensed the steam to produce the critical vacuum allowing atmospheric pressure to drive the piston down, drastically reduced the temperature of the cylinder.

Watt's key insight was that a separate condenser, leading off from the cylinder, would then allow its temperature to be maintained by enclosing it in a jacket of water at, or close to, boiling point. However sound the principle, Watt still had to apply all his skills as a craftsman to overcome the technical problems involved in constructing an engine considerably more complicated than anything ever contemplated by Newcomen and those, such as Smeaton, who had succeeded him. What is more, work on the separate condenser, in his workshop at the university, was taking up so much time that his own trade in the Saltmarket suffered.

At this critical time Joseph Black, ever a true friend, came to the rescue. He was free not only with advice – on such matters as latent heat, a phenomenon he had himself discovered – but also with funds lent to Watt to allow him to carry on his work with the condenser. Even more useful was an introduction to an Englishman, John Roebuck, already established as a captain of industry, as a result, first, of using a new method to produce sulphuric acid, and second, of being a pioneer in using a blast furnace to produce iron. The first enterprise brought him to Prestonpans, in East Lothian, and the second to the River Carron in Stirlingshire. As both locations were in Scotland, with Edinburgh between them, it was almost inevitable that an entrepreneur such as Roebuck should become acquainted with the city's leading scientist.

Watts' friendship with Black proved critical when Roebuck embarked on a third Scottish enterprise, the exploitation of the considerable coal reserves located close to the Duke of Hamilton's home, Kinneil House, west of Edinburgh on the south side of the Firth of Forth. With a lease of the mining rights from the duke, Roebuck soon discovered that the atmospheric engine he had installed at Kinneil was not up to pumping out the water that flooded into the mine.[16] Black, knowing of Watt's work on the separate condenser, brought the two men together, and in 1765 Watt moved his working base to Kinneil House, where he had the advantage of material supplied from Roebuck's Carron Iron Works.[17] Roebuck's contribution was to pay off some of Watt's debts (including part of what was owed to Black), with the prospect not only of being able to earn profits from Kinneil, but also of sharing in those to be earned from Watt's separate condenser once it came into general use with atmospheric engines.

By 1768 Watt's work at Kinneil had so impressed Roebuck as to justify sending Watt to London to petition Parliament for a patent for the separate condenser. Roebuck then agreed to pay off the remaining debts owed by Watt to Black (about £1,000) and also to meet the costs of the patent (about £120), in exchange for two-thirds of an interest in the patent once it was granted. Watt was in London in time to take the oath on the patent on 9 August, and returning to Glasgow by coach, he made a detour to Birmingham in order to visit Matthew Boulton (1728–1809) at Soho House.

Boulton and his partner John Fothergill had together built the Soho Manufactory, which opened in 1766, and by the time of Watt's visit two years later it was manufacturing a great variety of small metal objects, mostly for domestic use and known generically as 'toys', in premises where 600 highly skilled craftsmen were employed. The machinery was powered by water from the local Hockley Brook which had been dammed to provide the head of water for a vast overshot waterwheel. The atmospheric engine installed to pump water back to the reservoir in time of drought had already acquainted Boulton with the limitations of the original Newcomen design. When Watt, with whom he had an immediate rapport, showed him the patent for the improved engine incorporating the separate condenser, he was immediately interested. Once back in Glasgow, Watt suggested to Roebuck that he grant Boulton a licence for a one-third interest. By this time Watt had also submitted a new engine design for Roebuck's Kinneil coalmine.

Watt's patent for a 'new invented method of lessening the consumption of Steam and Fuel in Fire Engines' was sealed on 5 January 1769,[18] covering England, Wales and the American plantations. With no drawings attached to it and no application of principle of action submitted, it was arguably defective,[19] but by this time Roebuck was so convinced of the value of the patent that – with a view to exploiting the patent elsewhere in his own right – he offered Boulton no more than a licence to make the engine in three Midland counties.

Boulton's reaction to this offer, which is to be found in a letter to Watt dated 7 February 1769, is a classic document of the Industrial Revolution, whose spirit justifies quoting from it at length:

> the plan proposed to me is so very different from that which I had conceived at the time I talked with you upon the subject that I cannot think it is a proper one for me to meddle with as I do not intend turning engineer. I was excited by two motives to offer you my assistance which were love of you and love of a money-getting ingenious project . . . [To] produce the most profit, my idea was to settle a manufactory near to my own by the side of our canal where I would erect all the conveniences necessary for the completion of engines, and from which manufactory we would serve all the world with engines of all sizes. By these means and your assistance we could engage and instruct some excellent workmen . . . and execute the invention 20 per cent. cheaper than it would otherwise be executed, and with as great a distance of accuracy as there is between the blacksmith and the mathematical instrument maker. It would not be worth my while to make for three counties only, but I find it very worth while to make for all the world.

For some five years from the end of 1769 so little progress was made at Kinneil that Watt turned away from working on atmospheric engines to other activities, such as surveying the routes of possible new Scottish canals, which assured him a better living. A letter to another Birmingham friend, William Small, and dated 7 November 1772, shows how this was largely a matter of temperament:

> what I can promise to perform is to make an accurate survey & a faithfull report of anything in the engineer way ... [but] I can on no account have anything to do with workmen, cash, or workmen's accts, nor would I chuse to be bound up to one object that I could not occasionally serve such friends as might employ me for smaller matters ... I am not a man of regularity in Business & have bad health. Take care not to give anybody a better opinion of me than I deserve, it will hurt me in the end. We have abundance of matter to discuss tho' the damned engine sleep in quiet.

A week later, in a second letter, he added, 'In short I find myself out of my sphere when I have anything to do with mankind.'[20] If Watt was content to let 'the damned engine sleep in quiet', this was unthinkable for Roebuck, who by 1773, in face of mounting costs at Kinneil and an economic crisis in Scotland, was beset by creditors and quite unable to pay the fees agreed with Watt. In the end Roebuck transferred his property in the engine at Kinneil to Watt in exchange for a release from this debt. Roebuck however did his best to hold to his two-thirds interest in the patent, but in August 1773 he was forced to make a composition with his creditors, who transferred this interest to Boulton on much more favourable terms. This in turn led Fothergill to retire as a partner, so leaving Boulton and Watt as the exclusive owners of the patent rights. Tragedy then overcame Watt, with the death of his wife in September. The time had come to start a new life. On 17 May 1774, having satisfactorily wound up his work as a surveyor, Watt set off to join Boulton in Birmingham; arriving there with his family and belongings, two weeks later. This was the beginning of the most remarkable partnership in the history of the Industrial Revolution.

Boulton and Watt at Soho

Watt's first task in Birmingham was to set up the Kinneil engine – which after being dismantled had been sent down from Scotland – in space made available by Boulton in the Soho Manufactory. This was a considerable challenge, seeing how the engine had failed at Kinneil; it was also essential for further progress, because Boulton and Watt were anxious to secure a patent, with as little delay as possible, for an engine that actually worked. Able to devote his entire time to the engine, Watt found many defects, which he remedied one way or another, largely by trial and error. The most serious shortcoming was to be found in the block tin cylinder which had been installed at Kinneil. The problem was solved by John Wilkinson, of Bersham on the River Severn, where his ironworks were renowned for their capacity to bore cast iron cannons. Wilkinson, a master of his trade, was up to the challenge of producing a cylinder, with not only a perfect circular cross section – a result already achieved by Smeaton – but one which was truly cylindrical in its entire length.[21] The Kinneil engine was now ready to be installed wherever there was a market. Boulton was optimistic; the new engine was so great an improvement on any previous ones, particularly in the matter of fuel consumption, that it would to be economic to operate in places where the costs of running a Newcomen engine were prohibitive. At the same time, the engine could work on a much smaller scale, allowing work to be done off site at the Soho Manufactory, which previously had to be carried out locally. The obvious market – now wide open – was to be found in Cornwall's tin and copper mines; where Newcomen had failed, Boulton and Watt had discovered a new field to conquer.

Roebuck was the big loser, but not through any fault of his former partners. He was unlucky that Watt's engine failed to live up to expectations at Kinneil, so that the most ambitious of all his ventures led not to prosperity but, in 1773, to bankruptcy[22] – a tragic end for a man whose early successes at Carron and Prestonpans had qualified him for election to the Royal Society of Edinburgh.

If for Boulton and Watt there was still a long way to go, there was one matter that demanded the utmost priority; to secure the widest possible patent cover for the new engine. The strategy adopted was to extend the existing patent of February 1769. On 23 February 1775 Watt submitted a petition to Parliament, and after considerable opposition, on 22 May the bill for the extended patent received the royal assent. This was a triumph for both men; the original patent was extended for twenty-five years, and would also cover Scotland, where, in spite of Roebuck's failure at Kinneil, there was certain to be a market for the new engine.

On the basis of the extended patent, Boulton and Watt entered into a formal partnership agreement on 1 June, to remain in force for as long as the patent was valid. Boulton acquired a two-thirds interest, while Watt, with the remaining one-third interest, would also work for a fixed annual salary of £300.

For Watt in particular, this was the beginning of good times. Returning briefly to Glasgow in June 1776, he remarried, a step he reported as 'one of the wisest of my actions'.[23] His second wife, Ann McGrigor, was the daughter of a prosperous dyer who was so cautious that he wished to see the deed of partnership between Boulton and his prospective son-in-law before consenting to the marriage. No deed has ever been found, and Ann's father had to be satisfied with the story that it was in the hands of a London lawyer. The marriage went ahead and in March 1777 James and Ann Watt moved into a new home, Regent's Place, close to Soho, where James also carried on all his paperwork. By this time, two of Watt's engines had already been installed, one at a coalmine in Staffordshire, and the other at John Wilkinson's Broseley Ironworks in Shropshire, where it was used to power the draught needed for smelting.

The success of the new engine can be measured by the interest that it attracted outside Britain. This first surfaced in the form of underhand dealings by a French smith, J.C. Périer, who had obtained from the ill-fated King Louis XVI an *arrêt de conseil* 'empowering him to raise water from the Seine to supply Paris & erecting a company'. Périer, already acquainted with Wilkinson, and knowing that he had a Newcomen engine, visited him at Broseley just at the time that he was planning to install his new engine from Boulton and Watt. Realizing its great advantages, Périer tried to order a copy directly from Wilkinson, assuring him that Watt's 1775 patent did not extend to France.[24]

Wilkinson not only declined the order, but informed Soho, where another more honourable Frenchman, the Comte d'Heronville, had already made an approach with a view to installing an engine to drain land near Dunkirk. The Soho partners then responded by offering to install the engine themselves, provided that the Count, who under the *ancien régime* was well connected, obtained an *arrêt de conseil* which would protect their rights in France. This was granted for fifteen years, subject to a trial, either at Dunkirk or Paris, demonstrating the superiority of the new engine.

In the end nothing came of the Dunkirk project. Instead, a coalmine proprietor, M. Jary, from the far west of France, offered to install the engine, provided the requisite trial could take place on site. All this took place at a time when Britain and France were at war, but even so a contract was signed and the engine installed, to become the first of its kind outside Britain. Ironically Jary never paid a penny for his engine, no doubt using the war as a pretext. Périer, on the other hand, did order two engines from Soho for pumping water out of the Seine at Chaillot just outside Paris, where – much admired even far from the city – they proved to be a tremendous advertisement for Soho. What is more, Périer paid up, the least he could do given his earlier, questionable dealings with Wilkinson.

While all this was going on in France, British orders were coming thick and fast to Soho from London,

Cornwall, Fifeshire and many places closer to Birmingham. Continental interest in the new engine brought any number of visitors. If some, but by no means all, were no more trustworthy than Périer and Jary, Boulton, carrying on a practice long established at the Soho Manufactory, not only extended a warm welcome but became an intimate friend of many, such as Count Semyon Woronzow, who came to London as Russian ambassador in 1785. All this was the beginning of a worldwide business operation. A new era in the age of steam had started.

Although orders for the new engine came from many different places, of the forty new orders built by Soho by 1780, twenty were from Cornwall. Although Newcomen himself had set his sights on this county's mining industry, his engine, even though it improved in the course of fifty-odd years, made little headway there, simply because of its extravagant fuel consumption. Soho's new engine, however, was sufficiently economical to convince Jonathan Hornblower (an engineer who had already installed Newcomen engines in Cornish mines) that installing it could be justified if the right terms were agreed. Watt always wanted a contract based on the accurate measurement of the savings in costs realized, and this is what he had proposed to Hornblower, whom he saw as 'an unbelieving Thomas', as early as 1776.

The problem for the Soho partners was how to divide their time between Cornwall (where the booming market still required much attention) and Birmingham, the essential base for developing, improving and marketing the new steam engine, to say nothing of all the other products of the Manufactory. They were greatly helped by a remarkably talented young Scottish craftsman, William Murdock, whom Boulton had impulsively taken into his employment in 1777. Proving to be 'the most active man and best engine erector [Boulton] ever saw', he was sent to Cornwall where the volume of new construction would make use of all his skills. At the same time, in order to maintain their presence in this difficult, but extremely profitable market, the partners bought, at Cosgarne in the Gwennap Valley, 'a most delightful place, a neat roomy house with sash windows double breadth the front to the south, where they could' when circumstances demanded, take up residence.

The day to day operations were left to Murdock, by temperament a man well suited to dealing with both recalcitrant Cornishmen and erratic steam engines. Cornwall was always a potential source of trouble though; the mine owners, resenting the monopoly of the Soho partners over the only viable steam engine, were rightly seen by Boulton and Watt as only too ready, if the chance ever came, to ask the courts to annul their patents.

Thus it was not for nothing that Watt gave evidence on behalf of Richard Arkwright in the first of the patent trials related in chapter 4,[25] nor was his concern – when Arkwright's patent was finally overturned in 1785 – ill-founded. As he wrote to Boulton soon afterwards, 'Though I do not love Arkwright, I don't like the precedent of setting aside patents through default of specification. I fear for our own.'[26] They were all in the same boat, as Erasmus Darwin, a mutual friend, stated in a letter to Boulton of 26 January 1785, 'Tho' your inventions by draining Cornwal, have supply'd work to ten thousands – Mr. Arkwright has employed his thousands – I think you should defend each other from the ingratitude of mankind.'[27]

To judge from the record of their not always peaceful opposition, the mine owners of Cornwall were less ungrateful than the mill owners of Lancashire, but the cases were hardly comparable. In Cornwall Boulton and Watt had no proprietary interest in the mines where their engines were installed; Arkwright, on the other hand, had designed and constructed his water-frames for mills of which he was himself the owner, so he was doubly vulnerable – but at the end of the day he also became much wealthier.

By the 1780s, Watt, wiser than Arkwright and certainly less confrontational, had protected the position of the Soho partners by taking out two new patents, in 1781 and 1782. So much was going on at this time that both partners needed to be in Birmingham. The reasons are given in a letter Boulton wrote to Watt on 21 June 1781.[28]

> The people in London, Manchester and Birmingham are *steam mill mad*. I don't mean to hurry you but I think in the course of a month or two, we should determine to take out a patent for certain methods of producing rotative motion from ... the fire engine ... There is no other Cornwall to be found, and the most likely line for our engines is the application of them to mills which is certainly an extensive field.

In short, Cornwall as a market would sooner or later be saturated; but the rest of the world was wide open.

Although Boulton's prophetic judgement would determine the future course of the Soho partners, they had in fact been pre-empted when it came to the key invention for using the reciprocal motion of an atmospheric engine for driving a wheel – and any number of other wheels linked to it. This was already the model to be found in many mills and manufactories (such as that of Boulton and Watt at Soho) powered by waterwheels. Indeed, it would remain standard in many sectors, such as wool, or in many places, such as France or the United States, until well into the nineteenth century.

The problem facing the partners was that James Pickard, the owner of a Birmingham flour mill, and Matthew Wasborough, a Bristol engineer, had, by means of a crank and a connecting rod connected to the piston of an atmospheric engine, already produced an engine which was therefore the first in the field. What is more, on 23 August 1780, Pickard had obtained a patent for it.[29] On the other hand Watt's patent prevented Wasborough from incorporating a separate condenser in his engine.

In principle this should have opened the way for Watt and Wasborough to exchange licences, but Watt was resolutely opposed to this. As an inventor he preferred to accept the challenge of making a rotatory engine which did not incorporate Pickard's crank and connecting rod. In the space of little more than a year he developed several alternatives, to the point that on 25 October 1781 he obtained a patent for 'Certain new methods of applying the vibrating or reciprocating motion of steam or fire engines to produce a continued rotative or circular motion round an axis or centre and thereby to give motion to the wheels of mills or other machines.'[30]

Of these new methods only one was viable: this was the sun-and-planet gear, inserted by Watt into the patent at the last moment, very probably as the result of a suggestion made by William Murdock.[31] Its success was such that Boulton and Watt used it during the whole period of the patent, even after Pickard's patent expired in 1794.

The sun-and-planet gear was not Watt's only invention during the 1780s. In 1782, he patented a double-acting engine, with steam introduced into the cylinder on both sides of the piston head. While utilizing the power of both the upward and downward strokes of the piston effectively doubled the efficiency of the engine, the chain linkage between the piston and the beam – which had been standard since the very beginning of the Newcomen engine – could no longer be used. Quite simply, while a chain could pull a beam downwards, it could not push it upwards. A rigid link, such as would be provided by a metal bar between the top of the piston shaft and the end of the beam, would place intolerable stress on the vertical movement of the piston, particularly during the upward stroke. To overcome this problem Watt invented a much more complex linkage that provided the necessary 'parallel motion' – so that the unwanted horizontal forces on the top end of the piston shaft were negligible. A critical problem had been solved, for without this invention frictional losses would have made the engine much less efficient, to say nothing of the wear and tear on the piston and cylinder head.

Watt himself said, 'Though I am not over-anxious about fame, yet I am more proud of the parallel motion than of any other mechanical invention I have ever made.' However, it was not to be his final invention; there were continual improvements to the rotative engine, and even if many were the result of trial and error in installing and servicing the engines, some, such as the governor (which can be traced back to a drawing dated '13 Dec. 1788') were new inventions. In this case the invention, although it had the valuable function of ensuring that the engine ran at a constant speed, was never patented.

One idea, suggested by Murdock, was eschewed by Boulton and Watt. This was to use the rotative engine to drive a carriage. The partners had more than enough work on hand without venturing into this new field; their first rotative engine was bought in 1783 by John Wilkinson, who used it to work a tilt hammer at his Bradley ironworks. Other orders followed, including a significant one from the Albion Mill in London, where the engine, finally installed in 1788, was used for any number of purposes, such as unloading wheat from barges, hoisting sacks, sifting and dressing flour. In the centre of London it was regarded as a great mechanical wonder, until it burnt down in 1791. This was allegedly the result of arson, as many had reason to fear the potential success of large-scale, steam-powered flour milling. A new industry would arise in seaports, while local wind and watermills would lose their trade.[32]

To Watt, who, like Boulton, incurred a substantial loss from the fate of the Albion Mill, it was a question of pride going before a fall. The mill had taken four years to install, and during the whole time Boulton, ever ready to promote his business, allowed anyone interested to observe progress. This was too much for Watt who, in a letter dated 17 April 1786, wrote, 'I know you have been actuated by good motives in showing the mill, namely the desire of getting quit of part of the property we have in it & the hopes of making interest to get a charter, but I conceive these things will be better achieved by making it a mystery to the many & by the external appearance of the business.'[33]

Watt was always pessimistic; it was part of his nature. Left to himself, he was very soon content to call it a day, as is shown by an even earlier letter, dated '1785, Nov. 5',[34] 'On the whole I find it now full time to cease attempting to invent new things, or to attempt anything which attended with any risk of not succeeding, or of creating trouble in the execution. Let us go on executing the things we understand and the rest to younger men, who have neither money nor character to lose.'

If success must have been overwhelming for so humble a man as Watt, he was still set on a course where he could not avoid it – at least as long as he had Boulton at his side. The merits of the rotative engine became known far and wide, with prospective new business not only in France and the Dutch Republic but also in Connecticut on the other side of the Atlantic, which had been independent of Britain since 1781. Watt, who already knew such great British scientists as Joseph Black and Joseph Priestley, now started meeting some of their European equals, such as Antoine Lavoisier (the greatest chemist of the day) and Pierre de Laplace (an expert on celestial mechanics to rival Newton).[35] Watt also made a significant contribution to metrology by establishing horsepower as the unit of power, measured in the first instance by what a mill horse could deliver in one minute.[36] (It is fitting that with the introduction of the metric system the watt became the standard unit of power.[37])

While until the early 1790s Boulton and Watt flourished by installing state-of-the-art atmospheric steam engines in any number of locations, and for a variety of purposes, both home and abroad, they both realized that their business strategy could outlive its usefulness. What is more, with Boulton about to become seventy, and Watt sixty, before the end of the century, it was time to look after their posterity, for once all relevant patents had expired the manufacture of atmospheric engines would fall into the public domain – as it was with the original Newcomen engine until 1769.

In October 1794 a new firm, Boulton, Watt & Sons, was formed, with Boulton's son Matthew and Watt's two sons, James and Gregory, joining their fathers as partners. At the same time a radical new business plan was adopted; steam engines would be manufactured, as a complete unit, in new purpose-built premises. On land purchased in 1795 at a Smethwick site next to the Birmingham and Wolverhampton Canal, the Soho Foundry was built, with separate buildings for a boring mill, forge, smithy, turning, fitting, carpenters' shops, drying kiln, foundry and air furnace, all to be served by a new wet dock.[38] Of all the machines to be installed, the boring mill, adapted from Wilkinson's Brosely ironworks, was the most important. Brosely would also supply many of the skilled craftsmen who were essential if the new foundry was to be profitable.

With the operation of the foundry left to the younger generation, it continued to flourish and expand after the turn of the century, even though other firms were by this time free to compete in an open market. Success was the result both of the high engineering standard of its products and of a business organization far ahead of its day. From this point on, the older generation played little more than an advisory role.

3

THE RAW MATERIALS OF INDUSTRY AND INDUSTRIAL POWER

Wind and Water

Until the invention of Thomas Newcomen's steam, or 'fire' engine, at the beginning of the eighteenth century, wind and water were the only sources of power beyond that of the brute muscle of men or specially harnessed animals – horses and oxen or, outside Europe, buffaloes and elephants.

. While wind was indispensable for sailing ships, especially for long saltwater voyages, it was also useful on dry land for driving windmills, whether constructed for grinding flour, fulling cloth, sawing wood, pumping water. As a source of power, it was versatile; a windmill can be built almost anywhere. This is no guarantee, however, that the wind blows at the right force or in the right place, so the usefulness of a mill depends on the local occurrence of sufficient windy days to justify its intermittent use – which may be quite frequent – for its dedicated purpose.

While all this makes wind the optimal source of power for many traditional uses, both on land and sea, it is little use for any operation requiring constant power, such as providing the draught for an iron foundry. Even at sea, where there is no alternative, a ship cannot only be becalmed, but must take into account the strength and direction of the winds to be encountered at every season of the year along its chosen course. Until well into the nineteenth century, shipping schedules depended upon these critical factors, which in the great maritime cities, from Malacca to Mombasa, Antwerp to Havana, Liverpool to New Orleans, determined the familiar parameters of commerce.

At the end of the day, wind, as a source of power, was subject to one essential shortcoming: there was an inherent limit to the scale on which it could be harnessed. The length of a windmill's sails could not go beyond a critical threshold (which is far below that of the windmills now used to generate electricity). Old style Dutch windmills were never going to drain the Haarlemmermeer, a vast salt water lake between Amsterdam and the North Sea, however many might be built along its shores.[1] There was a critical limit to the area of sail a ship could carry.[2] With shipping this meant a drastic restriction on tonnage and cargo capacity; historically 3,000 tons was the displacement of the very largest ships.[3]

On the other hand, at a time when transport overland was often problematic, the constraint on the size of seagoing ships meant, in practical terms, that rivers remained navigable until far inland, so that such unlikely places as Cambridge and Florence were recognized seaports. Grain – which, as a result of a strong export market, had become a major bulk cargo for British shipping in the eighteenth century – was carried mainly in ships with less than a hundred tons displacement.[4] Such small cargoes were economic on terms inconceivable by today's standards, while both the small size of ships and the time needed for any voyage meant relatively large numbers at sea, with corresponding demands on manpower for crews.

At the same time, shipyards were numerous in the era of sail. Although the decline of the traditional industry with its own characteristic building materials of wood, rope, canvas – and to a limited extent iron or brass – was, as a historical process, part and parcel of the Industrial Revolution. It still survives worldwide, in its own microeconomic niche, with any number of yards meeting local demands for recreation, fishing or trade.

Harnessing the power of water was more complicated. The most efficient means was the vertical waterwheel, first exploited, if in somewhat rudimentary form, before the Christian era.[5] Until the age of steam it had no rivals when it came to the supply of concentrated intensive mechanical power, far beyond the capacity of any windmill. As one engineer, Biringuccio, noted in 1540, 'the lifting power of a [water] wheel is much stronger and more certain than that of a hundred men'.[6] Its power comes from the natural flow of an inland waterway, which is itself the result of gravity. This is then harnessed to drive a vertical wheel on a horizontal shaft located on the outside wall of a substantial building of standard design. The mill house design is universal throughout the western world, as are the proportions of the building, and – except to the eye of an experienced millwright – the same is substantially true of the machinery it contains.[7] The possible uses of a watermill are much the same as those of a windmill, with the critical, if inherently obvious exception of pumping water. Much more than with windmills, watermills can vary very greatly in size, according to the task to be performed, and to the rate of flow of the stream providing the power.

Long before the end of the eighteenth century, the 'overshot' waterwheel had become standard, largely as the result of a number of experiments carried out in the late 1750s by John Smeaton (1724–92), the 'father' of modern civil engineering. His results, published in 1759, were widely accepted and greatly influenced the future design of watermills. In the years after 1759, Smeaton (whose improvements to Newcomen's atmospheric engine are related in chapter two) was responsible for the construction of forty-three mills incorporating his overshot waterwheels. One of these, at John Roebuck's Carron Company ironworks near Falkirk, which was completed in 1769, generated the essential draught of air required by Scotland's first coke-fired blast furnace, adapting the model established by Abraham Darby II in England. The Carron Company, which was at the forefront of the British industrial revolution, prospered through its development and production of a new short-range and short barrelled naval cannon, the cannonade, which helped it become one of the largest iron works in Europe in the nineteenth century.[8]

The problem with overshot waterwheels was to find locations where a waterway could be dammed to provide a sufficient difference in water levels, above and below the dam, to allow for efficient operation. At the higher level – at some distance before the dam – a flow of water, sufficient to turn the waterwheel, was diverted along a wooden canal supported by trestles,[9] which ended just above the top of the waterwheel. Gravity then ensured a cascade of water powerful enough to turn the wheel. The water not required for the waterwheel was left to flow into what is variously known as a sluice or a race[10] – to follow its natural course to the lower level. There its flow would join that of the water used to drive the wheel.

A waterwheel has two key dimensions: first its diameter, which *a fortiori* is determined by the difference between the water levels above and below the mill, and second, its width, which is determined by the volume of water – measured as so many cubic feet per second – available. As a rough guide, it can be taken that for economic operation the diameter must be at least twelve feet, and the width, two feet. The diameter, in turn, decides how far upstream from the mill the water backup necessary to turn the waterwheel extends. This is also a question of the contours of the land through which the waterway flows. The matter is critical since it determines the location of the first possible site, upstream, for another mill. Where there is considerable local demand for the power provided by watermills, they will tend to be sited as close to each other as is possible allowing for the need for every one to have a sufficient backup of water.

The best place to study this phenomenon is in the eastern United States, where the use of water power goes back to colonial times. Although watermills were used for providing mechanical power from 1710 to 1940, the peak development, from 1780 to 1860, coincided almost exactly with that of the Industrial Revolution; the fact that in 1840 there were more than 65,000 watermills in some 872 counties reflects the scale of operations. Far from being evenly distributed, the watermills' locations were concentrated in certain areas, such as the 'mid-Atlantic Piedmont region . . . where stream gradients are conducive to milldam construction and shipping ports of the Coastal Plain are in close proximity'.[11]

The greatest concentration was reached in the drainage area of the Brandywine River in south-east Pennsylvania where the 1840 US Manufacturing Census lists 379 water-powered operations. Although stream gradients were relatively low, the general use of small diameter waterwheels[12] allowed mills to be sited at distances varying between 2.4 km and 5 km along the rivers in the drainage area.[13] The power provided was used for a number of different purposes; in addition to sawmills and gristmills, there were sixty watermills for the manufacture of paper, and the Hopewell Iron Foundry, in using a waterwheel to power the draught of air required for its operations, was doing no more than follow standard practice.[14]

Until well into the nineteenth century, the developing economy of North America relied on waterwheels for almost all its power – even for major operations such as the United States Federal Arsenals at Harpers Ferry in Virginia and Springfield in Massachusetts – but by the end of the eighteenth century such reliance was becoming extremely problematic in Great Britain. As the scale of industrial enterprise increased, finding locations on natural waterways suitable for watermills of sufficient power became increasingly difficult. When Richard Arkwright, in 1771, decided to build his vast mechanized cotton-spinning mill at Cromford, the suitability of the location for a large-scale watermill was a major factor in choosing this particular site adjacent to the River Derwent. Even so, in a region with relatively high average rainfall he was soon constrained to use steam power to pump water from downstream back to the reservoir above the mill. With this problem confronting other manufacturers besides Arkwright, the topography of British waterways threatened to become a critical factor in determining the location of new industry. As a result, sites well located in terms of access to markets or raw materials were in increasing measure ruled out for want of power.

In the one critical case – pumping water out of flooded mines – both wind and water were bound to fail as a source of power. Wind power could never meet the need for continuous operation, while water power was ruled out by the fact that the highest point of the whole complex of shafts and galleries constructed for exploiting a mine was the only possible site for the pumping machinery. So long as the essential mining operation was on a small scale, such as was the case with the tin and copper mines of Cornwall, the power of horses turning a purpose-built 'horse capstan' was sufficient to pump out such groundwater as accumulated in the underground workings. If this was common practice in the mining of base metals for almost the whole of the eighteenth century, it was clear, even at the beginning of the century, that it did not measure up to the demands of coal mining. Although this shortcoming was dealt with by the invention of Thomas Newcomen's atmospheric steam engine, a word must still be said about the economic background in the history of coal mining.

Coal and Coke

Even before the end of the sixteenth century it was becoming apparent that Britain, while long on coal and iron, was short on wood and water. True, a superficial survey of Britain might suggest that both wood and water were abundant in almost every part of the kingdom, but appearances were misleading. Taking first the case of wood, British resources – as in almost any other part of the world – consisted almost entirely of natural growth, rather than plantations. Wood from British forests had diverse uses, with the construction of buildings, machinery and ships competing with the demand for fuel, both for domestic use, and – as often or not in the form of charcoal – for industry (which, at least until well into the eighteenth century, was mainly to be found in cottages rather than factories).[15]

London led the way not only in recognizing a critical shortage of wood as a fuel,[16] but also in accepting that coal was a viable alternative. Coal was abundant in many regions, which were sufficiently accessible as to justify investment in the transport infrastructure needed to ensure that it reached places where the demand was greatest. In economic terms this linked the coalfields of north-east England to London. A steadily expanding system of wagonways enabled coal to be transported from the mines to rivers,[17] notably the Tyne and the Wear, which were navigable by sea going vessels; they then took a North Sea route to London down the east coast of Britain.

If conversion to coal solved the problem of domestic heating where wood from local forests was in short supply (as it was in London), the position in regard to charcoal, whose on-site manufacture devastated forests at an alarming rate, was more complicated, because coal from the mines was no substitute for it. The answer, by the middle of the eighteenth century, was to convert coal to coke, in a process analogous to the production of charcoal from wood.[18] By this time, however, the exploitation of Britain's abundant coal resources was frustrated by a hazard that established sources of mechanical power were unable to overcome.

As the demand for coal increased, mines went deeper. Inevitably, beyond a certain critical level, they were flooded by groundwater. The rich seams were there, but they were unworkable. By the end of the seventeenth century the problem was acute, and although pumping machinery had evolved to a state where, in principle, it should have been able to deal with flooded mines, in practice the horse capstan provided the only power available to drive. Although this method was still used, occasionally, until well into the nineteenth century, the quantity of water that had to be pumped out of an economically viable mine was more than horses could manage. What was possible for tin and copper was next to impossible for coal, which, by its nature as a combustible fuel, had to be won from mines producing in far greater quantities; where a mine's output of tin and copper was measured in pounds, output of coal was measured in tons. Similar proportions governed the volume of water to be pumped out, but teams of horses could never be multiplied on the same basis.

When it came to power, the inevitable location of the entrances to mineshafts high above the level of local rivers meant that coal – or for that matter any other mineral dug out of the ground – could be run downhill under gravity, a practice established in continental Europe at least a century before it was adopted by British coalmines.[19] This explains the development of the earliest railways centuries before the era of steam locomotion. All that was then needed was a navigable waterway at the bottom of the hill – not a great problem in early eighteenth-century Britain, provided that the mine itself was productive enough to justify this sort of infrastructure. Here the most formidable obstacle – flooding – largely disappeared with the adoption of Newcomen's atmospheric engine.

Iron and Steel

Before the end of the sixteenth century, British iron-founding was already emerging as a capitalist industry, with the ironmaster at the head of each separate foundry employing workmen, earning a fixed wage, dependent upon him for both markets and raw materials. While the industry has changed very considerably since then in its scale of operations and their concentration at a very small number of sites, the basic technology is substantially as it was before the industrial revolution. The same is true of its essential raw material, iron ore, or as it was known in the eighteenth century, 'ironstone'. In the course of the century there was, however, one critical and substantial change; coal (or coke made form coal by much the same process as charcoal is made from wood) replaced charcoal as the fuel used in the smelting process that separated iron from the ironstone. The result of this change was an industry supplied mainly by cheap and abundant materials, produced almost entirely in Britain, in place of costly materials which – even when not imported – were becoming increasingly scarce.[20] This transformation greatly extended the uses of iron both in construction and in the implements made from it. By the end of the century its extension to wrought iron, as well as to the standard cast iron, was a major development in an industry previously dependent on bar iron imported mainly from Sweden.

There is essentially only one way to make iron, and that is to apply intense heat to the ore in which it is found. Until the second half of the eighteenth century, this process still took place in furnaces – often of very considerable size – burning charcoal. These were 'scattered all over the country from the Scottish Highlands to the Weald of Kent, wherever there was a sufficiently large woodland to supply their voracious need for charcoal'.[21] Although in Britain such dispersion was already a critical constraint in the mid-eighteenth century, it was not so in the American colonies, where woodlands were plentiful and local populations relatively small; charcoal-burning for the Cornwall Iron Foundry, opened in southern Pennsylvania in 1742, required, at the peak of production, an acre of woodland for every day of operation, so that by the time it was shut down in the late nineteenth century its operation had consumed in all some 10,000 acres. Devastation on this scale was never going to be possible in Britain. What is more, the fact that in Britain iron ore and coal were often to be found in the same geological strata was an extra incentive, if any were needed, to convert from charcoal to coal.

This was easier said than done. Coal, as it comes from the mine, invariably contains volatile elements that rule out its effective use in iron founding. Charcoal overcomes this obstacle simply as a result of the process by which it is manufactured; this in turn points the way to solving the problem with coal. Submitting coal to extremely high temperatures – up to 2,000°C – not only drives out the volatile elements but also agglomerates the residue into a solid fuel suitable for an iron furnace. In principle the result is coke; not all coals produce this result, however, and some that do may still not measure up because of residual impurities, of which sulphur is the most obnoxious.

Where, in modern times, advanced chemical technology could accurately identify suitable coking coals, the eighteenth century had to rely on trial and error, though in practice this was still sufficient to reach adequate production levels at coalmines exploited to meet the needs of iron founders. The drawback to coke is that efficient combustion is much harder to attain than it is with charcoal.

To understand this critical limitation one must look at the manner of operation of blast furnaces used to produce iron. In material terms three things are needed: iron ore, flux and fuel. In addition a very strong draught of air is needed to ensure the heat necessary for the chemical reaction which fuses these three elements together. The whole process takes place in a roughly pear-shaped furnace, with a charge-hole open at the top and a crucible to receive the molten iron at the bottom. Some distance above the crucible, a pipe, known as a *tuyère*, provides for the input of air from a vast bellows.

Before beginning operation, small trolleys, fully loaded with either a mixture of ore and flux (the latter generally consisting of either limestone, or its essential chemical constituent, lime) or fuel, whether charcoal or coke, run gently downhill, under gravity, along a charging ramp to supply the furnace with the essential raw materials. The furnace then fills with the mixture of ore and flux, with the fuel on top of it. This is then set alight, and, helped by the draught of air from the bellows, a raging inferno is created, to be kept alight indefinitely to ensure continuous production.

Once underway, the noise created by this process, as it roars out of the charging hole, can be heard up to a mile away, and the light of the flames can be seen as far as five miles away.[22] The crucible at the lowest level of the furnace then fills with molten iron, which in turn is covered by a layer of slag – which is lighter in weight – compounded out of the flux and the unwanted elements present in the ore.

Once the molten iron in the crucible has reached a critical level it is tapped, to flow out of the furnace into a flat pig bed filled with sand,[23] and moulded so as to allow the stream of iron to settle into two rows of 'pigs', where it is cast into standard solid forms. These, when sufficiently cool, are removed to store, so that the pig bed can be reconstituted and the whole process repeated. At the same time, the slag is tapped at a higher level on the other side of the furnace, to become a by-product – with various low grade uses – of the whole process. Plainly, if the molten iron and slag were not removed, they would combine to reach a critical level at which the *tuyère* would be blocked, and the fire die down. This, needless to say, is never allowed to happen. On the contrary, as the molten iron and slag are removed, new wagonloads bringing either ore and limestone or fuel – as required – continue to feed the furnace. Continuous operation is essential if the process is to be economically viable.

For as long as iron founding was fuelled by charcoal, ironworks were confined to well wooded areas, where – by the eighteenth century – maintaining charcoal burning as a sustainable long term operation had become increasingly problematic. Two factors then constrained ironmasters to move their operations, as woodlands inevitably in the long run – were depleted. First, charcoal was so brittle that it was virtually non-transportable;[24] second, every ton of iron produced required up to ten tons of charcoal.

The challenge to substitute coke for charcoal was taken up by Abraham Darby I (1678–1717) some time around 1710. Darby, the first of three generations in his family to become an ironmaster, had originally worked with brass in Bristol, but in 1706 he conceived of the idea that he would do better by broadening his operations and relocating them in Coalbrookdale, in Shropshire, some 120 miles up the River Severn, where he had leased a semi-derelict blast furnace. There, as his account book for 1709–10 relates, he successfully used coke instead of charcoal to fuel the furnace. Even before the end of the seventeenth century, others had attempted the same transformation, and if they failed, Darby almost certainly learnt from their mistakes. Although he too had problems, these were resolved with such success that he was able to open a second blast furnace in 1715[25] – and he would certainly have proceeded further but for his untimely death in 1717.

The family did not let Abraham Darby I down. His son-in-law, Richard Ford, kept on the foundry until his son, Abraham Darby II (1711–63), was ready to start working there in 1728, going on to become a full partner in 1738. The two Coalbrookdale blast furnaces continued to operate with coke, ironstone and limestone supplied by local mining partnerships, and in 1743 Darby, to ensure continuous operation, installed a Newcomen atmospheric engine to pump the water that had driven the waterwheels – which powered the bellows providing the essential blast of air required by the furnace – back to the reservoir above the foundry. The pig iron was used mainly in-house for making cast iron household utensils, which were then sold wholesale to ironmongers throughout the West Midlands and the Welsh borders.

At the same time, Coalbrookdale became the principal manufacturer of cast iron cylinders for steam engines[26] in coalmines throughout Britain. This was only the beginning of a programme of expansion and innovation. A contemporary record of Abraham Darby II in 1753, in which he records spending six nights and days busy with experiments at the Coalbrookdale furnaces, suggests that he achieved a significant breakthrough in metallurgical technology.[27] This could then explain the fact that between 1755 and 1757 the partners blew in four new coke-fired blast furnaces at a new site two miles from Coalbrookdale, having leased mining rights and then worked the mines through sub-contractors. They were then led to marketing surplus coal to local brickworks and lime kilns, as well as constructing wooden railways such as had long been in use in the coalmines along the Rivers Tyne and Wear in north-east England. A forge was also set up to produce blooms, bars and plates of wrought iron for the market – possibly the first time this result was achieved with a coke-fired furnace.

In 1762 the partners also agreed to act as agent for selling the quality steam engine cylinders produced by John Wilkinson, who was to become the most successful ironmaster of the eighteenth century – and in 1775 the only manufacturer meeting the exact specifications of James Watt for the Soho Manufactory in Birmingham.

Abraham Darby II, who died in 1763, stands above his contemporaries in mid-eighteenth century Britain for his gift of combining managerial skills with technological innovation – an example later followed by Richard Arkwright in cotton spinning. Unlike Arkwright, he was described as 'small and slight of stature', and being, like all his relations, a Quaker, he was – if never as successful as Arkwright in material terms – a much easier man to deal with.

After his death, Abraham Darby II's operations at Coalbrookdale continued under the management of his son, Abraham Darby III (1750–89), now remembered mainly for the iron bridge – the first of its kind in the world – constructed across the River Severn, using cast iron from the same furnace as that in which Abraham Darby I had first used coke instead of charcoal in 1709. A cost overrun of some 500 per cent on the construction of this great monument of the Industrial Revolution – for which the original idea came from John Wilkinson and Thomas Pritchard, a Shrewsbury architect – apparently left Abraham Darby III hard up. His financial difficulties, however, could equally have been the result of his lifestyle; a comfortably furnished house,[28] luxuries bought from craftsmen in London and Bristol, the regular consumption of wine and Fry's[29] chocolate, his scientific experiments, hunting for fossils – on occasion exchanged with Erasmus Darwin – and keeping two spaniels as gun dogs. Although, at his death, his farm stock and the contents of his house had to be sold, the Darby family continued as ironmasters at Coalbrookdale until well into the nineteenth century.[30]

Although conversion to coke greatly increased production of cast iron with useful economies of scale, for many purposes wrought iron or steel was still required. Because savings in production costs were passed on to the consumer, a variety of household utensils, such as pots and pans, together with 'gates . . . nails, joists [and] pipes', which had previously been made of wrought iron, came to be made of cast iron instead. This was not possible however with 'plough-shares, hoes, tools of all kinds, locks and bolts and stirrup bits', for which only wrought iron was suitable.[31] The problem was exacerbated with cutlery and other steel goods, for which British iron ores were unsatisfactory; for such purposes ore of a suitable grade was imported from the continent, mainly from Sweden.[32]

This was also true of much of the bar iron needed for conversion to wrought iron. In metallurgical terms, the key factor was the chemical composition of residual material, comprising up to about 5 per cent of the whole, left in the iron after smelting. This depended both on the ore itself, whose composition varied from one region to another, and on the residual elements in the coal left after coking – of which sulphur, once again, caused the most problems.

For every type of iron or steel, trial and error had, even before the eighteenth century, led to a considerable practical knowledge of the location of the best sources of both coal and ore. Portsmouth, the site of the Royal Navy's most important dockyard, was a major user of wrought iron, a much more advanced industrial product. As with cast iron, the need to produce wrought iron independently of the availability of charcoal became every day more critical, and for much the same reasons. Production was a two stage process; the first stage, smelting, was the work of a blast furnace; the second, fining, was the work of a forge. By the end of the eighteenth century both stages were adapted to coke. Although the transition is difficult to trace in detail, by the end of the 1780s as much of the bar iron supplied to forges was made with coke as it was with charcoal. This result, however, depended upon a key innovation: the introduction of a refinery furnace between the operations of the blast furnace and those of the forge.[33]

The new intermediate stage was defined by the introduction of the reverberatory furnace[34] which, fuelled by coke, converted 'grey' or cast iron, into 'white' or wrought iron. The characteristic operation of a reverberatory furnace, keeps separate the burning fuel in the firebox from the metal smelted in the hearth. The heat required by the hearth is the result either of radiation, reflected from the roof of the furnace, or of convection brought about by contact with the hot exhaust gases from the fire. Here bituminous coal, rather than coke, is better than coke as a source of radiant heat. The smelting process, by its nature, largely prevents the impurities contained in the coal from mixing with the metal – a result that cannot be avoided with a blast furnace.

From 1760 onwards, patents granted for furnaces in which 'direct contact with iron and fuel was avoided',[35] led to the introduction of a number of industrial processes producing wrought iron for specific applications, such as the manufacture of nails. Here Richard Reynolds, in a letter of 1784, wrote that the nail trade, 'would have been lost to this country had it not been found practical to make nails with iron made with pit coal'. He clearly saw this as only the first stage, noting that 'we now have another process to attempt, and that is to make bar iron with pit coal . . .'[36]

In fact, the essential breakthrough had already been made by Henry Cort (1740–1800), who, as a young 'navy agent' in London, realized at an early age the need for improving the quality of the wrought iron required for naval ordnance. As a result of a fortunate marriage in 1768 to Elizabeth Haysham, the niece of William Atwick, owner of a forge at Gosport, just outside the naval base of Portsmouth, he was able, first, to invest in this enterprise, and then, in 1776, to take over its management. With his own mill at Fontley, in the same neighbourhood, Cort began to experiment with rolling and refining iron, a promising enterprise given the proximity of the naval dockyard. This led, in 1783, to a patent for the use of grooved rolls by which malleable bar iron, of a higher quality than that attained by forge hammers, could also be produced at a much faster rate.

A year later, in 1784, Cort took out another patent, this time for the use of coal for decarburizing pig iron (usually supplied by iron founders), so as to convert it into malleable iron bars. To achieve this result Cort used a reverberatory furnace, fuelled by pit coal, to produce a crucible of melted pig iron, which could be stirred by long rods introduced through apertures in the wall of the furnace. At a certain stage, indicated by the emission of a bluish 'flame or vapour', the melted iron was ready for an operation known as 'puddling'; skilled workmen standing close to the outside of the furnace, engaged in a process of 'raking, separating, stirring and spreading' the melted iron in such a way that it could be 'collected together in lumps, called loops, in sizes suited for the intended uses'. These were removed, at welding heat, to pass first under a forge hammer to be shingled into half blooms, and then through rollers to produce bar iron according to the specifications of end-users: '. . . by this simple process all the earthy particles are pressed out'.[37] Swedish iron ore was going to lose much of its British market.

The first joint application of the combined processes, at Richard Crawshay's Cyfarthfa ironworks in Glamorgan, came into operation in the late 1780s. This was only the beginning. Further success came when, in April 1789, the Navy Board, advertising for tenders for the supply of bar iron – to be used mainly for the making of anchors – stipulated manufacture according to Cort's patents.

Fate, however, was soon to overtake the inventor. In developing the use of his patents, Cort had taken on as a partner Samuel Jellicoe, son of Adam Jellicoe, deputy paymaster to the Royal Navy. Given the prospective finance promised by Samuel this seemed like a sound business alliance, but the money in fact came from sums wrongly advanced by Adam Jellicoe out of official navy funds. In 1788 the Admiralty discovered this and in August 1789 claimed to recover the vast sum of £27,500 from Cort who, as a partner of Samuel Jellicoe, was equally liable to repay it. Although the partnership's business had thrived, its assets were still insufficient to pay its debts. With his property and goods claimed by the Admiralty, he had nothing left to satisfy the remaining creditors and so was declared bankrupt in October 1789. Cort's debts were paid by his friends, who in 1794 also secured for him a government pension of £200 per annum. Nonetheless he remained an undischarged bankrupt until his death in 1800, leaving his wife Elizabeth, together with thirteen children, to survive him.

'Rolling' and 'puddling', the innovations in the production of wrought iron introduced by Cort, revolutionized the British iron industry. Following processes introduced by Crawshay, this was particularly true of South Wales, which in the last twenty-odd years of the eighteenth century became a major producer, mainly on the initiative of entrepreneurs from England who wished to capitalize not only on the vast local reserves of iron and steel but also on their accessibility to markets.[38]

In contrast to the considerable progress achieved by iron founders by the end of the eighteenth century, that of the steel industry, although significant, was relatively unimpressive. In its early days the industry owed much to an immigrant community of German steelworkers and sword makers in the neighbourhood of Newcastle – a location more convenient than any other for the importation of bar iron, the essential raw material for steel, from Sweden. The so called 'Newcastle' steel, which was suitable for making cutlery, shears and edge tools,[39] became the British standard in an industry that in the early eighteenth century shifted its base to Sheffield. That the name of this city would soon become associated with steel of the highest quality was largely the single-handed achievement of a clockmaker from nearby Doncaster.

Benjamin Huntsman, a man who, in spite of his very English name, was of German or Dutch ancestry, was intent on finding a better material for springs and pendulums. Before Huntsman's day the production of steel involved a two stage process working with Swedish bar iron. In the first stage, the alternative layers of bar iron and charcoal were packed into stone boxes, to be heated in a furnace for an entire week. The result was bars of 'blister' steel, of variable quality, which, in the second stage, were tied together in bundles, reheated and hammer-forged, to produce 'shear' steel. Because this process, known as 'cementation', was developed in Germany, the country had become Europe's main exporter of steel.

This was not good enough for Huntsman. To bypass cementation he developed a process, derived from his experience as a brass founder, by which, after some ten to twelve clay crucibles had been brought to white heat[40] in a furnace, they were each charged with something over 30 pounds of blister steel, in one pound lumps, together with a suitable quantity of flux. The result was comparable to that achieved in a standard iron foundry. In this case, however, there was no continuous operation: instead, after three hours in the furnace, the unwanted impurities, having fused with the flux, were skimmed off, with the molten steel then remaining in the crucibles ready to be poured into ingots. This final stage then produced the uniform high quality 'crucible' steel ingots which opened the way for Sheffield to grow from a small town into a leading industrial city with a worldwide reputation based on this single product.

Huntman's success was largely the result of his producing a clay suitable for the crucibles – capable of withstanding great heat for several hours – which his manufacturing process required. This new crucible steel was not only ideal for the watch springs and tools required by Huntsman's fellow clockmakers, but also for razors, penknives and other tools with a fine edge. By this stage Huntsman, although still selling cutlery and tools on a small scale, was concerned mainly to supply other manufacturers. When, locally, they proved to be reluctant buyers, custom was successfully sought abroad, from Paris to St Petersburg and any number of places in between.[41] Even in England, outside Sheffield, needle-makers in Redditch and Matthew Boulton in Birmingham became important users of Huntsman's steel.[42] Where the industry failed, however, was in producing steel on a large scale for industrial use; this had to wait until the middle of the nineteenth century, when, as related in chapter nine, new processes – associated with names such as Bessemer and Siemens – achieved this result.

4

COTTON AND WOOL: LANCASTER AND YORK

The Arkwright Empire

At 8 o'clock in the morning on Saturday, 25 June 1785, the case of *Rex* v. *Arkwright* opened in the Court of King's Bench in Westminster Hall, before Mr Justice Buller and a special jury. It was a cause célèbre; the defendant, Richard Arkwright was Britain's most successful businessman. The petitioners were business rivals, mainly from Lancashire, the county at the heart of England's cotton textile industry – and also where Arkwright himself had first set out on a business career, not in cotton spinning, where he made his fortune, but as a wig maker. Lancashire cotton spinners had long resented the way in which the fifty-three year old Arkwright seemed to hold all the good cards and to play his hand ruthlessly. The terms on which he granted licences for his latest inventions – without which no one could compete with him in Britain's expanding cotton spinning industry – were extortionate. By 1785 his competitors were ready to pay almost any price to defeat him in the law courts.

Although Arkwright had a genius for finding the right men to work with him, whether as craftsmen, foremen or business partners, his success made him more enemies than friends. If mobs burnt down his mills, he could always rebuild elsewhere; if business rivals pirated his patents, he did not hesitate to take court proceedings against them. Yet this proved to be his Achilles heel.

On that June morning in 1785, lined up against him in Westminster Hall, Arkwright's business rivals complained not so much about his business strategy, which was indeed revolutionary, but about the fees he had exacted for the right to use two pieces of textile machinery of which he claimed to be the inventor; a carding machine and the 'water-frame'. Arkwright's patent for the water-frame had been granted in 1769 and had transformed the industry of cotton spinning at a time when both the demand for its products and the supply of its raw material were rapidly increasing.

Arkwright, by pioneering the factory production of cotton yarn during the 1770s – while at the same time licensing his water-frame to competitors – was by 1780 far ahead of the field. This was what lay behind the court case in Westminster Hall, which having started at 8 o'clock on a Saturday morning, continued almost uninterrupted, under the indefatigable direction of Mr Justice Buller, until 2 o'clock the next morning. The trial, which lasted eighteen hours, was dramatic. A vast crowd of

actors included twelve of England's leading barristers –
six appearing on each side – witnesses to every stage of
Arkwright's remarkable career, and any number of other
interested parties. The trial was conducted in a corner of
a vast medieval hall,[1] where the public was free to come
and go. In the dark final hours candles provided the only
lighting, but no one was going to give up until the final
judgment came in the small hours of the morning.

Arkwright had brought the case upon himself. In 1781
he had proceeded against Charles Lewis Mordaunt, a
successful and well connected Lancashire mill owner, for
infringement of his carding patent, only to hear the Court
rule that it was void for being 'obscure and incomplete'.[2]
In 1783 he attempted to restore it by bringing an action
for infringement against a neighbour (and former High
Sheriff of Derbyshire), known throughout the county as
'Mad Peter Nightingale'. Arkwright had deliberately
chosen a soft target, and he won the action; the 1781
judgment was effectively reversed. It was to prove an
expensive and short-lived victory.

In an era without a Court of Appeal[3] other than the
House of Lords, it was no easy matter for Lancashire
cotton spinners to find the means of reversing the
Nightingale judgment. They found the right solution in
the writ of *scire facias*, by which a court could be
petitioned, in the name of Crown, to review an earlier
judgment of another court. Arkwright's victory over
Nightingale had been in the Court of Common
Pleas; the case that opened on 15 July 1785 was heard in
the King's Bench, the only court with the power to
accept the writ. The Crown's case was simple enough:
Arkwright was not the inventor of the machine he had

patented; he had stolen the roller-spinning invention from Thomas Highs through the agency of John Kay, while the crank and comb, which were essential components of the carding machine, had been invented by James Hargreaves. Conveniently for the Crown, Highs, Kay and Hargreaves' widow all testified in support of its case; like all too many others who had dealt with Arkwright they had a score to settle. At 2 o'clock on the morning of Sunday, 26 June, the jury, clearly directed by the judge, brought in a verdict for the Crown. The next morning the news reached Manchester, where it was received with general rejoicing.

But who was this Richard Arkwright, who had fallen so mightily before the forces of the law? Accepting that Britain's cotton textile industry was at the heart of the Industrial Revolution, then it must follow that he was its greatest hero. If this was the judgement of history, it was subject to many critical reservations. As any great man of his day, Arkwright left to posterity a number of portraits of himself, of which the best known, by Joseph Wright of Derby, shows, in the words of Thomas Carlyle (1795–1881), 'not a beautiful man, no romantic hero with haughty eyes, Apollo lip, and gesture like the herald Mercury; [but] a plain almost gross, bag-cheeked, potbellied Lancashire man, with the air of painful reflexion, but also copious free digestion'.[4]

Carlyle saw Arkwright as a 'Historical Phenomenon' who, by giving Britain the power of cotton, had provided the resources needed for the wars against Napoleon, in which the country was involved for almost the whole quarter century following Arkwright's death. In 1816, the year after the final defeat of Napoleon at

Waterloo, Sir Robert Peel[5] – who had been Arkwright's most formidable and successful business rival – described him as 'a man who has done more honour to the country than any man I know, not excepting our great military characters'.

Regard for Arkwright did not abate as the cotton industry continued to expand; in *North and South*, Elizabeth Gaskell's remarkable portrayal of a northern mill town at the beginning of the railway age, the mill owner (and one of the novel's leading characters), John Thornton, thinking aloud about his own livelihood, places it in the context of the 'great future . . . concealed in that rude model of Sir Richard Arkwright's'.[6] A short anonymous poem quoted at the head of the following chapter[7] (although not intended by Mrs Gaskell to refer to Arkwright) presents, nonetheless, a remarkably accurate summary of the sort of man he was:

There's iron, they say, in all our blood,
And a grain or two perhaps is good;
But his, he makes me harshly feel,
Has got a little too much of steel.

What was so distinctive about Britain's cotton industry in the middle of the eighteenth century? Why did Arkwright, as a young man, become involved in it? How then did he transform it – or in other words, what was the 'rude model' which John Thornton had in mind? Although in answering these questions other actors entered the stage, Arkwright never lost his leading role.

At the turn of the eighteenth century, the cotton industry was so backward and small that, unless protected, it could not compete, either in quality or price, with Indian calicoes and muslins.[8] By the end of the century it had become, in the words of one noted economist,[9] 'the original leading sector in the first take-off' of the Industrial Revolution, or to quote the Marxist historian Eric Hobsbawm, 'whoever says the Industrial Revolution says cotton'.[10]

Cotton is a natural fibre derived from a plant unsuited to cultivation in the temperate climates of northern Europe. Until well into the seventeenth century this meant that raw cotton for textiles made in Europe was imported mainly from such countries as Egypt and India. At this stage England was only just beginning to spin its own cotton yarn, which was used mainly to produce fustian, a cloth made with a linen warp and a cotton weft.[11] This was a cheap cloth, which, with the increasing urbanization of Britain, found its main market among men from the industrial working classes, such as Nick Higgins, introduced in *North and South* to represent the hands employed by John Thornton. While at this low end of the market it competed on price with pure linen cloth, the fact that it was no threat to wool and worsted at the quality end of the market meant, in the eighteenth century, that those who produced for this market did not see its manufacture as a threat. At this stage also, British spinners were unable to produce cotton thread strong enough to be used as warp – a deficiency which had to be overcome if weavers were ever to produce a pure cotton cloth.

Arkwright was born in Preston in 1732 and educated there. He first carried on his original trade as a barber in Bolton, some twenty miles to the south, on the way to

Manchester. The town was widely known as a 'Staple for fustians of divers sorts ... from all parts of the Country'.[12] Following his first marriage, five years after first coming to Bolton in 1750, he acquired as a brother-in-law Thomas Wood, a fustian weaver who, in 1776, was to take out a patent 'for carding and roving silk, cotton and sheep's wool'.[13] Although Arkwright's first wife died in 1756, the contact was maintained even after he married for a second time, in 1761. A year later he expanded his activities by becoming, first, a not very successful innkeeper, next, a skilful and highly regarded maker of wigs, and last, but not least, an inventor bent on developing a machine to spin cotton by rollers.

Even as a young man, Arkwright was known for his inventiveness and genius for mechanics. In Bolton he was able to realize that the introduction of large-scale mechanical spinning of cotton would greatly increase the production of fustian. What is more, if stronger yarn could be spun, the way would be open to produce pure cotton cloth. All this was sufficient incentive for Arkwright to turn his hand to invention, and with the help of a smith and a clockmaker he produced a prototype of the roller-spinning machine that would later make his fortune, at the same time transforming the British textile industry.

From the middle of the eighteenth century the process of spinning became an obstacle to the increase of production in the cotton textile industry. With the introduction of John Kay's flying shuttle (patented in the early 1730s), weavers just did not have enough thread to produce the standard wide cloth.[14] Little is known about John Kay, but for a Lancashire man from Bury, the 1730s

– when wool and worsted still accounted for the lion's share of English textiles – were not a good time for promoting a new invention. To judge from the way a mob of angry weavers wrecked John Kay's house in 1753, hand loom weavers apparently saw little future in increased production of fustian.

That the turbulent events of the 1750s were only the beginning of John Kay's troubles can be seen from a letter, with a much later date, written by his son to Richard Arkwright, relating how he 'was obliged to leave his native Country haveing spent large sums in lawsuits in defending his Patent against a combination of Weavers who had an intention to murder him, and it was with some difficulty that a workman he imploy'd escap'd with his live by being put in a Pack of Wool'.[15] If this was not encouraging to other inventors in the realm of textiles, the steady growth of the cotton industry not only led to wider adoption of the flying shuttle, but also encouraged those who made their living by spinning to look for ways of transforming their industry as Kay had done for weaving – taking care, at the same time, to avoid the trials that had forced him into exile. Richard Arkwright's success exceeded that of any rival. The first breakthrough came with the development – generally attributed to James Hargreaves[16] – of the spinning jenny in the 1760s.

The basic operation of the spinning jenny was that of the long established spinning wheel. Instead of a single spindle, the mechanical system of the jenny enabled a great number – more than a hundred by the 1790s[17] – to operate with a single supervisor. Inevitably the jenny, being cheap both to build and to house, was widely adopted, so much so that one manufacturer described its success in these words: 'From the year 1770 to 1788 a complete change had gradually been effected in the spinning of yarns. That of wool had disappeared altogether and that of linen was also nearly gone; cotton, cotton, cotton was become the universal material for employment'.[18]

The jenny, however, suffered from the same drawback as the spinning wheels it replaced; it could only work with coarse yarn, rated at a maximum of little more than 20 hanks (of 840 yards) to the pound.[19] If this was good enough for the weft of fustian (which by definition, had a warp of some other fibre, generally linen), there was no future for the jenny in an industry destined to produce high quality textiles with ratings measured in the 100s. What is more, the jenny, being mainly intended to make the work of domestic spinners more productive, was designed to be operated by hand. Later, with jennies built on a larger scale, this proved impractical, though horse power was still sufficient to drive them.

For Richard Arkwright this was not good enough. During 1767 he set about constructing a roller-spinning machine in Warrington, where he was assisted by none other than John Kay. Once the machine was completed, Arkwright took it first to Manchester, and then during the early months of 1768 – still accompanied by Kay – to Preston, his home town. At this stage Arkwright, for sound business reasons, decided to leave Preston and exploit his invention (which he patented in 1769) in Nottingham, where, in a converted brewery, and with a number of partners and a labour force consisting of John Kay,[20] a smith and a watch-tool maker, he set about installing a working roller-spinning machine. Arkwright had taken the greatest care in selecting his employees, knowing that any machine on the scale he envisaged could only operate satisfactorily if its numerous and intricate moving parts met the highest technological standards. This practice, to which he always held firm, was a major factor in his capacity constantly to outperform business rivals.

In 1771, with the new Nottingham mill still in its experimental stage, Arkwright decided to start again from scratch with a new purpose-built mill at Cromford, on the River Derwent,[21] some twenty-eight miles northwest of the city. This was a momentous decision, for where the Nottingham mill was powered by horses turning a capstan, Cromford was powered by water, allowing it to operate on a much larger scale. There, according to their lease, they had 'full and free Liberty Power and Authority . . . to Erect and Build one or more Mill or Mills for Spinning Winding or throwing Silk Worsted Linen Cotton or other Materials and also such and so many Waterwheels Warehouses Shops Smithies and other Buildings Banks and Dams Gails Shuttles and other Conveniences as they should think proper for the effectual Working the said Mills'.[22] Unwittingly, the conveyancer had drawn a charter for the Industrial Revolution.

Pride, as ever, goes before a fall. Until 1781 Arkwright, ever expanding his business operations, had the world of factory spinning – based on his water-frame – more or less to himself. It was not a peaceful world, particularly in Arkwright's home county of Lancashire. There, in 1779, he opened a new spinning mill at Birkacre, where by the autumn of that year 'part of the numbers of Spindles agreed for were at Work ... making Yarn or Thread of a superior Quality to any now spun from Cotton'. At a time when trade was bad as a result of the American Civil War, hand-workers of west Lancashire, who saw their livelihood in danger, revolted. On Monday, 4 October, a mob 'to the number of 4 or 5,000 with considerable Quantity of Fire Arms and other Offensive Weapons and meeting with little or no resistence ... broke into the Mill and destroyed all the Machinery then Attacked the Building with Pickaxes Hatchet & c to demolish it but at last as a shorter Method ... set fire to it had burnt it to the Ground'.[23]

By this time Arkwright had begun to sell water-frames and carding machines to potential business rivals, not only for considerable capital sums but also subject to licence fees for his patents. This was bound to be contentious, and (as related on page 81) in the Mordaunt case he lost his carding patent, although his position was in part restored by his court victory in 1783 over Peter Nightingale.

Given that the Mordaunt case had been taken to throw the carding patent open to all, it had led to a new industry in which £100,000 was invested in buildings and Arkwright machines, to provide employment for some 30,000 men, women and children. Since the terms on which Arkwright was prepared to license his patents provided for a 'Rate of 5s. Per Spindle per Annum ... if the [licensees] confine themselves to spinning by Day, and 5s. More if by Night'[24] his prospective income, at a time when spindles were already to be counted in hundreds of thousands, was simply colossal. It is not surprising then that rival cotton spinners moved heaven and earth to reverse Arkwright's victory over Nightingale.

The result was the case of 25 June 1785 at the Westminster Hall, where the judgment against Arkwright effectively placed every invention he claimed as his own in the public domain. It was, however, very late in the day; Arkwright no longer needed his patents to expand his business empire. The wealth already accumulated guaranteed him the capital required by every new venture. In a completely free market he was still stronger than any competitor – although some, such as Sir Robert Peel, were also making fortunes. By this stage also Arkwright was semi-retired; his sons had been schooled to take over and manage his business empire, which under their direction continued to flourish after his death in 1792.

Paradoxically, in the new world of cotton textiles produced by mills on the same vast scale as those built by Arkwright at Cromford, the cotton yarn essential to it was produced not by the water-frame (the machine whose invention was contested in the King's Bench in 1785) but by another spinning machine, Samuel Crompton's mule, which, combining the water-frame's advantages with those of the spinning jenny, explains the name given to it. Where the water-frame was designed to spin cotton yarn suitable for warp, the jenny produced yarn for weft: that the mule could spin yarn suited to both purposes, in a factory operation, was the main reason for the success of an invention that was never superseded.

Crompton, born in a village near Bolton in 1753, started his working life as a weaver when only eleven years old. At the age of fifteen he attempted to produce yarn suitable for warp, using a recently acquired spinning jenny – a breakthrough, which if successful, would enable the production of pure cotton cloth in place of fustian. This was first achieved some five years later in 1773, though not by Crompton. But this did not lead him to give up; indeed, he devoted almost the whole of the 1770s to inventing and then constructing a spinning machine that would overcome the limitations of the jenny. The prototype, constructed in 1778–9 to combine the spindles of the jenny with the rollers of the water-frame, was a forty-eight spindle machine used by Crompton to spin both warp and weft for his own use. At a time when riots were proceeding across Lancashire, to reach Bolton in October 1779, Crompton, who was naturally self-effacing – the very opposite of Arkwright – concealed his invention, which he never patented.

The mule's greatest advantage was its capacity to produce yarns almost as fine as those imported from the hand spinners of Bengal. By enabling both Lancashire and Scotland to weave muslin that could compete with Bengal, it created a whole new cottage industry in the 1780s, producing for the top end of the market. The much larger bottom end of the market, where Arkwright and rival mill owners made their fortunes, still operated with water-frames and spinning jennies, but the inherent superiority of Crompton's mule was bound to tell in the long run. Peter Drinkwater built the first mule mill in Manchester in 1789, complete with carding engines powered by steam. The use of a steam engine for driving a mule is first recorded, also in Manchester, in 1797,[25] although, as early as 1792, a mule driven by a water-wheel had been introduced in Lanarkshire.

By this time the mule was steadily moving down-market; if progress was relatively slow, it was because of the intricate operations required of the mule spinners. These highly skilled working men organized the first British craft union in 1792 – another breakthrough in industrial history.

In 1810 Crompton himself undertook the first census of British cotton spinning. When completed in 1811 it covered 650 mills, mainly in Lancashire. It revealed that 88 per cent of nearly four million spindles counted belonged to the mules of which he was the original inventor; although there were still any number of water-frames and jennies, these were clearly on the way out. Although he lived until 1827 Crompton profited little from his invention, other than by using it as an adjunct to his own trade as a weaver, for which he invented an improved loom in 1808. In character he was everything that Arkwright was not: 'shy', 'sensitive', 'diffident' and 'unworldly', he found solace in music and an austere contemplative religion that had room neither for field sports nor for lamb, veal and new potatoes. His invention finally reached perfection at the hands of Richard Roberts (1789–1864), who in 1790 took out his first patent for an automatic, fully power driven mule. This proved to be at best a prototype. It took another forty years, and £12,000 in development costs, before he was able to sell to the market – which by 1830 extended far beyond Britain – a fully automatic, self-acting mule, based on a design which held the field until well into the twentieth century. Roberts' profits never covered the costs incurred, even when his mule was driving half a million spindles worldwide. His problem was that he devoted too much time to invention, too little to business. It was by finding the right balance between the two that Arkwright became the king of cotton.

American Cotton

Following the independence of the United States of America, established by the Treaty of Versailles in 1783, the southern states of the Union soon became Britain's major supplier of raw cotton. On both sides of the Atlantic it had long been recognized that American plantation cotton would fetch a higher price if it could be shipped as lint, free from seeds. In 1793 this became possible with the invention, by Eli Whitney, a New England schoolmaster, of a 'cotton engine', which would achieve this result mechanically. Whitney's 'cotton gin' was a machine-powered, at least in its early stages, by a horse capstan, which removed, on the plantation where it was harvested, the mass of seeds embedded in raw cotton. This meant an immediate saving in the weight of the cotton bales shipped to England, and eventually to other European destinations, with a considerable price advantage to the importers – as was immediately reflected on the trading floor of the Manchester Exchange.

Whitney's invention not only provided an incentive for plantations, in such established states as Georgia and the Carolinas, to turn to cotton from rice, indigo or tobacco, but also – and critically in the long run – encouraged the settlement of new lands in the deep south, extending as far as the Mississippi River and beyond. The way forward had already been shown by Tennessee, where cotton was already cultivated when it was admitted as a state in 1796.

Where Tennessee led, the territories along the lower Mississippi were, sooner or later, bound to follow, but the way ahead was problematic until, with the Louisiana Purchase in 1803, the whole of the lower Mississippi, except for Florida (which belonged to Spain), became American territory. By this time cotton plantations were already developing upriver from Baton Rouge in Louisiana, but expansion inland was blocked by Native Americans, who occupied a relatively small corner of south-western Mississippi, more than half of Alabama and a considerable part of western Georgia.

In 1811, a powerful northern chief, Tecumseh, encouraged the southern Native Americans to defend their rights against American settlers. At the same time the Americans had chosen their own man to make the whole territory safe for settlement. When Tennessee became a state in 1796, it elected as its first Congressman Andrew Jackson (1767–1845), a young lawyer from North Carolina. A year later the state legislature elected him as one of two senators. After only one term in Washington he returned home to become both a major general in the state militia and a successful cotton planter and slave owner on his estate outside Nashville, the state capital.

Jackson was the man sent to defeat the Native Americans in the territory south of Tennessee. In the spring of 1814, commanding some 3,300 soldiers, he won a crucial victory in Alabama at the battle of Horseshoe Bend. This allowed him to dictate the treaty of Fort Jackson, which provided for some twenty-three million acres of Native American land to be ceded to the United States. This was all open to settlers, and they would not wait long in planting cotton. Mississippi became a state of the Union in 1817 and Alabama in 1819.

The economic geography of the southern states was transformed. Along the Atlantic seaboard, South Carolina and Georgia – the states most suited for the cultivation of cotton – lacking the great navigable rivers of tidewater Virginia, had problems shipping cotton down to harbours such as Charleston and Savannah. The Mississippi river, together with any number of its navigable tributaries, provided a far more extensive transport infrastructure. New Orleans, close to the mouth of the Mississippi, was already a port that handled considerably more traffic than any of its rivals, and Mobile, where the Alabama river reached the sea, would soon outrank both Charleston and Savannah. At the same time, the introduction of steamboats – well underway by 1820 – enormously enhanced the economic potential of the whole area.

The cotton plantations then rapidly extended westwards across a wide band of territory, some distance inland from the Gulf of Mexico and known as the 'cotton belt'; where the combination of soil and climate was ideal. East of the Mississippi, western Georgia, Alabama and Mississippi joined Tennessee as major producers of cotton, followed in due course, to the west of the river, by Louisiana, Arkansas and Texas. For the new settlers one long established principle was fundamental; cotton plantations could only work with African American slaves. Although until 1807, when the British Parliament outlawed the international slave trade, followed almost immediately by the United States, the American plantations and the British cotton industry effectively combined to finance the African slave trade, its abolition did not mean the end of slavery in the United States or, for that matter, in the British West Indies. On the contrary, the fact that the slave population of the United States maintained itself by natural growth favoured the plantations against potential competitors in the Caribbean.[26] Until 1860 the labour of millions of slaves in the southern United States was not only essential to the supply of raw cotton to the European textile industry – still dominated by Britain – but also allowed the United States to become much the world's largest producer of cotton (which is still its largest agricultural export).

In Britain, the importation of raw cotton increased at a phenomenal rate – from under 10 million pounds per annum in the early 1780s to ten times as much in the 1810s and fifty times as much in the early 1840s[27] – with almost all of it coming from the United States.[28] In the thirty year period, 1791–1821, the American cotton crop rose from 2 to 182 million pounds.[29] In both the United States and continental Europe cotton textile industries took for granted the almost unlimited potential of the plantations in the American south to extend the area cultivated in cotton. As new land was opened beyond the Mississippi, production continued to increase as new states entered the Union: in the course of time Arkansas, Louisiana[30] and Texas and even Missouri, all with abundant land satisfying the geophysical conditions requisite for cotton planting, became as important as the states east of the river.[31]

Steam Power in the Cotton Industry
The vastly increased capacity of the cotton industry on both sides of the Atlantic invites the questions when, and

to what extent, it had to turn to steam power. While in the United States the abundance of water power meant that this happened at a very late stage. In England on the other hand, Arkwright inquired about the possibility of installing a reciprocating engine at Cromford as early as 1777 after visiting the Boulton & Watt Soho Factory outside Birmingham – but not apparently for the purpose of powering the water-frames. Nothing seems to have come of this, but in the 1780s Arkwright was already experimenting with steam power at his Miller's Lane mill in Manchester.[32] Somewhat unwisely he did not order his machinery from Boulton & Watt, and he was left with an engine that could only be used 'to replenish his reservoir by pumping back into it water that had already passed over the waterwheel';[33] other mills occasionally used windmills for this purpose. At least in the opinion of James Watt, expressed in a letter to his father-in-law, Arkwright did not know what he was up to when it came to steam engines:[34]

> Some years ago he applied to us at two different times for our advice which we took the trouble to give him, in one or more long letters, which he never had the manners to answer but followed his own Whims till he threw away several 1000£s and exposed his ignorance to all the world, & then in disgust gave up the scheme ... Our rotative engines which we have now rendered very complete, are certainly very Applicable to the driving of cotton mills in every case where the conveniency of plaicing the Mill in a town or ready built Manufactory will compensate for the expense of coals & of our premium.

James Watt was quite right; steam-powered rotatory engines were well suited to cotton mills, and in the vast expansion of the industry described above would become indispensable, though the process was remarkably slow and lasted well into the nineteenth century.[35] This was, moreover, in a country not particularly well endowed with water power. In countries where water power was more abundant, steam power – as already noted in the case of the United States – was much longer in coming.[36]

In the end, economic factors overcame the conservatism of industry, for, as the bottom line insistently made clear, growing demand for power was accompanied by a steady fall in the unit costs of steam and an equally steady increase in those of water. In the conversion from water to steam, Lancashire cotton mills led the way, inevitably given that the flexibility of steam power enabled it to meet – far better than water power – the needs of the industry.

When, in 1835, a statistical analysis was made, for the first time, of the relative contributions of steam and water to power cotton mills; the ratio of one to the other was, in the north of England, 4.35 to 1, whereas in the Midlands it was the other way round, at 1 to 2.74, with Scotland, at 1.3 to 1,[37] somewhere in between. What really counted, however, was that some 84 per cent of all the mills were in the north – with the great majority in Lancashire. This concentration of industry was clearly far beyond the capacity of local rivers to supply water power, and that in a region containing vast reserves of coal.

At the same time, with Richard Roberts's recently invented automatic spinning, the output of labour was nearly fifteen times as much as it had been in 1780 when, with Crompton's mule, advanced technology was first introduced to the spinning industry, and 370 times that of Indian hand spinners at the beginning of the eighteenth century.[38] The fact that the number of mule-spindles had increased from 50,000 in 1788 to 4,600,000 in 1811,[39] confirms the phenomenal growth of the industry, which, needless to say, continued until well into the nineteenth century.

During the years of spectacular advances in spinning, these were not matched by similar gains in weaving, for which efficient power operated machinery only came into use in the 1830s. This may be because power looms were technically more challenging to inventors, but at the same time the labour force of hand loom weavers was much more resistant to change, despite the poor wages paid.[40] As late as 1833, when efficient machines had finally been developed, there were still only 100,000 power looms to set off against some 250,000 hand looms.[41]

In the years that followed, up to 1850, Lancashire, with integrated cotton mills accounting for 77 per cent of the increase in steam power over the whole of England, became ever more dominant in the industry. Nonetheless, although it reached an unprecedented level of concentration and specialization,[42] in 1856 only 35 per cent of the mills were engaged in both spinning and weaving.

After 1830, the rapid expansion of the British railway network, following the opening of the line from Liverpool to Manchester in that year, inevitably accelerated the conversion of industry to steam power. The fact that locomotives could for some sixty years only be powered by steam meant that railway engineers, led by such men as Robert Stevenson and I.K. Brunel, invested heavily in improvements in the technology of steam power – a process justified economically by the vast scale of railway construction.

British industry as a whole benefited from the technological progress achieved by the railways. Even more important, railways could bring not only machinery powered by steam, but also the coal to fuel them, to almost any location chosen for new plant. By the middle of the nineteenth century, the leading sectors of British industry, such as notably the Lancashire cotton mills, were well integrated into the new transport infrastructure. Needless to say, the new railways were useful not only for bringing capital goods and raw materials to new factories, but also for distributing their production throughout the nation – and further afield.

Wool and Worsted

Although in a study of the Industrial Revolution cotton comes first, there can be no doubt that wool – from sheep grazing in any number of different areas throughout the kingdom – is the classic British natural fibre. If its origins are lost in time, the wool export economy was always important in the recorded history of Britain, while those parts of the country dependent on it were also among the most prosperous. By early modern times, the export of raw wool, mainly to the Low Countries, had yielded to the export of finished cloth – which was entirely the product of a cottage industry employing, at least for some seasons of the year and in any number of different stages, millions of Britain's rural inhabitants.

By the eighteenth century the organization of farming in England, together with the proprietary rights to the land available for it, had long ensured that certain parts of the country, favoured by the right combination of soil and climate, were used for grazing sheep, which in turn supported the local production of woollen textiles. Long before the Industrial Revolution, local economies in the West Country, East Anglia and above all the West Riding of Yorkshire, were dominated by the production of wool and woollen cloth for external markets. Local agriculture was then essential for providing both a reserve of labour for this economy, and then feeding it. Indeed, at village level, the annual cycle comprised, according to the season, both working on the land and engaging in the many different stages in the production of woollen cloth. The complete process of manufacture, starting with the seasonal shearing of the sheep and ending with cloth ready for tailors, was extremely complex. In this process, spinning and weaving, the two operations at the heart of textile production, were both intermediate stages.

Wool, before it was spun, had to be scribbled and carded, in order to lay the fibres roughly parallel. This was achieved by working the raw wool between two cards with wire teeth, one fixed to an upright frame and the other free to move across it. The importance of this operation – which was generally repeated several times with ever finer rows of teeth – can be seen by the fact that in the west of England it was a separate trade for a very substantial part of the working popu-lation – so much so that in the West Country scribblers comprised as much as 10 per cent of the adult male workforce.[43]

Significantly, a scribbling engine patented in 1775 was one of the many inventions of Richard Arkwright, who – true to his own business interests – intended it to be used for cotton, not wool. Adapting the engine to deal with wool in the 1780s encountered considerable resistance, because of the threat to local employment. According to a petition published in Leeds in 1786, the introduction of machine scribbling would put out of work some 4,000 men and another 4,000 apprentices. Even so, by the late 1780s scribbling engines were used on a large scale in the West Riding, where they were sometimes combined with spinning jennies – another adaptation from the cotton industry – in water-powered mills. In increasing measure, the scribbling engines were run by joint-stock companies owned by prosperous master clothiers, who as often as not added these new operations to the work of established fulling mills – a critical stage in transforming a cottage into a factory industry.[44]

In the 1790s, attempts by master clothiers to work the same transformation in the West Country met with considerably greater resistance: this came to a climax in 1795 when, for the second year running, a poor harvest provoked local food riots. By May the discontent had spread to the wool industry, with scribblers at Westbury demolishing two scribbling engines. By August the local authorities in Wiltshire, unable to control the unrest, were asking the War Office in London for troops to maintain law and order. Although peace was finally restored when a troop of dragoons was sent in support of the local yeomanry,[45] the master clothiers remained extremely circumspect when it came to introducing new machinery.

While a number of factors relating to the organization of local society explain why mechanization in the wool textile industry (and the resulting factory production) were acceptable, if with some early resistance, in the West Riding where they were not in the West Country, the difference was critical for the future of both parts of the country. By the turn of the nineteenth century the West Riding, with the growth of new towns such as Leeds and Huddersfield, was a largely urban society, while the West Country remained rural, as it still is 200 years later. Who today would conceive of Westbury or Frome as comparable to Leeds and Huddersfield? Yet it was only towards the end of the eighteenth century that the West Country was being overtaken by the West Riding.

Where scribbling was an early stage in the manufacture of cloth, fulling was an equally important late stage, which followed weaving. This involved two operations; scouring and thickening. The purpose of scouring was to wash out impurities, a result achieved by trampling the cloth in water containing an appropriate solvent, which by medieval times had become a clay-like material known simply as 'fuller's earth'. For thickening, the foul liquid residue left after scouring was washed out with clean water, and the cloth then beaten by wooden hammers, known as 'fulling stocks'. This was a laborious process, carried out in Britain from the twelfth century onwards by watermills. With the mechanization of scribbling at the end of the eighteenth century, a position was reached in which the intermediate processes of spinning and weaving remained a cottage industry, while the initial processing of raw wool and the finishing of cloth were carried out in mills.[46]

Cloth, once fulling was completed, still needed to be 'dressed', and as often as not by the eighteenth century, dyed, before it could be marketed as a finished product. Because dying required heavy machinery, and depended upon imported raw materials, it was from the earliest days concentrated in relatively few separate enterprises, with a strong preference for a river site providing water for use both as a solvent and as power for a mill. The relatively high level of capital then required led dyers to include dressing among the services offered. The result was the emergence – in three leading mercantile centres of the West Riding, Halifax, Wakefield and Leeds – of a specialized dressing and dying sector within the wool industry.[47] This development foreshadows, once again, the ascendancy of the West Riding in the Industrial Revolution.

By the end of the eighteenth century, with scribbling and fulling – to say nothing of dying and dressing – powered in increasing measure by watermills,[48] the way was open to follow the example of the cotton industry and use the same power for spinning and weaving. This transformation, however, did not occur until well into the nineteenth century. One reason for this is to be found in the threat to their livelihood perceived by those accustomed to working in the domestic system. The opposition to innovation was strongest in Leeds, where finishing was geographically concentrated, in contrast to Huddersfield and Halifax where labour found it difficult to organize an effective opposition.[49]

Here also, as in many other matters relating to the British woollen industry, a distinction must be made between woollen and worsted, with each sector dominant in its own particular centre. Worsted yarn, spun out of long staple wool, not only produces – as any professional tailor can explain – a quite different kind of cloth, but does so as a result of its own distinctive technology. Worsted cloth belonged to the class of the 'new draperies', introduced by Protestant immigrants from the Netherlands who were invited in 1565 to settle in Norwich in order to stimulate its trade.[50] Its name derived from the parish of Worstead, in the centre of a rural area north of the city known for its well-fed sheep with their long staple wool.[51] Pre-eminent among the so-called 'Norwich stuffs' it accounted for much of England's export trade in the seventeenth century, and contributed substantially to the prosperity of the City of London,[52] where it was actively traded on the floor of the Royal Exchange.

During the second quarter of the seventeenth century, the development of worsted production in the West Riding, to the cost of the long-established Norfolk producers, was a key factor in the Industrial Revolution. That the West Riding had developed a better business model – involving collaboration between weavers, cloth-iers, factors and merchants, working in a market focused on local cloth halls[53] – was decisive in its favour, as was also, by the end of the eighteenth century, its proximity to the cotton textile industry, which much more than wool was always in the forefront of innovation. After all, Richard Arkwright's great mill at Cromford in Derbyshire was much closer to Huddersfield and Leeds than it was to Norwich. When it came to worsted, the West Riding won over East Anglia just as, with wool, it won over the West Country.

Since, in the West Riding, worsted only came into its own in the eighteenth century, its production was 'capitalist from the start'[54] and so less hampered by the conservative grassroots forces characteristic of traditional British woollen manufacture. It also helped that worsted, as a yarn, resembled cotton much more than wool did. With its fibres much better adapted to roller-spinning by water power, the first worsted spinning mill in the West Riding opened at Addington on the River Wharfe in 1787.[55] Here the wool industry lagged far behind, so that whereas hand spinning of worsted was rare in the West Riding by the 1820s, this was far from being the case with wool. In any case there was an intermediate phase around the turn of the century, when the local abundance of underemployed female labour led to technologically advanced hand operated spinning mules, with only eighteen to twenty-four spindles, being installed domestically. But from 1818 onwards high wool prices coupled with continuous innovation in worsted spinning, with 'massive increases in the number of spindles per frame and in the amount of yarn spun per spindle',[56] meant that the domestic spinners were no longer competitive. It also meant that the weavers, who still worked at home, could absorb only a fraction of the yarn produced by the spinners; the substantial surplus production found a ready market in other textile regions, not only in Britain but also in the rest of Europe. As early as 1774, Yorkshire woollens and worsted accounted for more than half the total of exports from the entire country.[57]

The position with wool spinners was quite different. Power spinning mules only appeared after 1830, and even then their dimensions were such that they could not attain the worsted spinners' economies of scale. Because both scribbling and fulling were already water-powered, mechanized spinning of wool – when it finally came – tended to make use of the same sources of power. (The fact that worsted does not require fulling made it a quite different case.)

In this realm the great innovator was the Leeds industrialist Benjamin Gott (1762–1840), but compared to Richard Arkwright, his great rival in the cotton industry, he was nowhere. Helped by a capital sum of £3,660 provided by his wealthy father, Gott, not yet thirty, became senior partner in one of the West Riding's principal merchant houses at a time when the local cloth industry was exceptionally prosperous.[58] In 1792, Gott – doubtless inspired by what Arkwright had achieved in Cromford – built the first large-scale woollen mill in the West Riding at Bean Ing, a greenfield site just outside Leeds. By doing so he took the almost unprecedented step from being a merchant to becoming a manufacturer.

When Bean Ing opened in 1793, it contained the whole range of machinery needed to produce and finish cloth. Although some machines were powered by a specially acquired Boulton & Watt steam engine, this was not used for the jennies, looms and finishing tools. A generation later, the mule spinners Gott had installed in his Bean Ing mill were still – as late as 1813 – operated by two boys; indeed there was no power at all in the spinners' rooms.[59] Even the rebuilding of the mill, after it had been destroyed by fire in 1799, did not provide the occasion for innovation. Indeed, in the wool industry mule spinning was only power-driven following the introduction of Richard Roberts's self-acting mule, after its first successful use by cotton spinners. By the 1830s, when Roberts's mule finally came into its own, steam engines, rather than waterwheels, were just beginning to be the source of power.

Gott had extended his empire to include three mills – all close to Leeds[60] – which in 1819 together employed more than 1,000 hands. Although Gott encountered little of the resistance, often violent, that had confronted Arkwright, the entire local cloth industry at the turn of the nineteenth century was much concerned by the way that he, and a number of other merchants similarly-minded, had become factory owners. Small independent clothiers rightly saw that this, in the long term, would destroy their livelihood. In the short term Gott was able to help them, by providing scribbling and fulling services at favourable rates, while at the same time, as a merchant, buying their finished cloth. True to his original calling, he always sold three times more cloth than his own mills produced. All this, however, was comparatively short-lived.

For the West Riding as a whole, the final result, by the middle of the nineteenth century, was a vertically integrated large-scale woollen industry, owned by merchant manufacturers, with mills located in rapidly growing towns such as Halifax, with the homes of hundreds of employees lining the hills above the central industrial area. By this time there was little distinction in outward appearance between Yorkshire mill towns and those on the other side of the Pennines, in Lancashire, where the whole industry was based on cotton. Even so, in Yorkshire the domestic weavers and spinners, particularly those of wool, survived well beyond the half century. Yorkshire was still much slower to adopt steam power, even in its relatively small cotton industry. Where, in Yorkshire, at the end of the 1830s, the aggregate horse power of the watermills still exceeded that of steam, in Lancashire – home to more than half of the cotton mills in the whole of Britain – it was less than 12 per cent.[61]

In Yorkshire's much older and more conservative woollen industry, steam power had still further to go, even at a time when steam accounted for some 72 per cent of the power used by the combined British textile industry – including not only wool and cotton, but flax, jute, hemp and China grass.[62] Whatever Leeds owed to Benjamin Gott, its debt was much less than that owed by Manchester to Richard Arkwright. On the other hand, there is no doubt but that the Yorkshireman was a much more agreeable man to deal with.

5

INVENTION, INDUSTRY AND THE MANUFACTURING COMMUNITY

Factories and the Men who Owned Them
In the course of the eighteenth century the large-scale manufacture of durable consumer goods to be sold – very largely in new trading outlets such as shops[1] – far from the actual location of the factories and workshops producing them, transformed the material well-being of countless British homes. Although inevitably the most lucrative market was to be found among wealthy families, including those of the court and the nobility, factory production would only make sense in the long run if consumer demand extended to countless relatively modest households. For this favourable development two conditions had to be satisfied, and both were. The first was a steady increase in spending power reaching down to all but the poorest homes. The second was the

improvement of the transport infrastructure to a level at which unprecedentedly large quantities of goods could be safely transported over long distances. The commodities subject to both conditions were not only durable; consumers also liked to spend their money on such luxuries as tea, coffee and sugar.[2] When, however, they preferred to buy ornaments for both their homes and their attire, or crockery to replace pewter mugs and wooden platters, specialist manufacturers were only too ready to satisfy them.

These were essentially new men – innovators on the British industrial scene – operating, more often than not, in towns with little history in any traditional sense of being the focus either of a local agricultural economy, or of the power of the church or state. Of these the two most significant (at least for this chapter) were Stoke-on-Trent and Birmingham, both located in the West Midlands, but separated along a north–south axis by a distance of about forty miles. In the course of the eighteenth century they flourished in a part of England made increasingly accessible, first by the construction of turnpikes to a standard adequate for the long distance all season transport of goods by wagon,[3] and second by canals linking up such major navigable rivers as the Severn, the Trent and the Mersey. These improvements in communication were no coincidence, but a response to the demands of manufacturers impatient to extend their markets. Their ambitions did not end with the coasts of Britain; the new waterways allowed new ranges of goods to be shipped to the New World from Bristol and Liverpool, and to continental Europe from Hull. Overseas trade also created much of the wealth available to be spent on new consumer goods, of which Birmingham and Stoke-on-Trent, each in its own way, were major producers.

Common to both these towns is an association with a particular class of manufacture. For Birmingham this included nails, locks, scythes, buckles and guns, or indeed almost any small industrial product made out of iron – so much so that as early as 1538, a local man, John Leland, wrote of the 'many smythes in the town that use to make knives and all mannour of cutting tooles, and many lorimers that make bittes and a great many naylors, soe that a great part of the towne is maintained by smithes who have their iron and sea-cole out of Staffordshire'.[4] At this time Birmingham was just one of a number of small towns, all close to each other, engaged in much the same line of trade, but by the beginning of the eighteenth century it led the field with hundreds of forges producing novelties and trinkets, made not only of iron, but of copper, brass, silver and gold plate.[5] With a population of 13,000 in 1730, it was already a large town by contemporary standards, and with every succeeding generation its population more than doubled.

Birmingham was not a borough, however, which meant that it was unrepresented in the Parliament at Westminster. This was in many ways a blessing in disguise, as can be seen from studying the politics of the borough of Coventry, barely twenty miles to the east, in the same county of Warwickshire. The two members sent to Westminster, chosen by procedures that were both corrupt and complicated, were generally ineffective in securing any advantage for their constituency, whether for the relatively few who were qualified to vote or for the large disfranchised majority.[6] At the same time, Coventry had to contend with the countless privileges long enjoyed by those with special interests, such as the local craft guilds.

Birmingham residents, on the other hand, enjoyed the much wider franchise of the county of Warwick, so that, if only by force of numbers, their voice counted for much when it came to choosing who would represent them in Westminster – indeed, it was accepted that one of the county members would act as their spokesman at Westminster.[7] At the same time they enjoyed freedom from interference from above, while at local level the absence of craft guilds left entrepreneurs free to conduct business in their own way. Another benefit was religious freedom – the result of the Toleration Act of 1689 – which allowed Baptists, Presbyterians and Quakers to worship in their own chapels and meeting houses, with their children educated in dissenting schools and academies. Although the principles uniting such dissenters – many of whom were successful businessmen – had hardly an echo in Westminster, they were not seen as a threat to eighteenth-century politicians of whatever party. Freedom to meet and exchange views, however critical of the established political structure, was seen as a price worth paying for the Birmingham dissenters' contribution to the steadily expanding national economy.

What was true of Birmingham was true also of Stoke-on-Trent, although the character of the town was quite different. To begin with it was not a town at all, but a conglomeration of the so-called 'Five Towns', of which, perversely, there were actually six: Tunstall,

Burslem, Hanley, Stoke, Longton and Fenton. Common
to all of them was the exploitation of the local resource
of brown and yellow clay, to manufacture, in many
different forms, what later came to be known generically
as 'china'. Although the actual processes of manufacture,
which were continually being improved, were introduced from outside Britain at the beginning of the
eighteenth century, nowhere were they applied on such
a scale and with such success as in the Staffordshire
'Potteries'. This made the whole area instantly recognizable from the vast kilns in which its products were fired,
and even more, at certain times, from what one contemporary described as a cloud hanging over the countryside, so thick 'as to cause persons often to run into each
other, travellers to mistake the road; and strangers have
mentioned it as extremely disagreeable and not unlike
the smoke of Etna or Vesuvious'.[8]

Although in the Potteries the dissenting influence was
less salient than in Birmingham, there was the same
climate of tolerance, which extended also to the cathedral
city of Lichfield and the county town of Stafford – both
incorporated boroughs sending their own members to
Westminster. If the county itself was one of large
landowners, they were only too ready to exploit the
wealth in natural resources embedded in their estates by
collaborating with the new industrialists in the Potteries.
In the mid-eighteenth century a Staffordshire millwright,
James Brindley, turned his hand to promoting canals and
converted prominent local landowners, such as Lord
Anson and Lord Gower, to the view that this was where
they should invest their money if they were to realize the
full value of their property. Here it also counted that the

two noble lords between them presented the two Members of Parliament for Lichfield. Such factors as this favoured industry, allowing local businessmen the same latitude as they enjoyed in Birmingham.

In the history of the manufacturing side of the Industrial Revolution, as it developed in the English Midlands, two names stand out: Matthew Boulton made toys in Birmingham and Josiah Wedgwood made china in Burslem, one of the 'five' towns of the Potteries. If neither was alone in his field, both were first among equals. There was, however, more to industry in the English Midlands than just toys in Birmingham or china in the Potteries; as in any industry, manufacturers were dependent upon the supply of raw materials, access to markets, skilled craftsmen and a generally favourable political climate.

Given how much was at stake, the strong community of interests among those active in promoting new manufacture and their proximity to each other at a time when travel was still slow and laborious, friendships were bound to arise, and in the course of time lead to some sort of organized fellowship. This, at least, is what happened in the second half of the eighteenth century with the Lunar Society, a remarkable collection of talented, successful, original and often controversial men. It all started informally in 1757 with a friendship between Matthew Boulton and Erasmus Darwin, who was not a manufacturer, but a doctor in Lichfield, where he had only recently set up his practice. The cathedral city, widely known for its horse racing,[9] was also a noted cultural centre, not least because David Garrick, England's leading actor, and Samuel Johnson, later to become famous for his dictionary, were among its native sons. Darwin who, after studying at Cambridge and London, had completed his medical training at Edinburgh – home to original and creative thinking at a higher level than anywhere in England – was an almost immediate success, both professionally and socially, in Lichfield. In Boulton he found a man no less gregarious and eager to reach out to the world at large; the friendship between the two was already very promising, and extended easily to their respective wives and families.

This was the beginning of a circle of friends, bound together by shared interests both in projects, such as the building of new canals, that would favour their business operations, and in science (then known as 'natural philosophy') and invention. The former brought Josiah Wedgwood, and the latter Joseph Priestley, the discoverer of oxygen, and William Small into the circle. Small had been appointed, at the age of twenty-three, professor of mathematics and natural philosophy at the College of William and Mary in Virginia. Returning to Britain in 1764, he decided to live not in London or Scotland, where he could continue his academic career, but in Birmingham, where – with a somewhat dubiously acquired MD from Aberdeen – he could buy an already established medical practice. There his patients included not only Matthew Boulton, but Boulton's friend, John Baskerville, England's greatest printer. Small was liked and admired by everyone who knew him on both sides of the Atlantic. At William and Mary College, one of his students was Thomas Jefferson (1743–826), who admired his gift for communicating his liberal views, but more critically he was also a friend of Benjamin Franklin

(1706–90), who came to spend some eleven years in England at the same time as Small returned home.

Franklin, whose inventions and discoveries in physics earned him a fellowship of the Royal Society, made his money as a printer in Philadelphia (where he was also the publisher of the bestselling *Poor Richard's Almanac*), and in this capacity he had already met Baskerville in 1758, at the beginning of an earlier two year stay in London as agent of the Pennsylvania Assembly.[10] Returning to England in 1764, he was invited to stay with Small in Birmingham, where, through Baskerville, he already knew Boulton. He was immediately welcome, as a sort of honorary member, to the circle of friends who would become known to history as 'the Lunar Men'.

The 1760s were troubled years for Britain. The end of the Seven Years War in 1763 left the nation heavily in debt, and it was little consolation that with victory Britain became, at the cost of France (and, with regards to Florida, at the cost of Spain), the owner of the whole of continental North America east of the Mississippi river, and at the same time the effective ruler of much of India. The accession of King George III in 1760 led, two years later, to an unpopular government under his former tutor, the Earl of Bute, which attempted to fund the repayment of the national debt by extending British taxes to the North American colonies. The result was uproar, both in the mainland colonies and in the islands of the British West Indies; collecting the taxes became next to impossible. In Britain, however, the threat of the North American colonists to boycott British goods led to a level of protest by manufacturers which the

Parliament at Westminster could not ignore.[11] Lord Bute's Tory administration fell in 1763, and two years later, in 1765, that of the Whig Marquis of Rockingham repealed the act that had taxed America.

By this time Franklin was back in England, where for the next ten years he continued in vain to protest against Westminster's pretensions to tax the American colonies without representation. When Lord Bute first tried to tax America, Josiah Wedgwood had warned that the government seems 'determined to conquer England in America . . . I tell them that the Americans will then make Laws for themselves & if we continue our Policy – for us too in a very short time'. Inevitably his voice, and that of many others of the same opinion, went unheard at Westminster. Franklin, his patience exhausted after the British Parliament, ignoring the interests of its North American subjects, had consistently tried to impose new taxes upon them, returned home in 1775 – to play a leading part in the deliberations leading to the Declaration of Independence on 4 July 1776.

At no stage did the chain of events – during the first half of the reign of George III (1760 – 1820) – relating to affairs in North America lead to any effective movement for the reform of the British Parliament. Although criticism of a constitution that denied representation to the great majority of the British people, as much as it did to the North American colonists, was widespread, particularly in circles such as those of the Lunar Men, substantial reform did not become an issue until the nineteenth century. Those in the vanguard of the eighteenth-century industrial revolution – whether or not they were Lunar Men – learnt from experience how to gain parliamentary approval when necessary, for such matters as new patents or land enclosures. Matthew Boulton and Josiah Wedgwood both had the supreme gift of being able to persuade the governing classes that they had a community of tastes and interests; offering their choicest products often opened the way to persuading the landed gentry that dominated Westminster of the advantages to be gained from exploiting mineral resources or building canals – both operations essential to the Industrial Revolution.

The absence of any significant movement for parliamentary reform did not necessarily mean that life in Britain was safe or peaceful. On the contrary, until well into the nineteenth century, hardly a year went by without riots and civil unrest, or at least the threat of them. The common British view that security was even worse in the colonies was mistaken, as can be seen from one of Franklin's letters:[12]

Do you Englishmen then pretend to censure the Colonies for Riots? Look at home!!! I have seen within a Year, Riots in the Country about Corn, Riots about Elections, Riots about Workhouses, Riots of Colliers . . . & c. & c. In America if one mob breaks a few windows, or tars and feathers a single rascally Informer, it is called REBEL-LION: Troops and Fleets must be sent and military execution talk'd of as the decentest thing in the World. here indeed one would think of Riots as part of the Mode of Government.

The forces of law and order were so little able to contain such events, that Parliament often regarded ever more stringent penalties as the only remedy. Once a few ringleaders were sentenced to death, or later – after Australia was established as a penal colony – to transportation, next to nothing was done about the underlying causes. Both Parliament and the people were ready to find scapegoats; in 1763 the trial of John Wilkes (a Member of Parliament bitterly critical of Lord Bute's plan to extend the excise laws) for seditious libel, led to mobs chanting 'Wilkes and Liberty' in the streets of London. Josiah Wedgwood, in London at the time, noted how 'It gives universal disgust here & is the general Topic of every Political Club in Town', but none of this was of any immediate help to Wilkes, who fled to France before the end of the year. Four years later he returned as a popular hero, first to be imprisoned and denied his seat in Parliament, but in 1771 he was elected High Sheriff of Middlesex, and in 1774 Lord Mayor of London and once more MP for the county. From such a chain of events Parliament itself learnt few lessons, and nor had anyone expected otherwise. Men could talk just as freely in the clubs and coffee houses as the Lunar Men did among themselves,[13] if only at a higher order of discourse – embracing such matters as the political philosophy of John Locke and David Hume or Voltaire's 'Enlightenment'. At this level it was a world of talk rather than action, as almost everyone who counted realized.

It was at this stage that the Lunar Men decided to give more structure to their meetings, by setting up a formal Lunar Society, so called because its monthly meetings were scheduled for the Sunday closest to the full moon – a common choice for such regular events, when they could well end after darkness had fallen. The decision was taken on New Year's Eve 1775, a year saddened for the circle of friends by the death of William Small. In the previous year James Watt, after joining Matthew Boulton as his partner at the Soho Manufactory, had been welcomed as a member, as was also, in 1775, William Withering, whom Boulton had appointed to succeed Small as his scientific adviser. In the succeeding years, absence from the Midlands, often for business reasons – such as called Boulton or Watt to the tin mines of Cornwall – meant that the strict timetable was honoured more in the breach than the observance.[14] When, however, the friends were able to meet together, they greatly enjoyed and profited from the time spent discussing the latest scientific discoveries as much as recent political developments.

For the Lunar Men it was important that they lived at a time when protestant religious dissent was tolerated; unlike Roman Catholicism it had no subversive political dimension[15] – except perhaps in Scotland. The position, with regard to both politics and religion – in a century during which Parliament and the Church of England were closely tied to each other at the summit of power and influence – became more uncertain with the American, and even more the French revolution, both of which enjoyed considerable popular support in Britain. As to politics, there was always strong opposition, both in Parliament and the country at large, to the Tory administration of Lord North (1732–92), who was Prime Minister from 1770 to 1782.

At least with the benefit of hindsight, saving the North American colonies was always a hopeless cause, but this was only recognized by Lord North after the decisive surrender of the British forces at the battle of Yorktown in 1781. This meant the end of his government, and, under the Whig administration that succeeded it, the Treaty of Versailles in 1783. This recognized the colonies' independence, at the same time drawing the boundaries of the future United States of America. Although the failings of Lord North's administration were often blamed on his close ties to George III (who greatly resented the loss of what he saw as *his* American colonies), its powerful Whig opponents did not exploit them in favour of the cause of parliamentary reform. Such men as the renowned parliamentary orator, Edmund Burke (1729–97), who had supported the cause of the American colonists, were not regarded as subversive. Burke himself played an important part during the 1780s in establishing the rapprochement between Britain and the United States that restored the lost North American market for British manufactures – a most welcome development to men such as Matthew Boulton and Josiah Wedgwood.

The position changed radically with the French Revolution. Even though the fall of the Bastille in 1789 led to widespread rejoicing in Britain, the way the revolution then progressed brought fear and anxiety to both people and Parliament. The execution of the French king, Louis XVI, at the beginning of 1793, followed by the reign of terror and declaration of war against Britain, turned popular support for French revolutionary ideals into paranoid hostility. As early as 1790 Edmund Burke, in a landmark publication entitled *Reflections on the Revolution in France, and on the Proceedings in Certain Societies in London relative to that Event*, saw the

French Revolution leading to the fall of civilization, the collapse of established institutions, the vandalism of culture and rule by 'calculators and economists'. The French were 'the ablest architects of ruin that hitherto existed in the world'.[16] All this echoed popular feeling, expressed in Birmingham, among many other places, by hostility towards dissenters.

Among the Lunar Men, many such as Boulton and Watt, and to a lesser extent Darwin and Wedgwood, maintained a low profile, but Joseph Priestley (1733–1804) chose otherwise. He preached in favour of the French Revolution, and at a time when Parliament was debating the repeal of the Test Acts (which denied political rights to non-Anglicans). Burke, speaking against the Bill, cited from Priestley's published works chapter and verse threatening destruction of the Church of England. On May Day 1891, Priestley, preaching in London to the mourners at the funeral of Richard Price, a well known dissenting minister, left no one in any doubt but that he saw the French Revolution as a 'good cause'. The defeat of the Bill to repeal the Test Acts was a decisive setback for political reform, and by the time Priestley returned to Birmingham, Louis XVI and his Queen, Marie Antoinette were imprisoned in Paris in the Tuileries Palace.

On 14 July, Priestley organized a dinner at the somewhat inappropriately named Royal Hotel, to commemorate the fall of the Bastille. There, after a first toast to 'the King and the Constitution', others followed to 'the National Assembly of the Patriots of France', 'the Rights of Man' and 'the United States of America'.[17] Prudently, Priestley himself did not attend, but even so a small mob gathered outside the hotel, and as the dinner guests – many of them Lunar Men – departed at about five o'clock they were pelted, somewhat ineffectively, with mud and stones. Later a larger and more unruly mob burst into the hotel, and finding that all the diners had departed, broke all its windows. They went on to destroy first Priestley's New Meeting House, and then his home, from which Priestley only escaped at the last moment. The next day other dissenters' houses were attacked in a rampage of destruction, including the place where Priestley had taken refuge. He and his wife escaped to London, while in the following days the riots spread to villages around Birmingham, finally leaving eight rioters and one special constable dead. Matthew Boulton, remaining in Birmingham, was relieved that both the Soho House and Manufactory were unharmed. George III was pleased with the outcome and Burke was delighted. Henry Dundas, the Home Secretary, was concerned that the mob would one day turn against the government – which it did two years later – and William Pitt, the Prime Minister, said nothing. His answer to Burke's concerns about what was happening in France – 'Never fear, Mr. Burke: depend upon it, we shall go on as we are until the Day of Judgment'[18] – was not a bad statement of the government's domestic policy as it was at that time. None of this achieved anything for the cause of reform, as was always the case with rioting and the wanton destruction of property. (On the other hand Pitt later fully supported the ultimately successful campaign of his friend, William Wilberforce, to abolish the international slave trade.[19]) Within two years, England, with Pitt still at the helm, was at war with France, as it would be – with one short break – for more than twenty years.

The Soho Manufactory

In the course of the eighteenth century, more than any other British city, the West Midland town of Birmingham established the Industrial Revolution as quintessentially industrial, commercial and urban. Its industry was known pre-eminently for the production of 'toys', a term embracing a wide range of small manufactured objects produced for a consumer market. The character of any number of small enterprises was defined according to whether they worked with gold and silver, tortoiseshell – or simply iron and steel for making such things as corkscrews, candle snuffers, watch chains, and above all buckles, which in the eighteenth century, were regarded as indispensable for both shoes and knee-breeches. In the second half of the century a young man, Matthew Boulton, soon became the leading manufacturer, having become both a partner and general manager in his father's toy-making business in 1749.

Boulton was not a man to let the grass grow under his feet. Even before he became his father's partner, he had, when only seventeen, produced a new enamelled buckle to be added the list of wares offered to customers. Once a partner, he not only continued to develop new products but also made two favourable marriages. The first, in 1756, was to Mary Robinson, a distant cousin and older daughter of an opulent mercer of Lichfield, whose family were also friends of Erasmus Darwin. Left a widower by Mary's sudden death – at much the same time as her father-in-law's death – Matthew Boulton then married her younger sister, Anne, a year later. Each of the two marriages brought the princely sum of £14,000 to Boulton, which he chose to invest in expanding the business he had inherited from his father, so that he could later say of himself that he had had the option of living the life of a gentleman but chose rather to become an industrialist.[20]

With this vocation, Boulton not only widened his product range, but also increased very substantially the scale of his operations. He had a remarkable talent for recognizing the creative genius of other men and of winning both their trust and their friendship. This gift led him to collaborate with Josiah Wedgwood in the production of cameo jewellery in steel set mounts, with master craftsmen from Sheffield in the production of Sheffield plate – in which a layer of silver was fused to domestic copperware to produce a silver sheen – and finally, and most successfully, with James Watt in the production of the world's most advanced steam engines.

In decorative ware Boulton was a recognized master in silver plate and ormolu. That his clients for ormolu included King George III and Queen Charlotte, who acquired pieces for both Windsor Castle and Buckingham Palace, is proof, if any is needed, that his talent for making good contacts extended right across society[21] – for he was also a very popular and caring employer.

With all these advantages, coupled with an exceptional spirit of enterprise, Boulton could hardly be content to operate on the same scale as his father. Setting his sights much higher, he took advantage of the fact that the Wyatt family, of Lichfield and Burton-on-Trent, were the leading architects and surveyors of the day. True to character, Boulton had good relations with many members of the family – indeed one, John Wyatt, was his London agent – and with their help he was able to move both his home and his business to a new site on Handsworth Heath in Staffordshire, some three miles north of Birmingham.

There, at the top of a hill, the Wyatts built a new home for him, Soho House, and then, in the course of the next two or three years, the Soho Manufactory which, when it opened in 1766, became almost immediately an industrial showpiece – a development which Boulton did everything to encourage. By this time he had also built dwellings for workmen, workshops and a warehouse. All this could only be justified by manufacturing on an unprecedented scale, with such humble objects as buttons for the mass market, and new designs launched to commemorate events such as, in Boulton's own words, 'every Birth Day of our Sovereign', at the same time presenting 'to such of the Nobility as we can make so free with (and such as are most dressy) some setts to garnish their Cloaths with on that Day'.[22] Well-regarded clients were sought out not only in London – where Boulton consistently undercut silversmiths and other craftsmen in fashionable markets – but were also welcome at Soho, which many were pleased to visit, often more than once.[23]

However, neither the splendour of the Soho Manufactory's toys, nor the distinction of many of those who bought them, was sufficient to make a profit for Boulton. With changing fashions, even before the end of the eighteenth century, the market was in decline. Boulton was saved, as an entrepreneur, by his partnership with

James Watt (described in chapter 2) in designing and installing steam engines.

Boulton was involved in any number of other ventures; these included operating a mint for copper coins which he had completed on a site next to the Soho manufactory in 1789.[24]

It was always accepted that the Royal Mint had a monopoly on the production of gold and silver coins, but by the end of the 1780s it was clear that satisfying the demand for copper coinage was quite beyond its resources. In principle Boulton was better able than any rival to fill the gap, but politics stood in his way until 1797, a year of great financial crisis for Britain, when the Treasury agreed to allow him to mint copper pennies – the famous Cartwheel coins which, by Royal Proclamation of 26 July, became legal tender for sums up to one shilling. In the following years the royal assent extended to halfpennies and farthings; by this time the Treasury had had enough and set about building an entirely new Royal Mint at Tower Hill in London, with the contract for the necessary machinery, worth £16,990, given to the new Soho Foundry on 30 July 1806. Quite simply, no other business in England was able to carry it out. Although the little building was not ready for operation until February 1810, six months after Boulton's death in August 1809,[25] at the end of the day, the Soho mint – however short-lived – proved to be one of Boulton's most successful business operations.

The British and European Pottery Industry
Next to iron and steel, the most remarkable industrial transformation of the eighteenth century was in the

production of pottery. In Britain, this is above all associated with the name of one man, Josiah Wedgwood, and that of the region, North Staffordshire, where he operated. Although the production of ceramics goes back to ancient times, it was only in the eighteenth century that it evolved from a cottage to a factory-based industry.

At the beginning of the seventeenth century the achievements of British industry in the world of pottery were modest. While village potters made earthenware, porcelain, which was of much higher quality, came from China, or in the form of Dutch imitations from Delft. Price alone dictated that it was to be found only at the grandest tables. From the earliest days of the century things began to change, both in Europe and in Britain. In 1709, Johann Böttger, an alchemist in the service of the King of Saxony whose remit was to find a way of transforming base metals into gold, found out, largely by trial and error, how to make Chinese porcelain from local deposits of clay.[26] His product, finally produced in the Saxon town of Meissen, rapidly became known as Dresden china, after the kingdom's capital city.

Although Böttger did his best to keep his process a secret, it had spread across Europe well before the half century. In particular it became established in such well known French centres as St Cloud, Vincennes, and above all, Sèvres.[27] On 1 April 1766 one of those involved in this process, Louis-Félicité de Brancas, Comte de Lauraguais, wrote to Britain's leading industrialist, Matthew Boulton, of Birmingham, offering to sell his patent rights.[28] There were already porcelain manufacturers in various British locations, but their product, for want of a suitable clay, was not a true porcelain. On the other hand, it did contain the essential ingredient, bone ash, and was much superior to earthenware, so that its manufacture did represent an important halfway stage.

The breakthrough in Britain was the discovery, in 1768, by a Plymouth chemist, William Cookworthy, that kaolin, a clay suitable for the manufacture of true porcelain (as made in China), was to be found locally.[29] His process for making porcelain was then patented on 17 March 1768. Although Cookworthy had for years been making imitation porcelain in Plymouth, because he did not have a local supply of coal he could only fire his kilns with wood. This shortcoming led him to move his manufacture to Bristol, where the absence of suitable local clay constrained him to work with an inferior substitute known as moor stone, or growan. In Plymouth he had clay but no fuel, while in Bristol the reverse was the case. Down on his luck he sold out to Richard Champion, a local businessman. In 1775 Champion applied to the House of Lords to extend Cookworthy's 1768 patent; the House, bombarded by pamphlets from Wedgwood and other leading Staffordshire earthenware manufacturers, restricted the exclusive use of the Cornish clay to the manufacture of porcelain. This was a victory for Staffordshire, where Cornish clay – deposits so abundant that they are still being worked in the twenty-first century – provided the highest quality raw material for the whole pottery industry.

Wedgwood, travelling in Cornwall, had by 1775 already realized the vast potential of its clay, noting at the same time the usefulness of Newcomen's steam

engines in local mines. Three years later a syndicate of
Staffordshire potters bought Cookworthy's patent from
Champion, who, with his capital spent, closed the Bristol
pottery; so putting an end to the manufacture of true
porcelain in Britain.[30]

In 1782 Wedgwood, ordering his first steam engine
from Boulton and Watt, became almost the first manufacturer in Britain to use steam power in a factory. What
is more, not only did Boulton already know about
porcelain as a result of the offer made to him by the
Comte de Lauragais in 1766, but he was a friend of
Wedgwood, who together with other members of the
Staffordshire syndicate exploited the patent rights
bought from Champion. With clay imported by sea and
river from Cornwall, and abundant local reserves of the
right coal for both kilns and steam engines, circumstances were ideal for a pottery industry producing all types
of earthenware. The way was open for innovations such
as double-glazed 'creamware', which, with a fine lead
glaze, was a close approximation to porcelain and first
appeared in the 1730s.[31]

The industry went from strength to strength. One
of the earliest innovations, introduced by Enoch Booth of
Tunstall some time in the 1750s,[32] was the practice
of twice firing clay articles. The biscuit ware produced
by the first firing was then ready for the application of a
variety of glazes. Wedgwood led the field in experimenting with many colour combinations. He worked with
raw materials from many parts of Britain, to the point
that at this death he left more than 7,000 specimens. Salt,
lead, glass, barium, flint, iron, cobalt, copper, manganese
. . . to name but a few of the materials he worked with,

combined to produce any number of different glazes, of which only relatively few had commercial possibilities.

But there were some remarkable successes, such as Wedgwood's 'Queen's Ware', introduced in 1763.[33] Wedgwood was not a trained chemist, but then neither was his friend, Joseph Priestley, now remembered as one of the founders of the science of chemistry for his pioneering work with gases. Wedgwood made sure that his sons received the best scientific education available in the late eighteenth century, and he himself spent some time in Edinburgh – a city not to his taste – so as to be close to such men as Joseph Black, the discoverer of carbon dioxide, at the university (where his son John was also a student). The company kept by Wedgwood also confirms how 'scientific advance in the eighteenth century came from the societies established in the Midlands and the North of England by craftsmen and industrialists – the Lunar Society of Birmingham, the Manchester Literary and Philosophical Society'.[34]

Wedgwood was only one among many innovators in pottery. Thomas Minton, who founded his own factory in Stoke-on-Trent in 1793, led the way in ceramic lithography, a process that allowed several colours to be applied to pottery at the same time,[35] and there were any number of other well known names, such as Spode, in what historically was the first instance of a major industry operating on a factory scale and producing for a mass consumer market. While this increased spectacularly in the second half of the eighteenth century – so that china plates came to replace wooden platters in even modest households – Staffordshire had to pay a high price for this success. It was not for nothing that the degradation of the local environment, a consequence of the operation of new factories, burning coal and powered by steam, led the region of the potteries to be known as 'the black country'. Even so, what was achieved in Staffordshire in the last quarter of the eighteenth century provided a model for modern industry, which, above all in the realm of textiles, would be at the heart of what we now know as the Industrial Revolution.

6

PEOPLE, POLITICS AND INDUSTRY

The Countryside and its People

It is easy to think of Britain – at the beginning of a long period of domestic tranquillity – in terms of a more or less uniform agricultural economy, supporting very large numbers of smallholders, with little diversity from one part of the country to another, in a traditional lifestyle. Such a picture is far too simple; in the early eighteenth century Daniel Defoe, in his portrayal of 'the Whole Island of Great Britain', shows how remarkably diverse, above all in terms of occupation, the nation then was.[1]

In many parts of rural Britain – still home to a substantial part of the population – the life of the common man and his family in their cottage was devoted to industry as much as it was to agriculture. This was particularly true of areas such as the West Country, East Anglia and the West Riding of Yorkshire, where the most profitable use of rural land was for grazing sheep. At the same time there were whole communities of miners and fishermen, whose lives were entirely divorced from the realm of agriculture.

Nonetheless, the cottage industries of the south, by failing to innovate, steadily declined, much to the benefit of the West Riding where (as related in chapter four) new textile mills bought raw wool from as far afield as the Scottish Highlands. New enterprise such as the manufacture of carpets, which began at Wilton in Wiltshire in 1720, could halt local economic decline, but even in this case the centre of the carpet industry had, by the end of the century, moved north to Kidderminster, in the industrial Severn valley (where it is still located). Quite apart from the wool-based industries, mining was expanding in response to market factors, and the extraction of coal and iron ore was (as related in chapter three) at the heart of the Industrial Revolution.

In a historical period with a steady secular growth in population, these processes meant that hundreds of thousands had to find not only new occupations, but also new homes – often far from where they had been born and brought up. If, in principle, legislation in the form of the Act of Settlements and Removals of 1662 should have checked this process, in practice it failed to do so. Business demand for labour as a factor in production was too powerful, and traditional employment opportunities too restricted. Urban populations, particularly in new industrial cities such as Birmingham of Sheffield, increased; rural populations and those of old market towns – typically cathedral cities such as Exeter and York[2] – which they supported, failed to do so. The results were often devastating.

Given the nature of the British economy at the beginning of the eighteenth century, the burden of taxation fell mainly upon land; or rather, upon those who owned it. In particular, the introduction of new land taxes at the end of the seventeenth century, together with changes in the political climate following the Glorious Revolution, show how landowners had to view their estates according to the money they could yield, rather than the number of tenants they could support. Because agriculture, in effect, became a business producing for the market, the factors in production had to be reduced to monetary terms, even at the level of labourers toiling in the fields.

Labourers were employed for a cash wage, generally by tenant farmers who could operate on a substantial scale, occupying their land according to the terms of a lease agreed with its owner. This was only possible by enclosing land at the cost of poor smallholders who lost their traditional rights.[3] That in the process many of them could no longer live in the countryside can be seen from the fact that whereas in 1688 nearly 90 per cent of the population were engaged in agriculture, by the 1760s this had fallen to less than 50 per cent.[4] This was the result of innumerable Acts of Parliament, so that by 1760 a total area of 338,177 acres – just over 1 per cent of all the land in England – had been enclosed.

Historians are divided on the question of the 'rights and wrongs' of enclosures; the populists blame them for the decline in the number of small farmers as a direct result of the loss of the commons that they had previously used for grazing, with the corresponding decrease of livestock – leading incidentally to less manure for their arable land. In this downward spiral they had little choice but to sell their farms to large landowners and find work in industry.[5] Others, noting how in certain critical periods, such as that of the long war against France (1793–1815), the number of small farms rose rather than fell, insist that the opposition to enclosure was by no means general. Men from the countryside, mostly young and unmarried, went into industry of their own free will attracted by higher wages;[6] which explains the steady increase of urban populations in a period when mortality exceeded the birth rate in new industrial cities.

Whichever view is taken, the fact that – as a result of enclosure – the extent of land devoted to market oriented agriculture increased, while the number of those working on it declined, could only mean that it was managed much more efficiently. This was essential if England was to feed its steadily increasing population, and it is significant that 1808 was the last year in which there was a surplus available for export. There was no doubt that by this time, the transition from an agricultural to an industrial economy was already far advanced.

Given the burden of taxation required to finance all the years of warfare, owners not only had a very strong incentive to increase the productivity of their land, but most of them actually achieved this result. The means adopted, for instance introducing fodder crops such as clover and turnips,[7] originated, as often as not, across the North Sea in the Netherlands, where they had been, locally, standard practice long before the eighteenth century.[8] The same was true of land reclamation which – as demonstrated by the draining of the fens in seventeenth-century East Anglia – created vast areas of rich new land open for agriculture; once again this was at the cost of traditional occupations such as fishing, poaching and water-fowling,[9] carried out by men, described by Lord Camden in the eighteenth century, as 'of brutish, uncivilized tempers, envious of all others'[10] and by Defoe[11] as 'famed for . . . idleness and sloth'.

All in all – and in spite of the shortcomings of such marginal groups as the unreconstructed fen men – the eighteenth century witnessed a substantial reduction in the labour required to produce a given quantity of grain, coupled with an equally substantial increase in the yield of a given area of land. This was partly the result of the steadily increasing use of burnt lime as fertilizer, made possible by the development of the coal trade.

While new crops made it much easier to feed livestock in winter, all season roads made it possible to bring cattle to London.[12] It is such networks, dependent upon wage labour, that characterize the changing material economy of eighteenth-century Britain, as well as the occupations of those involved in it. If then, the enhanced productivity of agriculture added mainly to the wealth of the proprietors – as they had always intended – it brought in its train the emergence of a cash economy, extending far beyond the agricultural sector and characterized, as already related on page 111, by the popular consumption of commodities such as tea and sugar.

Although, in the eighteenth century, the agricultural revolution led to a substantial decline in the numbers of those who worked on the land, European populations, including that of Britain, remained mainly rural. This was possible only because of an increase in the number of craftsmen and others engaged in domestic industry or, alternatively, transport.[13] In the household – by this time generally based on a nuclear family – all members, except for the youngest children, were expected to be wage-earners in one way or another. Although they worked as individuals rather than as members of a team,[14] their earnings were generally pooled to meet the consumer demands of the household as a whole.

Production typically consisted of clothing and textiles destined for the market, but it also included articles based on metal, leather, wood and ceramics.[15] This was an endogenous response to market opportunities, offered not only by the rapidly growing cities but also overseas, particularly in the North American colonies.[16] Because this fragmented organization of the household was essentially a strategy for preserving the status quo at a time when household resources in land were much depleted, often to vanishing point, it was bound to fail sooner or later. As a result, the cottage industries of rural England provided the Industrial Revolution with its workers, not its consumers.[17]

The New Middle Classes

Those forced by circumstance to leave the countryside provided much of the workforce in places such as the Staffordshire potteries and the coal and iron industry of the Severn valley, both of which were part of the process of diversification in the eighteenth-century British economy. Another result of this process was the emergence of the middle class as an important social category.

A typical middle class household could be recognized by both the employment of servants[18] and consumption patterns defined by goods – both durable (such as clothes) and for immediate consumption (such as food) – purchased outside. While the modest wages of servants were mainly spent on clothing,[19] their masters spent their money on custom-built furniture, porcelain tableware, large windows and curtains to match. In some instances, substituting articles (for example, carpets) of British manufacture for expensive imports from countries such as Persia added a new dimension to home furnishing.

At the top end of the scale, as it was at the beginning of the eighteenth century, Thomas Twining's tea house, opened in London's Strand in 1706, provides an excellent case study. Twining, born in 1675, started his life in trade working for Thomas d'Aeth, an East India Company merchant and tea importer, but by the time he was thirty he had sufficient resources, both financial and professional, to start out on his own. He bought an established coffee house and converted it to a tea house, serving a prosperous modern estate built to provide new homes after the great fire of London – many of which still survive as offices.[20]

This innovation was an immediate success, with ladies waiting in their carriages while their footmen fetched them Twining's tea. From this beginning the business expanded to sell tea and coffee 'dry'; an innovation that opened out the market, which in 1749, extended to the North American colonies, where the Governor of Massachusetts was one of the customers. By this time tea had become much cheaper in Britain and north-west Europe, the main consuming areas, with sales volume increasing many times over, as tea became affordable even among the poor.[21]

If the Twining family (which is still in business in the Strand in the twenty-first century) were unusually successful as shop keepers, this was partly because this type of business only came into its own in the late seventeenth century. Where the Twinings were in the vanguard, thousands of others followed in their train, not only in London, but throughout the kingdom and its North American colonies. Only the Dutch Republic – where, for example, the Twijnstraat in Utrecht, still a busy shopping street, is centuries old – had any claim to being ahead.[22]

Shops sold not only tea, but also sugar, coffee and tobacco, and at the luxury end of the market cocoa, leading a revolution in retailing achieved at the expense of traditional fairs and markets – which in the early eighteenth century still operated on a colossal scale. This can be seen from Defoe's[23] description of the Sturbridge Market held in early September on Cambridge's Midsummer Common, where he refers specifically to 'the shops ... [with] all sorts of trade ... goldsmiths, toyshops, brasiers, turners, milliners, haberdashers, hatters, mercers, drapers, pewterers ... all in tents and booths', but this, the retail side of the market, was nothing in comparison with the wholesale side, with its 'grocers, salters, brasiers, iron-merchants ... [dealers] in woollen manufactures ...' Where payment in the latter was by various forms of credit, in the former, it was made in cash.

In the course of the eighteenth century, the retail sector became separate, to become, in increasing measure, established in shops as they are known today, with fixed premises and opening hours throughout the week. Retail shops and tea and coffee houses were to be found in the same streets – a form of organization that transformed traditional market towns as well as London and other large cities.

New spas opened from the late seventeenth century onwards, as can be seen, for instance, in Tunbridge Wells' Pantiles.[24] Becoming accessible to visitors arriving by coach was essential to their success, and this in turn depended on roads being constructed to a much higher standard. This result was achieved by the turnpike trusts that transformed the British road network in the course of the eighteenth century, leading to a three-fold increase in traffic at steadily decreasing rates.[25]

Commerce and Finance

Such essentially commercial developments not only offered considerable wage employment outside agriculture, but also required an administrative infrastructure that depended upon typical middle class occupations, such as the keeping of accounts. Indeed, all this was only possible because of the development, from the later seventeenth century onwards, of new financial services. Modern banking, characterized by taking deposits, discounting bills and issuing notes, which first emerged in the Dutch Republic in the early seventeenth century, was established in London well before the end of the century, with the Goldsmiths' Company leading the way. Although such developments had their greatest utility in foreign trade, where they enabled debts to be discharged without shipping gold, it soon became clear that they could be equally useful at home, particularly if extended by such innovations as payment by cheque.

The Bank of England, established in 1694, became the model of central banking,[26] in spite of the somewhat remarkable fact that it was a public company – with its shares traded on the London Stock Exchange – until nationalization by the Labour government of the late 1940s. What counted was the fact the British Exchequer could safely entrust its own money to the Bank, which meant, in turn, that it could borrow on terms so favourable that interest rates fell from 14 per cent in the 1690s to less than 4 per cent in the 1750s.[27]

By this time British public finance had gained the reputation, both at home and abroad, of being more honest and efficient than in any other European country.[28] The Bank also became 'the bankers' bank', so providing centrally for the clearance of financial transactions. This was an extremely important facility given the way that commercial enterprises, such as Twining's Tea House, extended their business to include banking, to the point – noted by Lord Liverpool in 1825[29] – that 'any petty tradesman, any grocer or cheesemonger, however destitute of property, might set up a bank in any place'.

Next to banking, insurance against the risk of loss, whether by fire, shipwreck or whatever, was the most important financial service to be established, comprehensively, in the seventeenth century.[30] Like banking, the success of insurance not only reflected a secure and stable economic climate – at least by the standards of any earlier age in British history – but also helped create and sustain it. It helped that houses built of brick were less likely to be lost to fire, or, better ships – enjoying such navigational aids as Harrison's H4 chronometer[31] and ever more effective protection by the Royal Navy – shipwreck.

All in all, these new financial institutions, together with the other novel types of commercial enterprise, provided services to the middle classes – and indirectly, the servants they employed. At the same time, the new prosperity, coupled with the cost of the wars that had helped create it, meant new taxes; like the excise charged on commodities such as tea, which in turn needed a bureaucracy to enforce them – however ineffectively.[32] This led to a consumer society with unprecedented purchasing power, so that new industry, such as that pioneered by men such as Matthew Boulton and Josiah Wedgwood, had the benefit of a market waiting to be exploited – to say nothing of what could be exported overseas.

Even so, the market was one they themselves helped create, for eighteenth-century capitalism created both a new labour force of industrious workers *and* a new class of consumers.[33] In the course of time, the degree to which these two classes coincided became a measure of overall national prosperity, but this development belonged essentially to the nineteenth, if not to the twentieth century.[34]

Government by Landowners

Until well beyond the end of the eighteenth century, Parliament was controlled by great landowners who, insofar as they were peers, sat in the House of Lords. The seats in the House of Commons were, as often as not, in the gift of members of the House of Lords, who could bestow them, unashamedly, on members of their own families, including their own sons and heirs. The case of Lord North was but one of many; a great parliamentarian who, as Prime Minister from 1770 to 1781, is commonly held responsible, somewhat unjustly, for the loss of the American colonies – he was the son and heir of the first Earl of Guildford.

Sybil, or The Two Nations, published in 1845 and one of the great novels of the nineteenth century, whose author, Benjamin Disraeli, later became one of Britain's most successful Prime Ministers; provides us with a short sketch of this landowning class, known to history as the Whig aristocracy. At its heart were 'the families who in one century plundered the church to gain the property of the people and in another century changed the dynasty to gain the power of the Crown'.[35]

The first of these centuries was the sixteenth, when the Tudor court favoured its key supporters with the grant of estates plundered from the monasteries, and the second, the seventeenth, when the Dutch *stadhouder* William III was welcomed to England as king in place of James II, whose conversion to Catholicism had made his position as monarch so difficult, that exile in France was the only way of saving his line. William III's contribution to England – at least as seen by Disraeli – was a system of finance which, when applied to the much more considerable wealth of his new realm, would pay for the wars against France in which the Netherlands had long been involved.

A Parliament, whose members 'acted with minds open to everything except fundamental ideas', could not do without the 'moneyed men', however much, to quote the Duke of Newcastle, 'East Indians, West Indians, citizens and brokers ... are not very reputable and yet very troublesome Members'.[36] What really counted in Britain, as opposed, say, to France, was that traditional land-owners and newly successful businessmen recognized a community of interests, with many being ready to acquire and exploit a foothold in the opposite camp; for example, Lord Dundonald exploited the mineral re-sources of his near insolvent Scottish estate.

Such toing and froing, even if not general practice, was still a recognized formula for success.[37] Not only that, it was a process that created wealth far beyond the limits of the class represented in Parliament, while at the same time supporting institutions, such as banking and insur-ance, that played a key role in financing the Industrial Revolution. It helped also that a landed estate in England could be acquired by purchase as much as by inheritance, so that for instance, the nabobs and planters, such as the Beckford family from Jamaica, who acquired their wealth outside Britain, could, once home, use it for political advancement as well as lavish living.

After governing for nearly a century, the Whigs finally lost power in 1783 to a government led by William Pitt, who at the age of twenty-four became Britain's youngest Prime Minister. The oligarchy survived, but was transformed into a 'plebeian aristocracy' when Pitt 'made peers of second-rate squires and fat graziers'.[38] Although this practice, as noted by Disraeli, had its origins some time before Pitt's Tory government, his conclusion that it changed the character of those who sat in the House of Lords, as well as increasing their number, still stands. It was well into the nineteenth century, however, before it can be said to have changed the course of the Industrial Revolution.

The Human Cost of Revolution

The most familiar of all the images evoked by the Industrial Revolution are those that represent its human cost. Friedrich Engels' *The Condition of the Working Class in England* has long been recognized as central in the Marxist canon, yet the portrayal of this theme by the great fiction writers of the nineteenth century has better stood the test of time. Any comprehensive view of the century must take into account not only Benjamin Disraeli's *Sybil*, but also Charles Dickens' *Hard Times*,[39] Charlotte Brontë's *Shirley*[40] and, above all, Elizabeth Gaskell's *North and South*.[41] This title highlights the different worlds evoked by the two halves of England, with on the one side, the unspeakable horror of life in cheap back-to-back houses in Lancashire's new industrial towns, and on the other, the idyllic rural life aspired to by the southern gentry – and forsaken by the book's leading character. In the south of England, while the Lancashire textile industry boomed, the history of Norfolk illustrates how rural life was far from idyllic. The countryside lost its traditional worsted trade and Norwich, the county town, its silk industry. By 1850, together with much of the rest of East Anglia, Norfolk had become an overwhelmingly agricultural county, with many wage earning families subject to poverty worse than that of their compatriots working in the new factories of the north-west.

The problem was essentially demographic. In regions where the demand for labour in agriculture was less than that in industry – and less even than that required by prevailing levels of population growth – agriculture was stagnant and the consequence was rural squalor.[42] The result, in all too many cases, was emigration from rural areas in the south to the new mill towns of the north, a hard option in any case, which echoed a familiar definition of Calvinism: 'You will be damned if you do – And you will be damned if you don't'.[43]

In the Scottish Highlands a reverse situation had equally dire effects. Where the West Country and East Anglia lost their sheep, the great Scottish landlords responded to demand for wool by the new Yorkshire mills by dispossessing their tenant smallholders, who were numerous, to turn their land over to sheep, whose care required only relatively few shepherds. Some of the smallholders survived by means of seasonal employment outside the Highlands – an opportunity created by domestic service or the new railways in the south – but the majority had to choose between remaining in Scotland as impoverished coastal crofters or emigrating to newly opened regions of Britain's constantly developing overseas empire.[44]

As early as 1811, Lord Selkirk, an idealistic young Scottish peer, acquired a land grant of 116,000 square miles in what is now the Canadian province of Manitoba, from the Hudson's Bay Company (of which he was a stockholder), and opened it to settlers from Scotland and Ireland. Theirs was not an easy life, for the territory, located around the confluence of the Red and Assiniboine rivers,[45] was contested by a recalcitrant population of Métis – of mixed French-Canadian and native American descent – who had long exploited it for its natural resources in beavers and buffaloes.[46] In the end the Red River Colony not only survived but prospered, with the Métis finally dispersed by a British military expedition in August 1870.[47] Few identify the Métis among the losers from the Industrial Revolution, but if one follows the linkages from the Yorkshire woollen mills to the Scottish Highlands and across the Atlantic to the Red River colony, that is what they were.

All this was part of a process of globalization, without which the Lancashire cotton mills could never have thrived, but before looking further at what this involved for populations outside Britain – a subsidiary theme of the present chapter – it is right to look more closely at what Lancashire cotton involved for its own mill hands, whose commitment to work, in terms of time and participation by all members of the family, of both sexes and including children, went far beyond anything imposed upon them in the rural communities they had left behind.

After the introduction of gas lighting made it possible for mills to operate outside the hours of daylight, the hands were subject above all to the tyranny of the clock. What is more, they had no right to quit employment at a wage level so low that they played no significant part in the consumer economy fed by new industry. It was accepted that the purchasing capacity of the working population, with wages not much above the level of subsistence, could contribute little to economic development.[48]

It was only after the coming of the railways in the 1830s that this began to change – as can be seen from the way that hundreds of thousands came to London for the Great Exhibition in 1851. Even so, the alternatives to employment were dire: following the Poor Law Amendment Act of 1834 the workhouse – in which husbands, wives and children were forcibly separated, to live in conditions little better than those found in prisons – became the standard method of poor relief, and remained such until well into the twentieth century.[49] Prison, indeed, was also the fate, not only of those sentenced for crime, but for countless debtors who – as shown by Charles Dickens' *Little Dorrit* – had fallen on hard times through little fault of their own; and convicted criminals were transported in great numbers to Australia.

On the question of the human cost of the Industrial Revolution no one is more eloquent or better known than Friedrich Engels – long recognized, next to the prophet himself, as the leading Marxist theorist. Leaving aside Engels' ideas about the inevitability of a proletarian revolution, and the emergence of the bourgeoisie as the calculated oppressors of British working families, *The Condition of the Working Class in England*,[50] based on his own travels in the early 1840s, is unequalled for its comprehensive portrayal of the conditions of life of the poor in the new British industrial cities. It is significant that the book was written in German, Engels' first language, as if Engels intended to show the German business class how to avoid the evils of the British Industrial Revolution. Here he had little obvious success.[51]

In the preface to the German edition of his book, Engels records that, 'the root causes whose effect in England has been the misery and oppression of the proletariat exist also in Germany and in the long term must engender the same results'.[52] His readers hardly reacted in any constructive way.

As a revolutionary tract, however, Engels' book eventually succeeded beyond his wildest dreams, mainly due to fortuitous historical developments occurring after his death in 1895. It is to be noted that the first English translation did not appear until 1886, in the United States. In the present context, therefore, the focus is on what Engels observed and reported in the early 1840s and this is best summed up by some of Engels' own subtitles: 'General Description of the Slums'; 'The Interior of the Workers' Dwellings'; 'Overcrowdedness of Population'; 'The Clothing of the Workers'; and so on, with every subtitle being amplified by detailed and evocative descriptions of the circumstances to which it related.

This process was inevitably somewhat repetitive, given that the same situation was to be observed in one town after another. It may be taken for granted that Engels almost always saw the worst side of life, but in his day few others from his social background saw anything at all of the lives of the urban poor. As he said of Manchester, his own base in England, 'The town itself is peculiarly built so that a person may live in it for years, and go in and out daily without coming into contact with a working people's quarter or even with workers, that is, so long as he confines himself to business or to pleasure walks'.[53] The conclusion was always that 'thousands of industrious and worthy people – far worthier and more to be respected that all the rich of London – do find themselves in a condition unworthy of human beings'.[54]

Engels, however, depicts the stage, not the actors. Indeed, it was central to his thesis that individualism was denied any part in the world of the industrial proletariat. The working-class hero had no place among his *dramatis personae*, which explains why Dickens will always be a better read, as in his introduction to an 'anti-hero', Stephen Blackpool, in *Hard Times*:[55]

> In the hardest working part of Coketown; in the innermost fortification of that ugly citadel, where Nature was as strongly bricked out as killing airs and gases were bricked in; at the heart of the labyrinth of narrow courts upon courts, and close streets upon streets, which had come into existence piecemeal, every piece in a violent hurry for some one man's purpose, and the whole an unnatural family, shouldering, and trampling, and pressing one another to death; in the last close nook of this great exhausted receiver, where the chimneys, for want of air to make a draught, were built in an immense variety of stunted and crooked shapes, as though every house put out a sign of the kind of people who might be expected to be born in it; among the multitude of Coketown, generically called 'the Hands', – a race who would have found more favour with some people, if Providence had seen fit to make them only hands, or, like the lower creatures of the seashore, only hands and stomachs – lived a certain Stephen Blackpool, only forty years of age.

The 'hands' were Engels' proletariat, but Dickens makes clear that Providence had *not* seen fit to make them only hands. Stephen Blackpool was still essential to the story of *Hard Times*, even though:[56]

> He took no place among those remarkable 'Hands', who, piecing together their broken intervals of leisure through many years, had mastered difficult sciences, and acquired a knowledge of most unlikely things. He had no station among the Hands who could make speeches and carry on

debates ... He was a good power-loom weaver, and a man of perfect integrity. What more he was, or what else he had in him, if anything, let him show for himself.

The rest of the chapter shows how this was achieved. Coketown, as depicted by Dickens, was not unlike Manchester as seen by Engels from the Ducie Bridge. Dickens' essential point, largely disregarded by Engels, was that the industrial working class of nineteenth-century Britain was far from uniform, and that there were opportunities for an individual to change his position within it, or even to rise above it into the middle classes. At the same time, anyone who has visited a cotton mill knows that a power loom weaver has much more to do than simply look at a giant steam-powered machine producing yard after yard of cloth. If Stephen Blackpool had not been a *good* power loom weaver, he could have lost his job. So much then, for the condition of Britain's industrial poor at the height of the Industrial Revolution.

The Abundance of Labour

In the first half of the nineteenth century, the British economy willingly accepted the wisdom of Thomas Malthus' *Essay on Population*.[57] According to which, population, if unchecked, would increase at a rate beyond that at which the productive economy could sustain it. In other words, any attempt to improve the standard of living of the poor was bound to be self-defeating. If history soon proved Malthusianism to be mistaken, its underlying principles could still provide a pretext for doing next to nothing to improve the living conditions of the poor.

In practice, British enterprise, as opposed to that of the United States, could also draw upon a substantial reserve of labour, largely as a result of creating conditions outside industrial areas inimical to traditional occupations. If this was not deliberate policy, it was certainly convenient to industrial employers, as is made clear by the examples, given earlier in this chapter, from Scotland, East Anglia and the West Country.

After 1830, when the Liverpool and Manchester Railway opened, the construction of railways added a new dimension to this process, which peaked during the railway mania of the 1840s. The need for a vast, relatively mobile labour force to be employed in heavy construction work was met largely by gangs of Irish navvies. Others from Ireland found employment in Scotland's new woollen mills in Paisley. There had long been an Irish immigrant community in London, whose members, with a reputation for undercutting English labour going back to the early eighteenth century, were a focus of anti-Catholic sentiment.[58] Their presence owed everything to the better employment opportunities offered by the highly diversified local London economy. On any measure the Irish economy was always less prosperous than that of England, but by the 1840s it was in a state of secular decline for a number of reasons.

Where, in the context of eighteenth-century regional agriculture, traditional cottage industry had managed to survive in Ireland with the widespread cultivation of flax and the grazing of sheep supporting both home spinning of linen and wool and such local crafts as hand knitting, embroidery and lace making, and, at the same time, cattle as the source of leather for local shoe making, by 1830 none of these industries could compete with English towns such as Leicester, with much better access to the British market justifying investment at a level unaffordable in Ireland.[59]

Although, as a result of a steady increase in population, British demand for Irish grain, butter, pork and bacon – to say nothing of live cattle – doubled between 1800 and 1826, this was not sufficient to sustain, country wide, a one sector economy based on commercial agriculture. For one thing, land enclosure in Ireland worked, just as much as in England, to ensure that increased productivity did not require a proportionate increase in labour. The result was that a substantial part of a rapidly growing agricultural population was left to survive, as best it could, on the poorest land; with little prospect of finding a market for traditional crops such as wheat and barley, marginal cultivators turned to growing potatoes as a subsistence crop.

Potatoes – unknown in Europe before the discovery of the New World, where they originated – not only thrive in a wide variety of soils and climates, but are nourishing and simple to cultivate. It is no wonder then that by the end of the eighteenth century they were gaining ground at the cost of grain crops, or that in the course of the nineteenth, they came to be symbolic of rural poverty, as illustrated by Vincent van Gogh's famous picture, *The Potato Eaters*,[60] painted in 1885.

In the 1840s the choice of potatoes as the main crop of the poorest Irish smallholders proved to be disastrous; from 1845, the harvest was devastated by a fungus, *phytophtora infectans*, leading to over a million deaths in an already declining population, and the emigration of three million people. Of these, some joined the armies of navvies working in Britain, but most went to the New World. It would be an exaggeration to say that the Industrial Revolution in Britain caused the Irish potato famine, but the link is incontestable – as are the sufferings of millions of Irishmen that Britain did little to alleviate. That so many of them found a new home in the United States or Australia also had important political consequences for both countries.[61]

The Improvement of the Standard of Living: Protest and Politics

In due course both the urban working classes, and those that governed them, did take steps to improve urban living conditions, even though there was little dialogue between the two sides. If, by the end of the nineteenth century working class life was immeasurably better than it had been at the end of the eighteenth, the process of improvement was slow to get started. Until well into the century, civil unrest born of popular discontent provoked fear among the middle classes rather than improving the lot of the working classes. A feeling of insecurity was the order of the day.

The historian will recognize a number of familiar milestones along the way – the Gordon Riots, the Luddites, the Tolpuddle Martyrs, the Peterloo massacre, Chartism, were all significant incidents in a history of labour unrest. In the six days of the Gordon Riots in 1780, a London mob destroyed and plundered property in response to an anti-Catholic petition presented to Parliament by Lord George Gordon, a Member subject to mental derangement and religious mania. This mindless civil disorder on an unprecedented scale, while reflecting ingrained prejudice against Irish labour; achieved nothing positive for the class from which the rioters came. On the contrary, it merely strengthened the resolve of the governing classes to enforce law and order, as can be seen from the sentences – in twenty-six cases this was the death penalty – imposed on those later convicted by the courts for the part they had played in orchestrating the riots. In a sense the riots were an early warning that civil unrest was always just below the surface of urban poverty.

In the five years, 1811–16, such unrest manifested itself when textile workers in the Midlands, Yorkshire and Lancashire, following a mythical leader known as 'General Ludd', destroyed the machinery which they were employed to operate. The movement was organized in a number of cells, each with a specific industrial objective according to the character of the local textile industry, so that in Lancashire, for example, Luddites targeted power looms.[62] The background of poverty, and what it involved at local level, provides the background for Charlotte Brontë's *Shirley*:

> Misery generates hate. These sufferers hated the machines which they believed took their bread from them; they hated the buildings which contained those machines; they hated the manufacturers who owned those buildings.[63]

All this reflects the way that advances in mechanization threatened traditional forms of labour at a time when the war against Napoleon's France had led to trade depression – above all as a result of the loss of America, the principal market for the European woollen trade – unemployment and high prices. As seen by Charlotte Brontë, it was 'their infatuated perseverance . . . [of the tyrants who ruled Britain] in an unjustifiable, a hopeless, a ruinous war, which had brought the nation to its present pass'.[64] Not only the working men suffered; many employers also, 'shuddering on the verge of bankruptcy – insisted on peace, with the energy of desperation'.[65]

The essentially urban Luddite movement found a rural echo in 1830 when agricultural workers, led by a mythical Captain Swing, destroyed threshing machines widely hated for taking away winter employment. Setting barns and hayricks on fire, protesters also struck at the heart of English agriculture. Action only lasted for a few months, and repression, when it came, was just as brutal – with nineteen death sentences carried out – as it had been with the Gordon riots in London a half century earlier.

In the rural scene, the 'Tolpuddle Martyrs' of 1834 fared better; indeed, after being tried for administering unlawful oaths prohibited by an act of 1797, the six agriculture labourers, who formed a trade union lodge in the Dorset village of Tolpuddle, were sentenced – conforming to the standards of the day – to no more than seven years' transportation. Even so, this penalty for a peaceful, if organized, protest against a reduction in wages, provoked widespread support for a campaign of petitions and mass demonstrations; this was crowned with success when the six were pardoned in 1838.

The 'Peterloo Massacre' of 16 August 1819 had shown, however, that peaceful protest could still be met with brute force on the part of the authorities. The fact that the demonstration took place at St Peter's Fields in Manchester meant that many of the 30,000 people participating in what was planned as a broad based appeal for radical reform were artisans and labourers in the local cotton industry. It is true also that 'shorter hours, higher wages, a repeal of the Combination Acts and an end to capitalist exploitation',[66] were part of the reformers' platform. This was sufficient for the local justices to call out the yeomanry to arrest the leaders of the protest at what was, by any standard, an extremely large meeting.

The result was a near complete breakdown of law and order, only resolved after the yeomanry had opened fire, to kill eleven of the protesters and wound hundreds more. In spite of uniform condemnation by the press, the reformers – not the justices – were prosecuted by Lord Liverpool's Tory government – which then went in to pass the so-called 'Six Acts' to strengthen the forces of law and order in any future confrontation with reform agitation. However, the government did learn the lesson that yeomanry were not the appropriate local force for maintaining law and order. One man at least went further. In 1829, Sir Robert Peel persuaded another Tory government, led by the Duke of Wellington, to establish the Metropolitan Police to keep order in London; in 1833 other local authorities were permitted to set up their own police forces, following the London model, and after 1856 they were obliged to do so.

If, as related above, organized popular protest was often counterproductive in its attempts to improve working class life, it is still worth considering what, if anything, was achieved by the governing classes. Until well into the nineteenth century, government acted according to the principle that suppression, by means of new legislation, was the best way of dealing with popular agitation for reform. The Combination Acts of 1799 and 1800 represented an early stage in this process, which continued with new legislation, such as the Six Acts, passed in reaction to specific events.

On the other side, the Factory Act of 1802, which regulated the hours worked by pauper children in cotton mills, was followed by that of 1833 which extended regulation to children throughout the textile industry and also provided, for the first time, for effective means of enforcement. The Ten Hours Act of 1847 and the Factories Act of 1850 restricted the hours of female mill hands; the Factory Acts of 1844, 1847 and 1867 also extended the earlier legislation to other manufactures, including small workshops, outside the textile industry.

Shorter working hours were not the only result; factories also became much safer as a result of the mid-nineteenth century legislation. After the opening of the Liverpool and Manchester Railway in 1830, the continued expansion of British railways also brought in its train new safety legislation, with the first provisions for statutory safety inspection enacted in 1840; the Regulation of Railways Act of 1873 consolidated all existing safety legislation.[67] If the new laws were passed more in the interest of those who travelled by rail, than of those employed by the railway companies, the demands made of the latter led to a degree of professionalism and public recognition that made railway workers something of a working class elite.

In 1846, Sir Robert Peel, who had by then become Prime Minister, secured the repeal of the Corn Laws, partly in response to the agitation carried out by the Anti-Corn Law League, whose strongest support came from the Lancashire cotton industry. The result, as intended, was a substantial fall in the price of bread. Little was done to extend the franchise to the working classes until Disraeli's Reform Act of 1867, or to provide elementary education for their children until Gladstone's Education Act of 1870.

By this time the rising tide of progress, when it came to the welfare and prosperity of the working classes, was unmistakable. All this was in part a response to the way the industrial revolution was progressing in continental Europe. Prince Otto von Bismarck in particular had led the way, first in Prussia and then in a united Germany, in providing for the health, welfare and security of workers in an industrial complex which represented a clear challenge to Britain, not least in the critically important field of armaments.[68]

Another factor – also in part attributable to the growth of railways – was that business came to recognize the potential of the working classes as consumers of the goods and services it offered. The Great Exhibition of 1851 proved to be the supreme justification of this view of British society. At the same time, mass education and near universal access to postal, telegraph and rail services opened the way for the working classes to organize on a massive scale. Trade unions, in their modern form, go back to the 1850s, and were protected by law as a result of Gladstone's Trade Union Act of 1871.

The Economic Cost of European Colonialism

If there was little regard, at least in the early days of the Industrial Revolution, for the human cost in the nations, led by Britain, in which it unfolded, elsewhere the suffering of overseas populations far removed from the industrial world was very much greater.

The success of the Industrial Revolution depended on modifying the essential principle of free trade in such a way that the world was divided, economically, into two sectors. One, the dominant sector, was devoted to the manufacture of goods destined for export as much as for domestic markets, and the other, the subordinate sector, was exploited first for its raw materials, and then as a market for the manufactured goods made out of them. The dominant sector comprised a number of states, led by Britain – with a temperate climate and a long history of trade and manufacture – which, while constituting a community of economic interests, were in competition with each other to the point that where circumstances demanded, national interests could be enforced by war.

The military success of Britain in the long eighteenth century was closely tied to its being in the vanguard of the Industrial Revolution. Insofar as the subordinate sector – comprising the greater part of the world outside Europe and North America – had a community of interests, this was simply to preserve, if not develop, traditional economies, mainly in the tropics, without their being appropriated by European colonial powers.

Already, by the end of the seventeenth century, local interests in such important parts of the world as South and South-East Asia were subordinated, often quite ruthlessly, to those of by the British East India Company and the VOC,[69] its Dutch equivalent. (After considerable rivalry between the two in the seventeenth century, the former, by the eighteenth century, was dominant in India and the latter in the East Indies.[70])

In the New World the tropical economies that contributed most to the Industrial Revolution were in no sense traditional, but based on non-indigenous plantation crops capable of being exploited only by labour obtained from external sources. Tobacco was something of an exception, for it was indigenous to the New World, but the plantations, just as those with other crops such as sugar and cotton, still needed to import their labour from outside.

The history of cotton in the British economy illustrates how everything changed as the New World took over from the old as the main source of supply. Throughout the seventeenth century, Britain's main source of both raw cotton and cotton textiles was India, which also supplied, if to a lesser degree, France and the Netherlands. Because the trade was small compared to that in other traditional European textiles, notably wool and linen, it was not seen as a serious threat to their market. With the eighteenth century the position changed quite radically.

The key point here is that the exchange economy of the greatest interest to the cotton cultivating regions of India was one based on vertical integration, with finished cotton goods – such as, pre-eminently, printed calicos – being the main export. There is every reason to believe that left to itself this is the way that the local economy would have developed. Indeed, in the seventeenth century, this was accepted as the operating principle of the London-based East India Company, and it would have continued on the same course in the eighteenth century if circumstances had allowed. This is not what happened, for even raw cotton, as an alternative to wool and linen, was a threat to British agricultural interests, while competition by manufactured cotton goods threatened a long-established and mainly rural textile industry.

The outcome in Britain was a succession of compromises between conflicting interests. The outcome in India was the loss of the opportunity to develop an advanced industrial economy serving a worldwide market. Worse still, as British rule became more firmly established, as it did following Clive's decisive victory at Plassey in 1757, India not only lost much of its French export market, but had no choice but to become a captive market for British goods, including – in the long term – those produced by Lancashire cotton mills. All this, needless to say, was at the cost of local manufacture. This process intensified after the British government assumed direct rule in 1857 and foreshadowed what, in the twentieth century, came to be called the 'dependency model'.[71] In twentieth-century India this defined the essential background to Mahatma Gandhi's 'homespun' movement, which played a key part in the struggle for independence. The price paid by millions of Britain's Indian subjects was they were denied the opportunity to participate in a modern industrial economy, which, at the beginning of the eighteenth century, was – if hardly recognized by them – a reasonable prospect.

Slavery in the New World

Returning to the question of the human cost of the Industrial Revolution, there is one theme that cannot be overlooked. The forced transportation of native Africans from their homes in Africa to slavery in the New World, was an integral part of international trade from the seventeenth to the nineteenth century. From the middle of the seventeenth century, the consumer economy of Europe and to a lesser degree that of Britain's North American colonies, was focused on the produce of tropical plantations.

The logistics of transport before the railway era were such that the only economically viable location for a colonial plantation was one either close to the sea, or to a river accessible to seagoing vessels. On both sides of the Atlantic, the eighteenth century witnessed a steady popular increase in the consumption of five agricultural products which, for reasons of climate and soil, were little suited for cultivation in Britain and Europe north of the Alps – where, in any case, there was an increasing shortage of agricultural land. These five products divide into two classes, with coffee, tea and cocoa on one side, and sugar and tobacco on the other. The first three, which in the seventeenth century were affordable only by the upper classes, were acquired mainly by trade with local markets in the appropriate part of the tropics – which could be Arabia, China or Central America. Here the main problem facing European commerce was to find trade goods acceptable in these local tropical markets, which in practice meant manufactured products.

On the other side of the line, sugar and tobacco were quite a different case. For sugar, the areas most suitable for cultivation – taking into account the economic imperative in favour of transport by sea – were primarily the coastal areas of north-west Brazil and the Guianas in continental South America and of the Gulf of Mexico in North America, and then the countless islands to be found in the Caribbean Sea. Even in early European colonial times, almost none of the islands had any indigenous population, while such inhabitants as there were around the continental coastlines had neither markets, nor any potential as possible recruits for agricultural labour. Quite simply, sugar was not an indigenous crop.

With tobacco, which was an indigenous crop, profitable cultivation was restricted to a much smaller area in Britain's American colonies. This area, known as Chesapeake, was defined both by the eponymous bay and by the great tidewater rivers such as the James, the Rappahannock and the Potomac. Virginia, and to a lesser extent Maryland, became the main producers of tobacco for both the European and the colonial markets, with North Carolina joining them at a later stage.

What is more, because the popular demand for tobacco preceded that for sugar, it was Virginia that first experienced a critical shortage of plantation labour. In the colony's early days, attempts were made to solve the problem by transporting convicts from England or offering short term contract labour to poorer members of the English agricultural community.[72] Both expedients had only limited success, and although the first ship transporting Africans to be employed as unfree labour arrived as early as 1619, direct large-scale transportation from Africa had to wait until 1663, when the Company of Royal Adventurers into Africa was granted a monopoly of this trade.[73]

The majority of Africans shipped across the Atlantic to work in the New World were destined for sugar plantations. Here the Portuguese planters along the north-east coast of Brazil led the way, so that as early as 1630 it was accepted that African slaves were essential for cultivation of any labour-intensive tropical or semi-tropical crop in the New World.[74]

By the end of the seventeenth century British planters – after abandoning other unsuccessful agricultural ventures – had overtaken the Portuguese in applying this principle of labour deployment to sugar plantations in the West Indies, where, on the eve of the American Revolution, they owned some 1,800 plantations.[75] As for labour, some 1.5 million Africans had been imported by this time into the British islands,[76] to say nothing of the countless numbers who did not survive the notorious 'middle passage' across the Atlantic ocean. The increase in production was phenomenal, with economies of scale combined with more efficient management making possible the sale of sugar in Britain and northern Europe at prices affordable by the majority of the population.[77]

Slaves paid perhaps the highest price of all for the revolution in the cotton industry. By the end of the eighteenth century three-quarters of British imports of raw cotton came from slave plantations, whose productivity was increased enormously as a result of the introduction of Eli Whitney's cotton gin in 1793. Its success can be seen from the five-fold increase in British cotton imports between the mid-eighteenth century and the early nineteenth century, by which time three-quarters came from the United States. The consequences for the slave population of the United States – which on the eve of the Civil War in 1860 numbered nearly four million – were catastrophic, as noted by Preston Brooks, a congressman from South Carolina, quoted by Abraham Lincoln in 1858:[78] 'when this government was originally established nobody expected that the institution of slavery would last until this day . . . the framers of our Government did not have the knowledge that experience has taught us – that experience and the invention of the cotton gin have taught us that the perpetuation of slavery is a necessity'.[79] The British cannot escape responsibility, for in both North America and the British West Indies local black populations were the descendants of African slaves imported, initially, to serve British interests.[80] Harriet Beecher Stowe's classic *Uncle Tom's Cabin*, first published in 1852,[81] also has a place in the literature relating to the human cost of the Industrial Revolution.

7

RIVERBOATS AND RAILWAYS

The Steamboat Revolution

Steamboats came into their own just as steam power in England was transforming the manufacture of cotton textiles and the production of iron. The key breakthrough came as a result of using the rotatory engine, patented by James Watt in 1781, to drive the paddle wheels of ships.[1] British waterways, however, were not a promising market. The size and weight of even the smallest atmospheric steam engines made them unsuitable for the small ships used for coastal and inland traffic; ships would not only have to find space for the engine, but also for the fuel – which in Britain could only be coal. In addition, canals ensured that water born transport could bring to any factory both the raw materials on which it depended and the coal consumed by its steam engines; the standard narrow boats would have gained nothing by converting to steam power.

In North America on the other hand, the many great rivers flowing into the Atlantic, such as the Connecticut, Delaware, Susquehanna, Potomac, James, Savannah – and above all the Hudson – while accessible to ocean-going sailing ships, were ill suited to the small boats which in Britain were towed by horses. It was for these rivers, rather than any in Europe, that paddle steamers, with their rotatory engines, were developed.

The pioneer in this field was the Frenchman, Marquis de Jouffroy d'Abbans, who in June 1778 made an unsuccessful attempt with a steam-powered boat on the River Doubs. Five years later he did succeed, with his *Pyroscaphe*, which on 15 July 1783 made its way for fifteen minutes upstream on the River Saône. Revolution soon blocked further progress, leaving the field to American enterprise, and in 1790 John Fitch established an infrequent but continuing service on the Delaware river, linking Philadelphia in Pennsylvania to Trenton in New Jersey.

This was followed before the end of the century, by similar successes on the Connecticut and the Hudson. Steam navigation with a reliable service and fixed timetables had to wait, however, for Robert Fulton's *Clermont*, which was commissioned by Robert Livingston, who in 1798 had been granted a monopoly on steam navigation in the waters of New York state, provided he could operate a successful steamboat by 1805. Although the *Clermont* only entered service in 1807, Livingston's monopoly still held until it was overturned by the US Supreme Court in February 1824.[2] Every advance in water transport therefore, from Fitch to Fulton and beyond, was calculated to meet the traffic demands on the great rivers of the American east coast, which provided abundant incentives for improving on wind and sail.

Fulton was hardly an innovator; the *Clermont* had a twenty horsepower James Watt type engine driving a paddlewheel crankshaft. It was a flat bottomed 100 ton ship – designed for both passengers and freight – with which Fulton, a businessman as much as an inventor, operated pleasure trips on the Hudson river between New York and Albany. A contemporary called her 'a monster moving on the waters, defying wind and tide, and breathing flames and smoke'. Fuelled by pine wood rather than coal, the ship moved faster than any steamboat had before, attaining a speed of 5 miles an hour and travelling 130 miles on its maiden voyage. Within three months, it had earned $1,000 against the initial cost of $20,000.

Fulton's steamboats were, however, soon superseded by the development of high pressure steam engines. Watt himself had long known of their potential, but – cautious as ever – was inhibited by the danger in working with high pressure steam. History was often to prove him right. In the new age of steam locomotion, exploding boilers were an ever present hazard. The high pressure engine is a landmark in the history of steam, if only for its simplicity and versatility. For its romance, and even more for its importance in economic history, the adaptation of steam power to shipping in inland water-ways is an essential aspect of the Industrial Revolution. Its impact in Britain, though, was relatively modest, mainly because the canals were built on too small a scale.[3]

Thus during the first half of the nineteenth century, the United States led the field with steam-powered ships plying inland waterways. From the second decade of the century this innovation centred in the vast area drained by the Mississippi and its tributaries. Even more important, at least in the long run, were the five Great Lakes – Ontario, Erie, Huron, Michigan and Superior – which, except for Michigan, were shared with Canada. The Americans west of the Appalachians and the British in Canada faced essentially the same problem; that is to develop a vast region which enjoyed both considerable if unrealized natural wealth – in furs, lumber and minerals – and an even greater potential for agriculture and industry. Yet, in spite of the considerable advantages – long recognized in Europe – of transport by water over transport by land, the Great Lakes and the Mississippi river system did not, at the turn of the nineteenth century, constitute a viable communications infrastructure. Even so, in the first half of the nineteenth century, the economic demands of the new American states west of the Appalachians could only be met by developing transport by water along the Mississippi and its tributaries, and across the Great Lakes. At least in the case of the Mississippi this would have been impossible without steamboats.

Almost inevitably, the success of steamboat operations inland from the American east coast led those involved to turn their sights to the Mississippi and its tributaries, particularly since there was no practical alternative to steam when it came to propelling boats upstream. The challenge was first taken up by the same two New Yorkers, Robert Fulton and Robert Livingston, as had established, in 1807, with the *Clermont*, a regular steamboat service on the Hudson. With the Clermont as their model, they built the *New Orleans* in Pittsburgh, which, departing on its maiden voyage, in October 1811, took only ten weeks to reach the city after which it was named. In spite of this success, the *New Orleans* was ill suited to the Mississippi, where its hull was uncomfortably deep for the frequent shallow waters. Only able to operate profitably below Natchez, it was destroyed by fire in 1814; Fulton and Livingston both died a year later.

Meanwhile in 1807, Henry Shreve, who had much better first-hand knowledge of the Mississippi and its tributaries, had commissioned a boat that took into account their wayward character. Its first voyage was a spectacular commercial success. Commanded by Shreve, it first followed the Ohio river from Pittsburgh – close to where it had been built – down to Cairo, where the Ohio joined the Mississippi. There it turned upriver to load a cargo of lead from the mines on the Galena river,[4] far to the north of St Louis. This was loaded on to a specially constructed flat boat, to be towed downriver the whole way to New Orleans. Trans-shipped to a schooner bound for Philadelphia, the whole cargo was sold there at a profit to Shreve of $11,000.

In spite of this success, Shreve realized that this first boat, like Fulton's *New Orleans*, was not suited to the Mississippi. The solution was found in a boat with a flat bottomed hull, 136 feet long and 28 feet wide. Too shallow for bulky machinery, Shreve decked it over and put the engine and boilers on deck. He then covered it with a second deck, and above this he placed the pilot house, with two high smoke stacks just behind it for two separate efficient light weight high pressure engines,[5] each with its own horizontal boiler and piston for powering one of the side wheels. The *Washington*, a boat built on this design at Wheeling, on the upper Ohio, left the city on its maiden voyage on 4 June 1816, with Shreve as its captain.

One of the *Washington*'s two boilers exploded on its maiden voyage, leaving several dead and injured. Shreve recovered almost immediately, buried the dead, repaired the boat and sailed the rest of the way down to New Orleans without further incident. Once there he turned the boat around and steamed back to Louisville on the Ohio in a record twenty-four days – so removing all doubts and prejudices about the future of steam navigation.

Shreve had designed, built and captained the classic Mississippi paddle steamer, a model which remained standard for generations. Western steamboats, following his basic design, differed very substantially from the model which Fulton had brought from New York. With little resistance to wear and tear, they were short-lived and extravagant with fuel, but with their high pressure engines cheap to build. They were built to carry freight as much as passengers, who had to accept a safety record quite horrifying by today's standards. Boiler explosions and fires on boats mainly built of wood could destroy both cargoes and the lives of passengers in a matter of minutes.

This was a different world from that east of the Appalachians, where fast, comfortable and long lived passenger boats, with low pressure engines – built at much greater cost – dominated the relatively low volume of traffic. By the 1850s – by which time the voyage upriver took as little as four days – with a combined weight greater than that of all the vessels of the Atlantic seaboard and the Great Lakes, Shreve's steamboats were the most notable achievement of the American industrial revolution.[6]

By 1840 steamboats had reached their most advanced form, and with engines rated on average at three and a half times the power of those used by industry on land, accounted for three-fifths of all the steam power used in the United States.[7] In the 1850s New Orleans overtook New York in volume of shipping, with half of all American exports moving through it. By this time also, the economic development of the Mississippi and the Ohio extended along the whole length of both rivers, with St Louis – in the mid-nineteenth century the fourth largest city in the US – located at the point where the Missouri joins the Mississippi, as its hub. It is no wonder then that the river steamboat was admired and copied worldwide as far afield as Siberia, Latin America, Egypt and the Congo.

By 1840, however, the American transport infrastructure was transformed by the construction of railroads. In the mid-nineteenth century, river and rail traffic both complemented and competed with each other in economic terms. In broad geographical terms, the bias of the Mississippi river system was north–south while that of the railroads was east–west. In the early days before the Civil War (1861–5) river traffic dominated; steamboats had had, after all, a quarter century start on railroads, and it was only in 1852 that the Pacific Railroad Company became the first to complete a line west of the Mississippi.

The Civil War was fatal to the future prosperity of the Mississippi as a waterway; four years of war had effectively closed it to both sides. The cotton based plantation economy of the deep south lost export markets worldwide, which would never be fully restored, while the north, with its much more advanced railroad network, could take full advantage of the American industrial revolution and prosper by supplying mainly domestic markets.

In 1825, a generation before the Civil War, the transport infrastructure defined by America's inland waterways was transformed by the opening of the Erie canal, linking the Hudson river, just above Albany, to Lake Erie. This was, to quote from the standard history, 'an outstanding engineering feat'.[8] The boast, made in one of the speeches at the opening ceremony, that New York had 'made the longest canal – in the least time – with the least experience – for the least money – and of the greatest public utility of any other in the world',[9] was justified. At a time when British and continental canal traffic was at its peak, the scale of the enterprise far exceeded that of any European rival.

The strategic importance of the new canal derived from the fact that the four upper Great Lakes; Erie, Huron, Michigan and Superior, together formed one great inland sea,[10] reaching, just as effectively as the Mississippi river system, into the heart of America beyond the Appalachians. Remarkably few rivers flow into the lakes, so that a comprehensive system of inland waterways, linking them to the Mississippi river system, required the construction of canals inland from the lakes – a programme that was carried out, in a number of stages, in the thirty-odd years, following the opening of the Erie canal in 1825. The routes were chosen to link up, over the shortest possible distance, with navigable tributaries such as the Illinois and Wabash rivers. The short ninety-six mile Illinois and Michigan canal linking the Chicago river, at the foot of Lake Michigan, and the Illinois river at Lasalle, was undoubtedly the most important. The fact that it only opened in 1848 meant, however, that its usefulness was lessened by Illinois' rapidly developing railroad network.

Long before the opening of the Erie canal in 1825 – an enterprise that for political, as much as for geographical reasons, was the sole concern of New York State – entrepreneurs from other Atlantic states, such as Pennsylvania, Maryland and Virginia, were only too ready to compete with it, if they could find a way to do so. Apart from their quite considerable resentment of the economic benefits accruing to New York, they could also argue that the Erie canal did not, of itself, provide any direct access to the Mississippi river system. If this shortcoming could be overcome – as indeed happened in the second quarter of the nineteenth century – by canals linking the Great Lakes to tributaries of the Mississippi, the case for a canal providing a direct link between the Mississippi river system and the Atlantic states was still strong enough to convince any number of investors in these states that this was the right place to put their money. For one thing they could point to the fact that the Great Lakes were frozen in winter.[11]

The most promising route for a canal was one continuing as far as possible upstream alongside the Potomac river, starting at the point, just north of

Washington DC, where the river ceased to be tidal. In 1785 the idea of extending the navigation of the Potomac upstream had already led George Washington to found the Potowmack Company, but in spite of his conviction that waterways should be constructed to link the Eastern Seaboard with the Ohio river and the Great Lakes,[12] his own company achieved next to nothing. It was only in 1820 that the new Chesapeake and Ohio Company bought out the Potowmack stockholders, and proceeded – with Benjamin Wright, who had formerly held that office with the Erie Canal Company, as Chief Engineer – to plan the construction of a canal linking the Potomac with the Ohio. The fact that the Potomac was the eastern boundary, and the Ohio, the western boundary of Virginia, made the project particularly appealing to George Washington's home state.

On the other hand, the fact that nothing could be done without the cooperation of Maryland, on the other side of the Potomac, was almost certain to cause trouble. Although construction started with a groundbreaking ceremony by President John Quincy Adams on 4 July 1828, the project was already running into trouble in Maryland, and the canal, when construction finally ceased in 1850, had got no further than Cumberland, Maryland – and was already obsolete. With the Allegheny Mountains between Cumberland and the Ohio river, the canal had stopped far short of its intended destination. The failure of the enterprise can be attributed, in part, to the problem of finding a route across the Appalachians in an area where the mountains were a far more formidable natural obstacle than they had presented to the Erie Canal in western New York state. In 1828, the Erie canal – which had itself taken eight years to build – had already been open along its whole length for three years.

In the end, the other canals that opened up the vast lands in the new states beyond the Appalachians were also doomed. Long distance transport that required trans-shipment to vessels drawn by horses was never going to survive the challenge of the new railroads. By 1850 it was becoming clear that modern canals must be built on a scale to accommodate river – and even ocean going – steamboats. But by this stage, the United States as much as the United Kingdom had moved beyond the heyday of the Industrial Revolution.

One must therefore go back in time and look at the other side of steam-powered transport, defined by the successful introduction of steam locomotion and the construction of railways. While the United States led the way with riverboats, with railways, which came into their own a generation later, the United Kingdom was in the vanguard in an historical process which transformed, worldwide, the impact of the Industrial Revolution.

Steam-powered Transport on Land

Although William Murdock, the best 'engine erector' Matthew Boulton had ever seen, had suggested to him and his partner James Watt that their atmospheric steam engine might be used to power a carriage, his two employers did not buy the idea. Considering the state of even the best British turnpikes, and the size of even the largest wagons that could travel on them, there was no way that even the most advanced steam engine could be adapted to locomotion. Murdock's idea was a pipe dream; no wonder, then, that little came of it.

Somewhat paradoxically then, the invention of a satisfactory rotatory engine led almost immediately to its use in the transport of both coal and the men who mined it underground. An engine capable of winding an indefinite length of cable on a drum that rotated on a horizontal axis, if used for hauling cages up mine shafts, could raise far heavier loads than the machinery (for which horses provided the motive power) used for this purpose before the introduction of steam power. The same was true when it came to hauling wagons uphill, and it was this – as much as any other factor – that in the early nineteenth century was to lead to the invention of steam-powered locomotives. They were not designed, however, to run on roads, but on rails.

Coal mining provided both the historical background, and the rationale for such a development. For geological reasons, coal seams, like many other sources of mineral wealth, occur mainly in hills, so the transport of coal from any given mine can usefully be by a wagon on wheels, carrying its load downhill, under the force of gravity. The final destination will then be some water-way, accessed by a staithe, that is a dock built to be accessible by wagons.

In 1603, Huntington Beaumont, born into a family of mine owners in England, applied the key principle, 'before you buy a mine, buy a road', and was able to lay down a railway on which carriages would carry coal downhill from his new mine at Wollerton Lane in Nottinghamshire to a staithe on the River Trent. The true character of this innovation is reflected in the words of a court claim against Beaumont after his original fifteen year lease had expired:

> The said Huntington Beaumont hath used new and extraordinary invencions and practises for the speedy and easy conveyance away of the said coales, and especially by breaking the soyle for the layinge of rayles to carry the same upon with great ease and expedicion – and by drawinge of certain carrylaggs laden with coales upon the same rayles.[13]

Although Beaumont's innovations led him in the end to bankruptcy, the technology he introduced was soon adopted elsewhere. For the mine owners of north-east England it became so indispensable that by the beginning of the nineteenth century, a vast network of railways brought coal down from the richest mining area of England[14] to its two main rivers, the Tyne and the Wear. The ultimate achievement was that of the Tanfield wagon-way; carrying about half the Tyneside traffic and a third of the total traffic of the north-east coalfields, wagons ran at an average interval of forty-five seconds, a rate four times higher than the average for all wagon-ways.[15]

In early days the rails were wooden, but in the course of time cast iron took over. With the transport of coal from the mines organized in this way – and there was really no viable alternative – the profitability of a proposed mine depended as much on the local topography as it did on the expected yield of the seams underground. By the beginning of the nineteenth century the existence of rich seams beyond the reach of any viable extension of a railway network dependent for its motive power entirely upon gravity or traction by horses was a major factor in the search for some better method.

With the exception of the use of rotatory engines to hoist skips up mine shafts, Boulton and Watt made no direct contribution to the development of steam-powered locomotion, but the rapid introduction of their engines in factories resulted in a demand for the transport of coal and other raw materials. The vast expansion of both mining railways and the British inland waterway network at the end of the eighteenth century created a need that became steadily more difficult to satisfy.

Not surprisingly, many potential inventors – on both sides of the Atlantic – contemplated the prospect of adapting the steam engine to locomotion. Indeed, as shown by the steam-driven mechanisms already in use for hauling both wagons and boats uphill by means of a cable wound around a drum connected to an engine,[16] the first step had already been taken. The breakthrough came when the engine itself became part of the transport – representing the ultimate in locomotion. Only when this was achieved were the limitations on distance – inherent in all cable systems – overcome.

The problem was that the atmospheric engine, even with all the improvements resulting from Watt's inventiveness, was never going to be suitable for mounting on a vehicle that would travel over land. The dimensions of a dedicated track, even when it was one with iron rather than wooden rails, could simply not be increased to cope with a wagon carrying any existing model of an atmospheric engine. The best any such wagon might achieve would be to move itself along a level railway – a result actually achieved experimentally before the end of the eighteenth century. What was required was a locomotive with a surplus of power sufficient to pull a train of wagons – itself a recent innovation in short-distance transport from coalmines.

On 24 March 1802, a critical step in this direction was taken by Richard Trevithick (1771–1833), an engineer whose long experience of Boulton and Watt atmospheric steam engines in mines in his home county, Cornwall, had led him not only to experiment with high pressure engines, but also to use one to provide the motive power for a carriage. For this purpose he was granted Patent No. 2599, entitled 'Steam engines – Improvements in the construction thereof and Application thereof for driving carriages'. This followed a not very successful demonstration of a prototype on Beacon Hill, just outside Trevithicks's home town of Camborne, on Boxing Day, 1801.

Success came at last on 21 February 1804, not on a road but on a cast iron plateway[17] linking two ironworks in South Wales – where the rolling mills were already powered by stationary steam engines installed by Trevithick – to the Glamorganshire canal. Trevithick produced a locomotive that ran successfully over a distance of nearly ten miles from one of the ironworks down to the canal. Not surprisingly, there was some damage to the track, but Trevithick's locomotive had the advantage that it was downhill all the way. However, he was too busy building and marketing his stationary engines to have time to spare for the development of locomotives.[18]

Nevertheless, it was soon recognized that the basic principle of Trevithick's invention was sound, and mine owners at the other end of England, in both the West Riding of Yorkshire and Tyneside, competed to adapt his locomotive to hauling wagons loaded with coal. Finally, the owners of the Killingworth Colliery on Tyneside believed that their engine wright, George Stephenson, could produce a viable locomotive, taking advantage of the fact that the wagons transporting coal from their mine already ran on rails. Stephenson, employing skills laboriously acquired by working with steam engines, produced a locomotive for Killingworth, which had its first trial run on 25 July 1814. Named *Blücher*,[19] and running on Killingworth's cast iron rails, it overcame the defects of all its predecessors in steam locomotion – so much so that one admirer noted in 1821 that 'the locomotive engine of Mr. Stephenson is superior beyond all comparison to all other Engines I have ever seen . . .'[20]

George Stephenson, soon to become known to history as 'the father of the locomotive',[21] was a man of humble origins but with a remarkable gift of perseverance. Every day, as a boy growing up in a poor Tyneside coal mining family, he saw wagons drawn by horses and running on wooden rails – the classic scenario described above. Inevitably he too went into mining, where his earliest ambition was to become an engineman. Starting as a fireman, he rose, after three years, to be a 'plug man', responsible for the operation and repair of a pump engine in Killingworth. Then, aged eighteen, he realized that he would go no further without learning to read and write, so he took lessons (also in arithmetic) three nights a week after work.

Once into his twenties Stephenson soon gained the reputation of being able to make repairs to machinery where others had been defeated; in one case making it possible to reopen one of the Killingworth mines after it had been flooded for a year. At the age of twenty-eight he was appointed engine wright to the mine, becoming responsible for all the steam-powered machinery. From almost his first day his innovations substantially reduced working costs – an achievement much appreciated by his employers. It is not surprising then, that they entrusted him in 1814 with the construction of a locomotive to haul wagons on the railway down to the River Tyne – where by this time, the rails were made of iron, not wood.

The *Blücher* was the result. Its success, which was immediate, was achieved by both better design and better machining. Stephenson, having seen all too often how mining machinery failed because of poor workmanship, set unprecedentedly high standards of precision. At the same time he was continually improving every part of his locomotive. The engine itself, the wheels (made from malleable instead of cast iron) and the springing (essential on the uneven tracks) all received attention. The same was true of the rails, together with the chairs and sleepers that supported them.

Although Stephenson's reputation for thoroughness soon led to commissions to lay down new railways throughout Tyneside, these were all private undertakings following the established pattern of moving coal from mines down to the river. This, however, was hardly a transport revolution. A new perspective on the potential of railways with steam locomotives was needed. This was also found in the coal mining region of north-east England, and realized in practical form with the opening of the Stockton and Darlington Railway on 27 September 1825.

The Stockton and Darlington Railway

In spite of the considerable extent of the mining railways of Tyne and Wear, and the improvement in their operation as a result of Stephenson's locomotives, there was, at the turn of the nineteenth century, no concept of railways constituting a public utility offering transport facilities, even if only for a restricted market. The success of stagecoaches in providing for the transport of passengers on the newly constructed turnpikes, which by the end of the eighteenth century effectively constituted a nationwide system, had no parallel when it came to the transport of commodities by rail. On the contrary, the construction of the British canal system in the last quarter of the century would seem to have pre-empted any need for an alternative nationwide system for the surface transport of goods.

If, in the north-east, the mining railways assured coalmines of access to two of the main rivers, the Tyne and the Wear, a third river, the Tees, was much less favoured, even though it was navigable by sea going traffic to the port of Stockton – some fifteen miles inland – which had pretensions to rival Newcastle-upon-Tyne. There – and in Darlington, some twelve miles further inland – prominent local citizens, in the years after 1800, coveted the right to transport coal from the rich Auckland coalfield in the centre of County Durham.[22] Their first step was to improve the navigation of the Tees by building a new cut. To celebrate its completion a dinner was held at Stockton Town Hall on 18 September 1810. There the possibility of a direct line of communication between the Auckland coalfields and Darlington came up for discussion.

Given the economic climate of the day, the majority in a straw poll would probably have been in favour of a canal. Times however, were changing, and a strong new faction, headed by Edward Pease, a Quaker banker and woollen merchant from Darlington, argued in favour of a horse tramway. For some years surveys were carried out by both sides; the issue came to a head in 1818 when the canal faction adopted a recommendation for a direct route from Stockton to Auckland that took no account of Darlington. An alliance led by Edward Pease then appointed as its own surveyor, George Overton, whose unrivalled experience with the cast iron tramways serving the coalfields in South Wales included the construction of the Pen-y-Darren line which, in 1804, was the scene of Robert Trevithick's triumph with a steam locomotive. Overton, who had written shortly before his appointment that 'Railways are now generally adopted and the cutting of canals nearly discontinued',[23] left no one in doubt about where he stood.

The canal faction reacted by switching their support to a tramway that would follow the same route as they had proposed for the canal: this was tantamount to surrender, and in the end the two sides jointly presented the Stockton & Darlington Bill, based on the route proposed by the railway faction, to Parliament – only to see it defeated as a result of the opposition of two substantial local landowners, Lord Eldon and Lord Darlington. Overton, who had never encountered such difficulties in South Wales, contained his exasperation and surveyed a new route acceptable to the noble landowners. The end result was the Stockton & Darlington Railway Act which received the royal assent on 19 April 1821.

The passing of the act left Edward Pease and his supporters in a commanding position, from which they offered George Stephenson (now joined by his son, Robert) a contract for providing steam engines for hauling the trains of coal wagons on the new railway. Because of the topography of the route between Auckland and Stockton designated in the Railway Act, the mode of operation planned for the new line was somewhat involved. At its western end, the Etherly and Brussleton inclines were judged to be too steep for locomotives, so provision was made for winding engines, with horses drawing the wagons along intermediate sections of track. Then, on the eastern side – from the foot of Brussleton bank – two steam locomotives designed by Stephenson, the *Locomotion* and the *Hope*, would take the wagons the rest of the way, over relatively flat country, to Stockton. They were duly constructed by the Stephensons' factory in Newcastle and brought laboriously by horse-drawn wagon to the new railway's New Shildon workshop in the middle of September 1825.

The line was ready for traffic on 26 September, with the formal opening the next day. This started at Witton Park at the western end of the line, with ten loaded coal wagons from the nearby Phoenix pit ready to be drawn by horses to the foot of the Etherly incline. There the steam bank engine successfully wound them up to the top, so that they could run down the other side under the force of gravity. Once they were down at the bottom, the process was repeated – with a wagon loaded with flour added to the train – up and over the Brussleton incline, but this time the *Locomotion* was waiting for them at Shildon Lane at the foot of the bank on the east side. The locomotive was already coupled to a train consisting of the *Experiment*, a specially designed passenger carriage built for the occasion at the New Shildon works, together with twenty-one new coal wagons converted to carry passengers. Then, hitched to the wagons from the Phoenix pit which had already completed the first part of their journey, the train went on its way to Stockton.

Tickets were allotted to 300 passengers, but almost as many again clambered on to the train; after one or two mishaps – corrected by George Stephenson with the help of his brother, James – the train reached the junction with the Darlington branch line at midday. There, six of the coal wagons from the Phoenix pit were uncoupled so that their contents could be distributed to the poor of Darlington, while two new wagons – one carrying leading citizens from the town and the other, the Yarm town band – replaced them. Along the line, tens of thousands had gathered to see the unprecedented spectacle.

At quarter to four this incredible train reached its final destination at Stockton Quay, to be greeted by a seven gun salute – repeated three times – church bells pealing, the town band, supported by the Yarm musicians, playing patriotic music, and a cheering crowd estimated at 40,000. The guests of honour made their way through the general pandemonium to the town hall for an official banquet that lasted until midnight, when the last of twenty-three toasts was drunk to George Stephenson.

The Liverpool and Manchester Railway

Even before the Stockton & Darlington Railway opened, George Stephenson was involved in a much larger project; the construction of a railway linking the seaport of Liverpool with Manchester – the centre of England's booming cotton industry – thirty miles away. The background was quite different: between the two cities the Bridgewater canal, opened in 1761 and built by the third Duke of Bridgewater for the transport of coal to Manchester from his mines at Worsley, already provided a transport link. In the early nineteenth century this did not (at the rates demanded by the Bridgewater Estate) satisfy the requirements of Liverpool businessmen concerned to transport raw cotton imported from the southern states of America to the mills in Manchester. The Manchester mill owners felt the same way. A railway was the obvious alternative to the canal, and who better to build it than George Stephenson? The new Liverpool Railway Company appointed Stephenson. His first task, the survey of possible routes for the new railway, was immediately opposed by the Bridgewater Estates, supported by Lord Derby and Lord Sefton, whose land would be crossed by whatever route was chosen.

Even without such opposition the choice was bound to be difficult. The thirty miles of country between

Liverpool and Manchester contained a remarkable number of natural obstacles. If the civil engineering problems involved in the route finally advised by Stephenson, which included the construction of a mile long tunnel, a cutting and a viaduct across a swamp, were severe, they would have been even more so on any alternative route.

Stephenson did not give up in face of the opposition, and when the Bill was presented a second time to Parliament it went through to become the Liverpool & Manchester Railway Act of 1826. Even so, when Parliament considered the grant of finance, the advice of the seventy-two-year old Thomas Telford, the leading civil engineer of the day, was negative. At this late stage it was not even clear whether the line would be worked with horses, winding engines or locomotives – or, as in the early days of the Stockton & Darlington Railway, some combination of these three options. Telford was, however, persuaded to advise positively after the company had promised a firm decision in favour of one form of traction and Stephenson had signed an affidavit binding himself to complete the railway in 1830.

Finally, in 1830 the Stephensons won round the Railway Board, which, taking into account expected 'improvements in the construction and work of locomotives', had already decided, on 20 April 1829, to offer a prize of £500 for the best locomotive. If this produced a winning entry of such merits as to make clear the superiority of locomotives, the issue would be decided in favour of steam traction. On 31 August 1829 this led the Liverpool & Manchester directors to resolve 'That the place of tryal for the Specimen Engines on the 1st

October next be the level space between the two inclined planes at Rainhill; and that the Engineer prepare a double Railway for the two miles of level, and a single line down the plane to the Roby Embankment'.

A locomotive entered for the trial had to meet very narrow specifications, and even before the conditions of the trial were made public, George Stephenson, in partnership with his son Robert, had set up new works in Newcastle to manufacture what proved to be the prototype of the modern locomotive. Their work went so well that even Robert Stephenson, a born pessimist, was able to claim that, 'On the whole the Engine is capable of doing as much if not more than set forth in the stipulations'.[24]

The Rainhill trials were finally held five days late, on Tuesday, 6 October 1830. The scene along the prescribed course would have been appropriate to a racecourse, with a grandstand at the midpoint and thousands of spectators along both sides of the track. Beside the *Rocket*, entered by Robert Stephenson, four other locomotives competed, although only two of them, the *Novelty* and the *Sans Pareil*, were a serious challenge. Even so, when it came to the actual trials, their performance was so far behind that of the Stephensons' *Rocket* that they did not even meet the minimum specifications.

When it came to the turn of the *Rocket*, it weighed in at 4 tons, 5 cwt – well under the prescribed limit – and in just under an hour, with its steam pressure built up from cold to 50 lb, was ready to be coupled to two wagons loaded with stone and to start its first lap. Stephenson prudently decided not to use full power, although he allowed it to increase during the last three laps in the first half of the trial. Having completed this without any mishap, the *Rocket* was ready for the second half. This went so well that in the last lap – towards Manchester – the driver gave it full regulator, to achieve, with a time of 3 minutes, 44 seconds, an average speed of just over 24 mph. For the full course of 60 miles the *Rocket*'s average speed was just under 14 mph – safely beyond the 10 mph prescribed by the trial rules.

Although the judges reported to the directors that the *Rocket* had demonstrated 'in a very eminent degree the practicality of attaining a high velocity even with a load of considerable weight attached to the engine', the owners of the two competing locomotives proved to be poor losers. To satisfy them, the trials were extended with further demands made upon the Stephensons. The new trials only confirmed the immense superiority of their locomotive, so that 'there could be no more talk of horses or fixed haulage engines. The battle for the locomotive had been most decisively won and it was as an exclusively locomotive-worked railway that the Liverpool and Manchester went forward to completion.'[25]

As a result of the Rainham trials the railway not only purchased the *Rocket*, but ordered six similar locomotives, all of which were delivered in the summer of 1830. The official opening of the Liverpool & Manchester Railway on 15 September 1830 was not the same happy event as that of the Stockton & Darlington some five years earlier. Because the Prime Minister, the Duke of Wellington, had agreed to attend, the day's programme was extremely elaborate, and the plans went complete awry after the unfortunate local MP, William Huskisson, had stepped unwittingly into the path of one of the trains involved. Severely injured, he died later in the day, leaving those staging the event to sort out a chaotic situation in which many of the trains taking part ended up in the wrong place. The Duke, at least, did complete the journey to Manchester, to be met by a hostile mob on his delayed arrival.

It was decided to return to Liverpool immediately, and the Duke himself did not even leave his carriage. Clearing a path for his train back to Liverpool inevitably added to the chaos so that only three, instead of seven, locomotives were in Manchester to bring trains carrying ordinary passengers. The only solution was to couple the carriages together, to make trains far longer than their engines were designed for – but the gradient of the Whiston incline was too much for them.[26] The male passengers had to get out and walk, in darkness and in pouring rain, but once they rejoined the trains at the summit, they had an easy run to the Liverpool terminus, where, at 10 p.m., cheering crowds were waiting to greet them. Among the railwaymen, everyone from George Stephenson downwards had kept his cool, and the day was saved, with poor Huskisson as its only casualty.

The next day the first train ran according to the timetable, carrying 140 passengers, and the line is still in business. Incontrovertibly, the age of railways had arrived – however many problems remained to be solved.

Railroads in America
The success of the English railways was soon noticed, on both sides of the Atlantic, by entrepreneurs intent upon

escaping the limitations of the existing transport infrastructure. The appeal of railways was particularly strong
in places deriving too little benefit from inland waterways. In the United States this meant, above all, harbour
cities such as Baltimore, which while accessible to the
Atlantic Ocean, were not at the head of any useful
navigable river. In 1827, a group of merchants met there
to organize the Baltimore and Ohio Railroad Company
(B&O). Its purpose, which was essentially the same as
that of the Chesapeake and Ohio Canal Company, was
to provide a transport link between Chesapeake Bay and
the Ohio River. The prospect of a canal leading to a new
port on the Potomac close to Washington – with the
advantage of the direct link to the Ohio – challenged the
supremacy of Baltimore. For the second largest city in
the United States this was incentive enough to promote
a railroad. The problem was that for much of the way to
Ohio, the valley of the Potomac was the only viable
route. Upriver from Point of Rocks, a Maryland township some forty miles north-west of Washington, there
were any number of points where there was hardly room
for both a canal and a railroad.

The result, which was in the interests neither of the
canal nor the railway factions, was a critical loss of
construction time during some five years of litigation
and political lobbying, allowing 'New York and Philadelphia [to forge] ahead as commercial centers at the
eastern end of a rich and growing western trade via
improved transportation systems'[27] – mainly consisting,
it need hardly be said, of inland waterways. Critically for
the future development of the American transport
infrastructure, the Chesapeake and Ohio canal failed,

while the railroad – by reaching the Ohio river, at Wheeling, Virginia, in 1852 – eventually succeeded. In doing so it had to cross the Buckhorn Wall, a natural feature at an altitude of 2,500 feet in the heart of the mountains, which would have been an almost insurmountable obstacle to canal builders.

Compared to what had already been achieved in Britain, followed by much of continental Europe, this may seem like slow progress, but the problems inherent in the topography of the hinterland of Baltimore could not be solved by engineering practices established by the Stephensons. First and above all, was the matter of distance; that separating Baltimore from the Ohio river – the intended destination of the railroad – was hundreds of miles greater than the length of any railway contemplated in Britain. When the B&O reached the Potomac river at Point of Rocks, Maryland – completing the essential first stage on the way to the Ohio – the total length of its track already exceeded the combined mileage of the Stockton & Darlington and the Liverpool & Manchester railways in Britain.

By this time, the directors of the B&O were laying the rails on wooden ties, in preference to the Stephensons' stone blocks, and equipping rolling stock with wheels with flanges on the inner edge fixed to rotating axles – both innovations eventually becoming standard worldwide. At the same time the cost of constructing any line across the Appalachians with the slight gradients and curves which were standard in Britain was prohibitive. The standard B&O locomotive, with its weight evenly distributed over at least four driving wheels and a swivelling front bogie designed to deal with the sharpest curves, was much more powerful. It was much more extravagant with fuel, but in contrast to Europe, the first American railways – constructed at a time when coal mining was little developed – followed the example of American steamboats and burnt wood, which was just as abundant along their lines as it was along the rivers. Later, when they did eventually switch to coal, this had already proved to be as abundant in the regions where they operated as it was in Britain. In the American case, as earlier in Britain, a number of important lines, such as the Lehigh Valley Railroad in Pennsylvania, were constructed specifically to serve coalmines.

The pioneer railways, the Liverpool and Manchester on one side of the Atlantic, and the Baltimore & Ohio on the other, were soon joined by countless others – so much so that by the half-century, railways accounted for more than half of all new capital investment. This was true not only of the English-speaking world of the North Atlantic, but of any number of other states, some of which, such as France and Belgium, lost hardly any time in following the road pioneered by Britain. The factor demands of the new railways, in materials, labour and capital, were on an unprecedented scale and they were by no means confined to specific demands of track and rolling-stock. Railways required civil engineering on a massive scale, particularly when local topography was adverse. Good surveying could make all the difference when it came to the profitability of a new line, a lesson continually hammered home by the great British civil engineer, Isambard Kingdom Brunel.

8

THE AMERICAN WAY

The Legacy of Revolution

A world accustomed to the vast scale of American industry in the twentieth century could easily assume that the United States, in the eighteenth and nineteenth centuries, was in the vanguard of the industrial revolution. This, however, is mainly true only of its final phase, characterized – on both sides of the Atlantic – by the massive increase in steel production made possible by the revolution in production methods during the 1860s and then a generation later, by the use of electric power. Significantly, the four years of the Civil War, 1861–5, also define a watershed in American economic history, with the Union victory in 1865 opening the way for expansion on a massive scale, with the base of the national economy shifting decisively from agriculture to industry.

During the thirteen years between the American Declaration of Independence in 1776 and the adoption of the federal constitution in 1789, the Industrial Revolution in Britain was well underway. During the colonial period Britain was always the main source of manufactured goods imported into North America – so much so that in 1772 the colonies accounted for more than a third of the British export market.[1] The steady growth of the American market was made possible by a vast increase, not only in the number of ships engaged in the Atlantic trade, but also in their size. One result was a fall in the rates charged for both passengers and freight, so that for instance, in 1770 the price of an emigrant passage from Europe was half what it had been in 1720. At this stage, just before the American Revolution, the Atlantic was not so much a barrier as a bridge between Britain and its North American colonies. By the early 1750s, according to a recent German immigrant, 'it is really possible to obtain all things one can get in Europe in Pennsylvania, since so many merchant ships arrive there every year'.[2] Inland from Pennsylvania, across the Allegheny mountains, was a largely undiscovered world – which in any case belonged to France until the end of the Seven Years War (1756–63).

From the seventeenth century onwards, the exchange economy of Britain's American colonies was based on the export of plantation crops, of which tobacco, in the years leading up to the war of independence, was the most important. The fact that Chesapeake Bay, together with rivers flowing into it such as the Potomac and the James, were accessible to ocean going ships, meant that the richest plantations were either in Maryland, along the shores of the bay, or in tidewater Virginia. Not only was the plantation economy totally dependent on slave labour, but the international slave trade was a major part of both the British and American economies.

In principle, American ships were barred by the British Navigation Acts from the trading on their own account. The fact that the prosperity of the port of Providence in Rhode Island (a New England colony without any plantations) depended largely on this trade, shows how ineffective the British navy was in enforcing the law, and here Providence was by no means alone. Britain was supplied with commodities such as tobacco, which could not be produced by domestic agriculture, while at the same time it had privileged access to a rapidly expanding market for its own manufactures.

If all this was the basis of colonial economic policy, as decreed by the government in London, the reality on the other side of the Atlantic was somewhat different. New England and the mid-Atlantic colonies – which, throughout the eighteenth century, were home to more than half the British population of North America[3] – were not suited to plantation agriculture. The result was that, except for timber and shipping, these northern colonies produced little that Britain needed. Instead their export economy depended largely on supplying lumber, fish, livestock and provisions[4] to Britain's West Indian colonies. Later in the century,[5] with wheat added to the list of American exports, southern Europe almost rivalled the West Indies as an export market. In both the West Indies and southern Europe, the American exporters were paid by bills of exchange, drawn on London, which in turn could be used to pay for imports from Britain.

The overseas demand for American wheat led not only to increased production in the mid-Atlantic states, but also to wheat supplanting tobacco on many Chesapeake plantations. This transformation had two important consequences; first, there was a significant decrease in the demand for slave labour and second, New England lost population to the mid-Atlantic states.[6] New York, and even more, Pennsylvania, had the great advantage of being able to offer new land for cultivation – but not of plantation crops. The free colonists, including many who remained in New England, enjoyed a level of prosperity unknown in the European countries that they, or their ancestors, had left behind. The necessities of life were abundant. Local forests provided lumber to build homes and firewood to heat them, while the grains, vegetables, milk and meat of a plentiful diet could be bought cheaply[7] by those outside the agricultural community.

The war of independence (1776–81) inevitably meant a major disruption of the commercial ties between Britain and North America. The economic consequences, on both sides of the Atlantic, were severe. Where in Britain the loss of the American market was a blow to manufacturers, those fighting for American independence had difficulty finding substitutes for British goods, which, with the loss of the British export market, they could not easily afford. In particular, because the Atlantic colonies never had an arms industry, the American colonists were left to fight the British with arms they had earlier imported from Britain. One of George Washington's priorities, once he was elected President according to the new United States Constitution of 1789, was to set up a federal arsenal,[8] which made a significant contribution to the American industrial revolution.

When peace came with the Treaty of Versailles in 1783, both sides soon realized how much it was in their own interest to restore the old commerce. Well before the end of the eighteenth century, the new United States was once again an important market for British manufactures, paid for mainly by the export of plantation crops. By this stage however, a radical change in the American export led plantation economy was well underway.

While in the last twenty years of the century, the demand for American tobacco – the mainstay of the plantation economy of the Chesapeake and the Carolinas – declined, the importation of cotton into Britain increased eightfold.[9] This was the result both of the new British inventions which were then revolutionizing cotton spinning and, in America, of Eli Whitney's invention of the cotton gin in 1793, which allowed the plantations in the southern states to produce lint to be tied up in bales ready for shipment to any destination, including the new Lancashire cotton mills.

There was however, a key distinction between the two classes of invention. Where the water-frame, and other British machinery designed for cotton spinning, could most profitably be used on a large scale that could only be achieved in a factory, Whitney's gin was designed to operate where the cotton was harvested. Its scale of operation was therefore much smaller, and the power needed to drive it could best be supplied by a pair of horses.[10]

Efficient operation on plantations – which varied considerably in size – continued to depend on the exploitation of slave labour. If, then, cotton was at the heart of the British Industrial Revolution, on the American plantations the case was quite different; the vast gains in production could only be achieved by increasing the labour force of enslaved Africans. The cotton gin, by enabling a more refined product to be shipped, saved labour not in the American south, but in its export markets, which meant, above all, Lancashire. While tobacco was most profitably planted in the Chesapeake and the Carolinas, the land most suitable for cotton was in the Deep South, particularly in the new states of Louisiana, Mississippi and Alabama that were admitted to the Union in the first twenty years of the nineteenth century. (At a later stage this meant that owners in Virginia and Maryland – as they switched from tobacco to wheat and cattle – sold their slaves to planters from the Deep South.[11])

The success of cotton in the southern states came, however, at a high price. After the introduction of Whitney's cotton gin the organization of the plantations required practically no innovative technology. The only exception is to be found in the shipment of cotton bales to market, which, from 1811 onwards, depended on the operation of steamboats on the navigable rivers of the American south. Of these, the Mississippi and its tributaries, such as the Cumberland, the Tennessee and the Arkansas were much the most important. This hardly supported any local industry, for the riverboats were mainly built in northern states – to which we must now return to discover where and how the industrial revolution ran its course in the United States.

At the end of the eighteenth century, the American population was overwhelmingly rural. While in modest settlements small-scale manufacture, carried out by countless saddlers, hatters, blacksmiths, weavers, cobblers, carpenters, bakers, apothecaries and many others producing for local markets[12] flourished, only six towns with a population larger than 8,000 were reported in the first US Census of 1790, and the largest of these, New York, had only 33,000 residents. The twenty largest towns were all Atlantic seaports, and it was only in the early nineteenth century that large inland cities emerged; of these, the four largest in 1830 were on major rivers, with Albany on the Hudson, and Pittsburgh, Cincinnati and Louisville on the Ohio, economically much the most important tributary of the Mississippi.[13]

The emergence of new inland cities reflected the importance of waterways to the industrial development of the United States. There were three essential categories: navigable rivers, small rivers suitable for the construction of watermills and canals. Until well into the nineteenth century, these comprised two separate systems. The first 'Atlantic' system was that defined by waterways, including countless tributaries of main rivers, which, sooner or later, flowed into the ocean at various points along the coast between Massachusetts in the north and Georgia in the south. The second was defined almost entirely by the 'Mississippi' and its many eastern tributaries.[14]

Until the early 1800s only the Atlantic system counted in the American economy, to which it was absolutely indispensable. To begin with, the great navigable rivers – Merrimack, Connecticut, Hudson, Delaware, Susquehanna, Potomac, James, Savannah and so on – were essential both to foreign trade and to communication between the Atlantic states (which in 1800 still accounted for more than 90 per cent of the US population).[15]

The early historical development of steamboats reflects the importance not only of these great rivers but also of the coastal sea lanes, which until the construction of canals in the early nineteenth century were the most important commercial link between them.

While the riverboats in the Atlantic states represented the beginning of the industrial revolution in America, one fact was still critical; none of them burnt coal. Whereas, in eighteenth-century England, the steam engine was indispensable for coal mining (which also provided its fuel), the economy of the Atlantic states of America had little if any need for coal. This was just as well given that such seams as had been discovered consisted mainly of anthracite. The richest of these, at Summit Hill in eastern Pennsylvania (overlooking the Lehigh River) was only discovered by a local millwright in 1791.[16] In spite of its proximity to the factories of Philadelphia – then the second largest city in the US – the transport costs, involving nine miles of precipitous wagonway and then the rapids of the fast flowing Lehigh, were prohibitive.

What is more the Philadelphia manufacturers did not know how to burn it, with one of them observing that 'if the world should take fire, the Lehigh coalmine would be the safest retreat, the last place to burn'.[17] If coal were needed, it would be much better to import bituminous coal from Britain, where it was the fuel par excellence of the industrial revolution. In any case, charcoal, produced from local woodlands, was readily available and suitable for almost all industrial processes. For most of these, as the next paragraph explains, the motive power was not provided by fire, but by water.

Next to the great navigable rivers, countless minor rivers, mostly tributaries but with some, such as the charmingly named Brandywine, flowing directly into the ocean, were intensively exploited by the construction of watermills. The origins of the vertical waterwheel are to be found in antiquity.[18] The power that it can deliver is measured by the product of the height of the head of water and the rate of its flow.[19] The ideal river for waterwheels is one with a relatively steep gradient (which will make it unsuitable for navigation), draining an area with a relatively high level of precipitation. Inevitably therefore, climate and geography limited the number of mills that a single stream could power.[20] While this limit was low in England, in the United States, with a much lower population density and abundant new land open to settlement, the limit was more than high enough to allow the almost unrestricted exploitation of water power. Even so, in settled agricultural areas close to big cities such as Philadelphia, only a few miles separated the watermills along many rivers.

In 1797 the Brandywine valley, which drained the larger part of Chester County, just outside the city, contained sixty watermills providing the power for the manufacture of paper[21] – at that time essentially a low tech craft industry offering few economies of scale. Waterwheels were just as important for providing power to saw mills[22] and for milling wheat. Such usage was typical of the whole Piedmont area of the mid-Atlantic states, where recent research has shown how next to nothing survives of the natural river system as it was encountered by the first settlers. Hundreds of waterwheels, with their weirs and dams, created a quite different system, and although many of the dams were breached even before the end of the nineteenth century, with more following in the twentieth century, the original river system was not restored anywhere.

American Iron Founding

Iron ore was first discovered in the Atlantic colonies at a very early stage. By the beginning of the eighteenth century it was clear that the most abundant reserves of iron ore were in Pennsylvania; in 1716 Thomas Rutter opened the colony's first iron forge on a tributary of the navigable Schuylkill river, which in 1720 was converted into the Coalbrookdale Foundry.

The most successful of the early entrepreneurs, however, was Peter Grubb, a stonemason, who having started mining ore in Lebanon County, in the eastern part of the state, during the 1730s, founded the Cornwall Iron Furnace in 1742 – choosing this name to recall the English county where his immigrant parents had been born and brought up. The site was well chosen because the Cornwall Banks proved to be the most important and largest iron ore deposit in Pennsylvania.

By this time the favourable prospects of American iron led to British government concern about the threat that it represented to the export of British manufactures. In 1750 the Parliament in Westminster passed the Iron Act of 1750, which, while encouraging the colonies to produce pig iron and iron bars for export to England where they were in short supply, prohibited not only their export beyond the British Empire, but also the construction of furnaces and mills, which would produce more advanced iron products for the local American market. In effect, what the British government gave with one hand, it took away with the other. It all made little difference in the long run; American manufacturing industry in the mid-eighteenth century, scattered in small units across some thirteen colonies whose population (a fraction of that of Britain) was mainly engaged in agriculture, was never a serious threat to British exporters. In any case, with revolution coming in 1776, the writ of Westminster only ran for less than a single generation.

By the end of the eighteenth century, the Grubb family had sold out to Robert Coleman, whose successful exploitation of the foundry led to his family becoming the wealthiest in Lebanon County. As the centre of a model industrial community, the Cornwall Iron Furnace attracted considerable notice from outside, and it is now open to visitors as a state historical park. The Cornwall operation was one of the best of many similar iron furnaces which, by the end of the colonial era, smelted one seventh of the world's iron. In Pennsylvania, the heartland of the iron industry, it employed some 2,000 men, equal to 1 per cent of the entire population. Inevitably, by this time the restrictions in the British Act of 1750 were honoured more in the breach than in the observance, so that the American market enjoyed an increasingly wide range of locally manufactured iron products. Remarkably – seeing that it never used any fuel but charcoal[23] – the Cornwall Iron Furnace continued to operate until 1883, by which time it was hardly visible in the vast American iron and steel industry as it had developed after the end of the Civil War.

Most significant advances in American iron production had to wait until well into the nineteenth century.

Thomas Lewis, in 1817, was the first to produce coke in America, for an iron rolling mill in Fayette County, Pennsylvania, just south of Pittsburgh. Lewis was brought from Wales, where he had learnt the relevant technology, by Isaac Meason, who had been an ironmaster since 1791. In spite of the best efforts of Lewis and two of his brothers who had come with him, Meason's innovation had little success; partly because of the poor quality of the local bituminous coal, and partly as a result of the poor transport infrastructure – a common reason for failure in the early days of the American industrial revolution.

The next important landmark, in 1837, was the Lonaconing Iron Furnace, which was just over the state line in Maryland. In this case, the furnace fuelled by coke operated according to plan. The site was determined by the local abundance of iron ore, limestone, water and coal. The fact it was also close to Cumberland – which in 1850 became the end point of the Chesapeake and Ohio canal – meant that the canal, still under construction when the Lonaconing furnace went into blast in 1839, was a good customer for iron dowels used in buttressing its walls. On the other hand, a canal still more than ten years from completion was of little help in bringing supplies to the furnace, or carrying its finished products to all but local markets. In 1837 it had only reached Williamsport, almost exactly halfway between Georgetown (where it began) and Cumberland: this meant that some twenty tons of machinery ordered for the furnace from the West Point Foundry in New York City had to be carried by wagons over the seventy-odd miles between Williamsport and Lonaconing – an extremely costly operation.

Production started in May 1839 at some forty tons of cast iron per week, with each ton requiring seven tons of coal. Peaking at seventy-five tons, it was more than sufficient to satisfy local demand, which, although including farming implements, mine car wheels and track, and household utensils, still left over a large quantity of pig iron which was more difficult to sell at a profit. The best market was the Baltimore and Ohio Railroad (like the canal, still under construction), which was offered pig iron at $29 per ton. Since this involved transport over a distance of nearly ten miles down, the Georges Creek Valley to Piedmont on the Potomac river – the nearest point on the route of the railroad – it was hardly a paying proposition. The answer was to build a railroad linking Lonaconing with Piedmont, and this was completed in 1853, two years after the Baltimore & Ohio had reached this point on its way to the Ohio river at Wheeling, Virginia. Although the new railroad was years too late to help local iron furnaces – the last of which shut down in 1855 – it had a sound future in the transport of coal, with some 225,000 tons in 102 car trains carried in the same year. It is still, if somewhat intermittently, in business.

The Cornwall and Lonaconing Iron Furnaces have their place in history because they were both among the first of their kind in North America. If Cornwall stayed in operation for far longer, this was because its location better fitted its market, while at Lonaconing too much weight had been given to the accessibility of the natural resources upon which it depended at a time when the local transport infrastructure did not measure up to its needs. Cornwall finally failed because it was too conservative, relying on charcoal as its fuel at a time when industry had long solved the problem of burning the anthracite of eastern Pennsylvania. In this, Lonaconing, judging the future of American industry correctly, was much more innovative; with its much shorter life it paid the price of being ahead of its time.

In Pennsylvania, as in other future industrial states such as Ohio, it was not so much the anthracite east of the Appalachians as the vast bituminous coalfields west of the mountains – which extended as far south as northern Alabama – that would count in supplying the fuel for new industry. When in 1758 – at a critical early stage in the French and Indian war – the French abandoned Fort Duquesne, located at the point there the Allegheny and Monongahela rivers join to form the Ohio, and left its smouldering ruins open to British occupation; they unwittingly surrendered one of the world's richest seams of coal, whose greatest width, 190-odd miles, was in western Pennsylvania.[24] In the same year as the French departed – abandoning the whole territory west of the Appalachians to the British – a Philadelphia newspaper noted that 'this valuable Acquisition lays open to all his Majesty's subjects a Vein of Treasure which, if rightly managed, may prove richer than the Mines of Mexico'.[25]

Almost on the same site as Fort Duquesne, the British established a trading village that they called Pittsburgh in honour of their Prime Minister. When the revolution came some eighteen years later, Americans who had already claimed their own freedom to disregard the long-standing British embargo on settlement west of the Appalachians, lost little time in turning the village into a boom-town – in spite of the fact that it was twenty days by packhorse from Philadelphia, at a time when there was no alternative transport across Pennsylvania.

There was no stopping the growth of Pittsburgh, which was already phenomenal during the American Revolution. The publication of the first newspaper west of the mountains in 1786 was just one sign of the prosperity enjoyed by its growing population. From the beginning, the production of glass and iron – two fuel intensive industries – depended on coal and steam power, so that Pittsburgh became the first of all American cities not to rely on wood and water for heat and power. By 1817 its population, of around 6,000, provided the labour for some 250 factories, which if not already steam-powered, would soon become so.[26]

Since at this stage in history there was still no efficient transport infrastructure linking western Pennsylvania with the east coast, the only market for its steadily widening range of new manufacturers was down the Ohio river from Pittsburgh, where the relatively new states of Kentucky and Ohio were, respectively, on its left and right banks. Stoves, essential for domestic comfort in the harsh winters, were much the most important product.[27] With the introduction of steam-powered riverboats in 1811, access to the steadily expanding market created by thousands of new settlers ensured the continued prosperity not only of Pittsburgh, but also of other major river towns such as Cincinnati in Ohio and Louisville in Kentucky.

In the generation before the 1820 Census, the extent both of American land and population more than doubled,[28] with the gain attributable in both cases mainly to the territory beyond the Appalachians and north of the Ohio river – which, in the first twenty years of the nineteenth century, had been organized into the new states of Ohio (1803), Indiana (1816) and Illinois (1818). It was no accident of history that in the remaining years of the century these three states, together with western Pennsylvania, would become the heartland of industrial America – if only to become, by the end of the twentieth century, its rust belt.

It is something of a paradox that western Pennsylvania and the lands beyond (which depended upon British victory in the French and Indian War (1756–63) to become American territory by virtue of the Treaty of Versailles in 1783) was where modern industry took off in the US, when eastern Pennsylvania – a British colony since the seventeenth century – could claim if it wanted to the advantage of almost every innovation of the industrial revolution. The paradox is to be explained, at least in part, by the fact that the coal in the west of the state was bituminous (as it was also, for the most part, on the other side of the Atlantic) while that in the east was unfamiliar anthracite. The anthracite region was not part of the original colony, but belonged to Native American land purchased from the League of the Iroquois for £500 in 1749.[29] Much of this extremely hilly country was drained by the tumultuous, and relatively short, Lehigh river a western tributary of the navigable and much longer Delaware river,[30] which it joins some 100 miles north of Philadelphia.

The frequent rapids of the Lehigh made it an obvious river to be explored for good sites for watermills, so it is perhaps not surprisingly that it was a millwright who, in 1791, discovered a massive outcrop of anthracite at

Summit Hill, close to the river. Its exploitation was however, extremely problematic, for the reasons given on page 205.

The first attempts to exploit the Lehigh valley mines, made before end of the eighteenth century were futile; most of the anthracite was lost when boats capsized in the rapids, and there was no market for the little that actually made it to Philadelphia. Some years then passed before a new entrepreneur, Jacob Cist of Wilkes-Barre, having recruited a local labour force and with a new lease of Summit Hill, mined sufficient coal to fill four arks on the Lehigh river. Only one ark reached Philadelphia, but this time there were willing buyers of its cargo; the two owners of a local rolling mill, Josiah White and Erskine Hazard, after much trial and error, found a way of burning anthracite to heat the iron to be used for making wire and nails. Having solved the technological problem, they then saw their future in exploiting Summit Hill; by doing all that was necessary was to make the Lehigh navigable. With the necessary approval granted by the Pennsylvania legislature in 1818, White and Hazard, after building twelve dams, completed their operation in 1820, so making it possible to safely ship anthracite to Philadelphia in a day and a half.

In Philadelphia the prejudice against anthracite, both as an industrial and a domestic fuel, was overcome, but a new problem arose. In spite of its new dams, the Lehigh was still not navigable upstream; the current was simply too strong. This meant that as every ark reached its destination, its wood was sold, leaving the crew to walk home – an uphill journey lasting several days – with its metal parts. These would then be incorporated in a new vessel. The process was not only wasteful of labour, but of the wood from the forests surrounding Summit Hill. While the exploitation of labour was sustainable – at least in the social conditions of early nineteenth-century Pennsylvania – that of wood was not. The solution was to be found in the construction of canals, which from the 1820s onwards became a major enterprise, not only in eastern Pennsylvania, but throughout the nation. In 1825 the Schuylkill canal opened – just ahead of New York's Erie canal – to link Summit Hill with the navigable Schuylkill river, which flowed into the Delaware at Philadelphia.

In 1827 construction started with a new Lehigh canal and by the end of the 1830s a network of canals shipped freight across the eastern states, and much of this was anthracite. Soon though, even the canals were not good enough for demanding industrial users; they froze in winter and ended up short of the pitheads. The only way forward was to build railroads, and in 1827 White and Hazard – following the example of the British mine-owners[31] – laid a track from Summit Hill down to the Lehigh river, where wagons carrying coal would descend under the force of gravity, to be drawn by mules on the return journey back to the mine. This, as in Britain, was only a temporary phase; in the 1830s haulage was taken over by locomotives burning wood in spite of the abundance of coal. By the end of the 1830s the extensive mining area of the Lehigh valley was criss-crossed by railroad tracks operated by five separate companies,[32] and still most of the traffic was coal.

The breakthrough came when White and Hazard persuaded David Thomas, a Welsh ironmaster who had succeeded in smelting iron from anthracite, to build a furnace close to their mine.[33] This had the great advantage that the low sulphur content of anthracite allowed it to be used without first being converted to coke. By the end of the 1840s the way pioneered by White and Hazard had led to some sixty anthracite furnaces operating in eastern Pennsylvania. The number more than doubled in the 1850s, making this small corner of the state the heartland of American heavy industry by the beginning of the Civil War. By this time too, the new railroads crossing the Appalachians made it economical to import coke from the bituminous coalfields of western Pennsylvania, with the result that the iron industry in the east adapted many of its furnaces to burn a mixture of coke and anthracite. At the same time the railroads opened the rich Atlantic coast market to almost every form of business enterprise west of the Appalachians, although the full potential was only realized after the Civil War.

The Small Arms Industry

With such familiar names as Colt and Winchester, nothing in the American industrial revolution achieved such renown, worldwide, as the manufacture of small arms. From the end of the eighteenth century its prime locations were in the broad valley of the Connecticut river, where the full potential of the vertical waterwheel as a source of power could be realized better than in any other part of the United States. Although small arms never accounted for more than 1 per cent of the total production of American industry, the industry was technologically advanced and led the way in establishing the production of machines with interchangeable parts, precision engineering and the manufacture of machine tools,[34] while at the same time adapting what was essentially a craft industry to the factory floor.

Before 1800 the United States had imported most of its arms mainly from France,[35] but the war of independence made clear the advantages that would flow from domestic production. On the initiative of George Washington, a federal arsenal was established on a site next to the Connecticut river at Springfield, Massachusetts. In 1795, and with its capital raised by federal government, it not only dominated the small arms industry but also provided an example that others could follow.

The incentive to do so was strong. Steadily expanding frontiers beyond the Appalachian mountain chain, and across the broad Mississippi catchment area, meant not only wars against Native Americans (which continued until almost the end of the nineteenth century) but also, in the 1840s – on a much larger scale – against Mexico. The Mexican war was the making of Samuel Colt (1814–62), a native son of the state capital, Hartford, on the Connecticut river. Although his six-shooter revolver was eventually to make him immensely wealthy, success in his early years as an inventor and entrepreneur did not come easily. Brought up to be a farmer like his father, while still a teenager Colt decided he wanted to be an inventor, setting his sights quite specifically on making a gun that could fire 'five or six times' – an idea he got from listening to soldiers in the local tavern. Sent to sea at the age of eighteen by his father, he came up with the idea of a revolving cartridge barrel by observing how, once a ship's wheel was at rest, one of the six spokes was always held in a direct line by a clutch. Before the end of the voyage he had made a wooden model of a revolver.

Once back home, Colt received money from his father to make two prototype revolvers, but both failed because the finance was only sufficient to pay low-level mechanics. After this setback, with the help of skilled gunsmiths he managed to build a pistol, and applied for his first patent. When the application was held up in America, he travelled to England where the patent was granted. On returning home, he set up a factory in Paterson, New Jersey, to make – in the words of the American patent that soon followed – a 'revolving breach-loading, folding trigger firearm named the Paterson Pistol'.

With his first patents Colt himself claimed to have done no more than adapt an English invention, 'Collier's revolving flintlock'. His great innovation was to have all parts of every Colt gun machine made and interchangeable. Nonetheless his pistol was the first practical revolver and the first repeating firearm. With both political and financial support, the Patent Arms Manufacturing Company of Paterson, New Jersey, was chartered by the New Jersey legislature on 5 March 1837, but the enterprise was slow to start because Colt's backers failed to fund the new machinery needed to make the interchangeable parts. In spite of the popularity of Colt's revolvers and new revolving muskets, with the American soldiers who were fighting Native Americans in Florida in the first Seminole War of 1837, the Paterson factory still had to close after the government failed to pay for the weapons.

The war, however, proved to be Colt's salvation ten years later, when in 1847 Captain Samuel Walker of the

Texas Rangers, who had acquired Colt revolvers produced for the Seminole War, ordered a thousand more
for use against the Mexicans. After that Colt never
looked back. He built the Colt's Patent Fire Arms
Manufacturing Company factory at Hartford, his home
town, and it was the pistols made there that established
the 'Colt 45' as the standard revolver. Colt's timing could
hardly have been better. With the California gold rush
and western expansion sustaining demand, the Hartford
factory continued to expand. With a virtual monopoly,
Colt had a worldwide market and, at a time of mounting
international tension, no great power could afford to
deny his small arms to its soldiers. Demand also reached
new heights in the American Civil War.

By this time Colt had built the Colt Armory, a much
larger factory, on land next to the Connecticut river. He
was a model employer, maintaining a ten hour day,
company housing, washing facilities and a daily one-
hour lunch break. He died in 1862, in Hartford, so never
saw the end of the war for which he had provided
hundreds of thousands of weapons. His estate was
valued at some $15 million, a colossal sum for the mid-
nineteenth century, but for all his success he personally
never got anywhere near to Florida, Texas or California,
or any of the states where the reputation of the revolvers
was made.

Besides Colt, other well known names such as
Winchester and Remington were part of Connecticut's
armaments industry. Eli Whitney, after becoming famous for his invention of the cotton gin, also went on to
become a major player in this field.[36] Together they
accounted for much of the prosperity of such cities as

New Haven, Middletown and Hartford, to say nothing of Springfield in Massachusetts. Except for New Haven, which was on the coast, these towns, together with the locations of any number of smaller firms, combined the advantage of navigation on the Connecticut river – open as far inland as Hartford to ocean-going ships – with that of the water power which could be tapped along its tributaries.[37]

Particularly in the early years, the Salisbury Hills in the border area common to Massachusetts, Connecticut and New York, were a source of iron ore for founding in the armament factories, while local woodlands could supply not only the walnut wood for rifle stocks but also the chestnut for charcoal burning. In the course of time walnut had to be imported from Pennsylvania, while small quantities of bituminous coal from Virginia came to be used instead of charcoal. On the other hand, up to the time of the Civil War, local water power was used throughout the whole industry during a period in which major technological advances radically changed the nature of the final product. If such innovation did not depend upon steam power, this is about the only respect in which the industry can be labelled as 'backward' – although it is as well to remember that the riverboats were steam-powered from a very early stage.

When, after 1830, the manufacture of machine tools developed as a separate industry – and one with an important future – in the Connecticut valley, it did rely largely on steam power,[38] but otherwise steam engines were used only as a standby. It was not until 1855 that the conservative management of the Springfield Armory finally recognized the advantages of steam when frost or drought prevented the operation of waterwheels. It also counted that by 1830 the opening of the Schuylkill and Lehigh canals[39] made the vast anthracite resources of the Lehigh valley affordable in New England.

Until 1830 the Connecticut valley small arms industry relied on imported steel from Germany and Britain for the manufacture of certain key components in its guns and rifles. The reason was simply the relatively poor quality of American steel, which in any case was in extremely short supply. Essential tools, such as files (of which many were required), anvils, planes, chisels and certain raw materials needed in only small quantities, were imported, mainly from Britain, right up to the Civil War.[40] On the other hand, the precision engineering and interchangeable parts developed not only by the small arms industry, but also by the American manufacturers of locks and clocks – and later of sewing machines and typewriters – was far ahead of anything on the other side of the Atlantic. In woodworking also, American innovation constantly produced machinery designed to reduce labour costs in such occupations as the manufacture of wood screws and nails.[41] From an early stage, economies in the use of labour were welcomed on the American shop floor, where European labour would see them as threatening its livelihood – a distinction that in the long run would account, as much as any other factor, for much higher levels of profits and productivity in the United States. As one observer noted as early as 1839, 'In Europe work is often wanting for hands ... in the United States hands are wanting for the work'.[42] In short, labour was a sellers' market; Americans always had the option of moving on to new land, with the prospect of earning more as cultivators than they ever would in a factory.[43]

The American Textile Industry

The scene shifts at this stage to the other side of the Atlantic, where, in 1810, a wealthy Bostonian, Francis Cabot Lowell, was visiting the new British textile mills in the course of travels undertaken primarily to improve his health. He was already discussing the possibility of starting similar operations in New England with American friends who were also travelling in Britain, but at this stage it was still cheaper to import cotton textiles from old England – and this indeed was a major part of Lowell's own business in Boston. The Americans had to be extremely circumspect, since it was illegal to export from Britain either models or designs of what they saw. Nonetheless, once back home in Boston, Lowell was able to sketch from memory the machinery he had observed so accurately, that with the help of Paul Moody, a skilled mechanic, it could be reproduced in New England.

This was just as well, because the character of the local textile economy changed completely with the outbreak war between the United States and Britain in 1812. Facing the ruin of his import business, Lowell, together with other wealthy investors in his social circle, founded the Boston Manufacturing Company in 1813, with an authorized capital of $400,000. Their purpose was to set up a textile mill in Massachusetts operating with substantially the same machinery that Lowell had so carefully observed in Britain.

There was however, one important difference; the American investors did not propose to work with steam power. Instead, by means of a public stock offer, they raised a capital sum of $100,000 to build a mill at Waltham to be powered by the flow of water in the Charles river. In this way the Boston Manufacturing Company became the first enterprise to transfer raw cotton to cotton cloth in one mill. This led to an entirely new method – known as the 'Waltham System' – of recruiting a labour force consisting mainly of young 'Yankee' women who lived in company dormitories and even attended churches supported by the company.

At a time of war with Britain, the plantations in the southern states were only too willing to supply raw cotton to the new American company. But then, when peace came in 1814, the company had once again to compete with imported British textiles. Lowell's reaction was to go to Washington and persuade the US Congress to enact a protective tariff. This was his last success; he died in 1817 at the young age of forty-two, leaving as his legacy the foundations of the American textile industry. The expansion which he had envisaged could not however, be realized on the Charles river, as its capacity to supply the essential water power was simply too small.

The directors of the Boston Manufacturing Company were not going to give up; they plainly had to move elsewhere, and where better than the network of canals bypassing, in one way or another, the Pawtucket Falls of the Merrimack, a river carrying down from New Hampshire a volume of water with much greater potential energy. The company bought up the old Proprietors of Locks and Canals, thus acquiring the right to harness the power of the Merrimack river. In 1822 the directors bought a considerable area of farm land in East Chelmsford as the site for their new operations, setting up at the same time the Merrimack Manufacturing Company to carry them out. A new Merrimack canal was built so as to make use of nearly the whole of the 32 foot head of the Pawtucket Falls for the new mills, the first of which became operational on 1 September 1823. Next to the female labour force, which was organized on the basis already established at Waltham, a large number of men – many of them Irish immigrants – were employed in the vast engineering works. A new town, built to provide homes for the labourers, was incorporated in 1825 and given the name 'Lowell' in honour of the man who, as much as anyone else, had conceived the whole project. The Waltham System became known as the 'Lowell System', and with the expansion of the American textile industry, Lowell's population eventually increased to more than 100,000.

By 1850 the success of the Lowell System had led to the city becoming not only the second largest in Massachusetts – with the state's economy now based on industry as much as on agriculture – but also the largest industrial centre in the US. In 1835 the opening of the Boston and Lowell Railroad made the Middlesex canal obsolete. The fact that steam-powered locomotives were part of the everyday scene did not lead to steam power being used by local industry. This had to wait until the 1860s, by which time its economic advantage for both the textile mills and the other industries attracted to the city could not be gainsaid.

The Lowell textile industry thus provided the model for new mills throughout New England, a welcome development at a time when the decline of local agriculture had led many residents to move west, to farm new land beyond the Appalachians.[44] The success of New England textiles can be seen from the increase in value of total production from $32,000,000 in 1830 to $115,700,000 in 1860.[45] Economy of scale is reflected in the fact that an increase of only 30 per cent in the number of mills was accompanied by a substantial fall in unit product price.[46]

All this was part of a historical process which led the United States to become, by 1860, the second nation in the world in manufacturing.[47] Significantly, some 71 per cent of all manufacturing employment was still to be found in New England and the North Atlantic states[48] where textiles were the major industry. This was also critically important for factories making textile machinery, which in the first half of the nineteenth century constituted the most important sector of the American manufacture of industrial plant. It was not only size however, that counted. The textile mills and the manufacture of textile machinery played a crucial part in training the men who later made most of the tools for the machine tool and locomotive industries at the heart of the American Industrial Revolution.[49]

In the very long term the New England textile industry would lose out to new mills in the southern states, so that whatever its historical role as a flagship of the American industrial revolution, the legacy of the vast investments made in the mid-nineteenth century came to be represented in the twentieth by any number of abandoned mills located along great rivers such as the Connecticut and the Merrimack. From the very beginning also, the industry depended on the technology developed – largely during the eighteenth century – in Britain.[50] Here Lowell, in spite of his careful observations of British textile manufacture, was not the first in the field. Samuel Slater, an Englishman, was twenty years ahead of him when in 1790, with the hope of winning one of the prizes offered by the Philadelphia Society for Promoting Agriculture and Domestic Manufactures, he opened a water-powered spinning mill in Pawtucket, Rhode Island, with machinery based on what he had seen while working in the Arkwright factories in England.[51] Lowell's legacy was to be found in the integrated production made possible by the vastly increased scale of the new textile industry.

The development of the textile industry owed its success then, to four factors: the first was the access to capital investment provided largely by the wealthiest families, including the Lowells,[52] in New England; the second was the tariff protection granted by the US Congress in response to Lowell's original petition in 1816; the third was the steady expansion of the domestic market during a period 1820–60, when the US population increased from ten to thirty million; and the fourth was the remarkable supply elasticity of the southern cotton plantations.

Agricultural Machinery

Because agriculture in America was short of men, while in Europe it was short of land, there was a strong incentive to develop better tools and machinery for use on farms. The need was also the result of an essential long-term transformation of American agriculture from the 1830s onwards. A landmark event was the final defeat of the Native Americans in the Black Hawk War (in which Abraham Lincoln, who never saw action, played a minor part) in 1832.

The result was that more than a million acres of land in northern Illinois became available for settlement.[53] Unlike most of the land cleared for settlement in the early years of the Union, which was mainly forest, this new land was open prairie. The challenge facing settlers was to plough heavy soil in which tough deep rooted grass had grown for centuries. The incentive to overcome it was the prairies' vast potential for cultivating wheat on a breathtakingly large scale. Illinois, after all, was just the beginning of the prairies; no one fully realized in these early days how far they would extend westwards. Opening up the land for sowing wheat was, however, almost beyond standard American ploughs (which were little more than European models adapted over the course of time by local blacksmiths).

The solution to the problem was John Deere's steel plough. John Deere (1804–86) was a blacksmith and part-time smallholder in Vermont, who, needled by creditors and confronted with one setback after another, left his home state for frontier Illinois. There, as one of many new settlers from New England, he soon discovered the shortcomings of the standard American plough on the heavy prairie soil and using a broken saw blade from a local sawmill he created the first ever steel plough. Realizing its potential, John Deere decided to exploit his skills as a blacksmith to produce steel ploughs for the market.

With new partners bringing in finance and steel imported from England – still the only dependable source in frontier America – John Deere's business expanded to the point that, in 1848, it was able to move to a large new factory in Moline, Illinois, where proximity to the Mississippi river assured good transport and reliable water power. In 1854, completion of the Rock Island Railroad linking Chicago with the Mississippi, once again improved market access. At the same time, by taking advantage of the growth of America's own steel industry in Pittsburgh, it became possible to make new ploughs with steel rolled to John Deere's own specifications.

In due course new products were added, almost all for use in agriculture and other operations such as construction. New plants were built, first in the United States and then later overseas; transforming Deere & Company (as it was finally known) into one of the largest multinational corporations (with its distinctive 'deer' logo) in its field. John Deere, like many successful men of humble origins, such as George Stephenson, took pains to ensure not only a better life for his family but also their continued involvement in the business. His son Charles, after graduating from Bell's Commercial College in Chicago – an institution that would now be a business school – took over the business, aged twenty-one, in 1858, and remained at its head until well into the twentieth century. The problem with recounting the life of John Deere is that he was almost too good to be true; trustee of the First Congregational Church, co-founder of the First National Bank, a two term mayor of Moline, he did all the right things.

Deere was not alone in establishing the primacy of Illinois as the state for manufacturing agricultural machinery. The state owes as much, if not more, to his equally well known contemporary, Cyrus McCormick (1809–84), the son of Robert McCormick, a prosperous Virginia farmer, miller, and almost inevitably in his day, slave owner. At a time when wheat was beginning to be cultivated on a large scale, reaping and binding, essential processes in harvesting, were a considerable bottleneck in the production process – just as spinning had been in the textile industry half a century beforehand. As early as 1815, Robert McCormick, at his 532 acre Walnut Grove farm, had begun work on a horse-drawn reaper, but after years of failing to produce a satisfactory model he finally gave up in the early summer of 1831. His twenty-two-year old son Cyrus refused to accept defeat, and with the help of one of the slaves working on the farm, he produced a new and workable harvester in time for the harvest.

Having succeeded where his father had failed, Cyrus McCormick spent another three years improving his invention, so that it was ready to be patented in 1834. By this time, he was busy converting the blacksmith's shop at Walnut Grove into a factory, but progress was slow among Virginia's conservative farmers. In the 1840s – some ten years after the original invention – sales took off and Cyrus McCormick, with an eye to the main chance, moved his operation to Chicago where the vast prairie wheat fields on the city's doorstep were a much more promising market for his 'Virginia reaper'. Like John Deere in Moline, Cyrus McCormick, once in Chicago, could not put a foot wrong, but the subsequent history of his business was somewhat different. In 1902, it was bought up by J.P. Morgan, one of the best known names on Wall Street, to become part of International Harvester, a giant Chicago based multinational corporation devoted mainly to the manufacture of agricultural machinery.

Inventions in this field, such as those of John Deere and Cyrus McCormick, played a major part in the expansion of American agriculture in the second half of the nineteenth century, so that the prairies became not only that nation's breadbasket, but that of Europe's industrial states – with the United Kingdom in the vanguard – where local grain harvests were no longer sufficient to feed rapidly increasing urban populations. At the same time, if much more slowly, American agricultural machinery began to appear on European farms, but for want of capital for investment this transition only became significant in the twentieth century; by then harvesters were no longer drawn by horses, but were part of a self-contained unit with its own petrol or diesel engine.

9

EUROPE JOINS THE PARTY

Britain and Europe

Any history of the industrial revolution in continental Europe must take into account three interrelated factors. First and foremost, the example of Britain was an incentive difficult to ignore for any state concerned for its economic future.[1] Second – largely as a result of wars fought on their own territory – the division of Europe into separate sovereign states, as it was at the beginning of the critical hundred years from 1770 to 1870, was quite different to what it would be at the end of this period. Third, although Britain, in times of both war and peace, was inextricably involved in this process of transformation, no foreign army was ever seen in the nation itself. During the long period (1793–1815) of wars with France, Britain was not even a combatant in many of the battles, so that inevitably its economy suffered far less than that of France,[2] to say nothing of the many nations from Portugal to Russia, and Egypt to Denmark, in which Napoleon at one time or another fought his battles and devastated the countryside. At the same time, Britain, by blockading continental rivals (mainly France and the Netherlands) and destroying their shipping, ruined many of their merchants, while continuing to develop its own connections in South America, Africa and the Orient.[3]

True enough, Britain had fought and lost the American War of Independence, but this was a setback from which it recovered in a remarkably short time. The crucial fact is that the historical process, in which Britain outclassed all its rivals both politically and economically, continued until well into the nineteenth century. Indeed, its two great rivals at the end of this century, Germany and the United States, did not even exist as independent sovereign states in 1770. The transformation of Europe during the period 1770 to 1870 is therefore a crucial factor in its industrial history.

The decisive event was the Congress of Vienna of 1814–15, which determined the political geography of Europe following the final defeat of Napoleon at the battle of Waterloo in June 1815. Although France had been defeated, the main objective in Vienna was to contain it for the indefinite future. This was achieved by: strengthening Austria, Prussia and Russia with the addition of new territory; creating a new united kingdom of the Netherlands, comprising what are now the kingdoms of Belgium and the Netherlands, under a Dutch king; guaranteeing the neutrality of Switzerland, to which new Protestant French-speaking cantons had been added; and sidelining Spain and Portugal, which, with their hold on their American empires becoming every day more precarious, could hardly be counted as great powers.[4] Ten years later, in the Treaty of Malacca of 1824, the United Kingdom restored to the Netherlands the greater part of the Dutch overseas empire in the East Indies, while retaining for itself the Dutch mainland territories in Malaya, together with North Borneo, Ceylon, Natal and the Cape Colony. Although the United Kingdom acquired no new territory in Europe, overseas its only rivals were the Netherlands, Spain and Portugal – all countries which, after the ravages of Napoleon, retained little of their past imperial power.

In one critical case, the political line-up agreed at Vienna did not hold. Uniting Belgium and the Netherlands into a single kingdom proved to be an arrangement unsatisfactory to both sides. In 1830 it became unstuck when a new provisional government in Brussels proclaimed the independence of Belgium. A year later, this became a new kingdom under Leopold of Saxe-Coburg, an uncle of Prince Albert, consort to Queen Victoria. The Dutch finally accepted this partition in 1839, and with a new king, Willem II, the Netherlands was once more divided into two parts – as it had been since the end of the Thirty Years War in 1648.

Although this chapter cannot cover every instance of the industrial revolution in Europe, its varied character will be shown by a number of special cases. The first is that of France, the classic European great power. The second comprises three small states, Belgium, the Netherlands and Switzerland, effectively reborn after the Congress of Vienna. The third relates to the kingdoms of Prussia and Piedmont, from which the new great powers of Germany and Italy emerged in the decade which ended with the year 1870. These examples will show how, in Western Europe, the second third of the nineteenth century was a critical period of expansion and development.[5]

Even in the early days of the eighteenth century, there were also important events, incidental to the industrial revolution, which took place outside Britain; for example, Böttger's success in discovering the secrets of Chinese porcelain. From close to the end of the century, another instance was the success of two brothers, Joseph and Etienne Montgolfier, in launching a hot air balloon from the small French city of Annonay on 4 June 1782, an event today commemorated by a plaque reading 'ICI EST NEE LA NAVIGATION AERIENNE'.[6] This overstated the case, since the balloon was unmanned. Even so, in November 1783 another Montgolfier balloon transported two other men, the Marquis d'Arlandes and Pilâtre de Rozier, over a distance of seven and a half miles. By the end of the century balloon travel led to the invention of the parachute by Jean Baptiste Olivier Garnerin and his brother André Jacques Garnerin, with the latter, in 1797, being the first person actually to use one – needless to say, by jumping out of a 'Montgolfier' – and make a safe landing.

In 1790 the process invented by the French chemist Nicolas Leblanc for producing soda ash by combining sulphuric acid with common salt, opened the way for the synthetic alkali industry – which in the nineteenth century became a major part of the industrial scene worldwide. Thus European inventions continued to play an important part in the nineteenth century, particularly in fields such as industrial chemistry, which became important only at a relatively late stage in the industrial revolution. The most important contributions came from France and Germany, where local inventors were often the first in the field. In France, M.E. Chevreul's discovery, in 1813, that glycerine was a constituent of all animal fats revolutionized the manufacture of soap, while his compatriot, Philippe Lebon, had already, in 1801, used gas to light his house and garden in Paris. (In this field, however, Britain and the United States were way ahead when it came to developing a mass market.)

In the realm of optics, the multifaceted lighthouse lens invented by Augustin Fresnel (1788–1827) – which allowed a narrow beam of light to be projected over great distances – after being first introduced in France in 1822 became standard throughout the world at a time when more lighthouses were being built than ever before in history.[7] This invention had great benefits for navigation at sea, although it was Fresnel's purely theoretical work that earned him an enduring international reputation as a scientist.

If the manufacture of the Fresnel lens was outside the mainstream of the industrial revolution, its widespread use contributed significantly to the development of the precision glass industry. The British Chance Brothers and Company, located just outside Birmingham, has had a pioneering role in the production of glass on an industrial scale since Fresnel's day. A measure of its reach is provided by Oregons's Heceta Head lighthouse, on the American Pacific coast, which still operates with a Fresnel lens made by the company in the early 1890s.

Throughout the nineteenth century, Britain was all too often the country where European inventions and scientific discoveries were adopted by industry, so much so that many leading figures, such as Wilhelm Siemens in steel and electric power generation, Ludwig Mond in industrial chemistry (both from Germany) and Guglielmo Marconi (from Italy) in wireless, deliberately chose to establish their industrial base there.

In Germany, the explorer Alexander von Humboldt (1769–859) brought the first sample of guano (bird droppings consisting of metabolized fish from the oceans) to Europe from the Pacific in 1804, after observing its use as fertilizer by peasant farmers in South America. Exploring the properties of guano opened up an entirely new field in which Justus Liebig (1803–73) – generally acknowledged to be the father of organic chemistry – was the first to establish a university-based research laboratory, where his own work was largely directed to meeting the needs of agriculture and medicine. Liebig, by showing how essential elements in plant nutrition could be produced industrially, opened up a new field of manufacture of artificial fertilizers, in which Britain, rather than Germany, led the way.

While the 'electro-chemical battery' was invented by an Italian, Alessandro Volta (1745–1827) in 1800, it was a new, much improved zinc-carbon battery, based on the same principles and invented by the German chemist Robert Bunsen (1811–99), that opened the way, mid-century, to large-scale production by electrolysis of metallic elements such as aluminium (1852), magnesium (1851) and chromium (1852).

The second half of the nineteenth century also witnessed a Europe-based revolution in explosives. C.F. Schönbein (1799–1868) in Switzerland and A. Sobrero

(1812–88) in Italy – both working with a mixture of nitric and sulphuric acids – led the way, in 1846, with the former inventing gun cotton (aka nitrocellulose), and the latter, nitroglycerine. In 1864, Alfred Nobel (1833–96) in Sweden discovered how to stabilize nitro-glycerine with a sedimentary rock known as kieselguhr and produced dynamite, thereby revolutionizing the explosives industry, in which he himself made a considerable fortune.

France

Despite being decisively defeated at Waterloo, France – as we have seen – simply had to be reckoned as one of the great powers. Any number of factors – historical, demographic, geographical and cultural – counted in its favour, and so it would be with industrialization. At the end of the eighteenth century, France could rightly claim to have existed for nearly a thousand years as an independent sovereign state.[8] At the end of the seventeenth century it was not only unrivalled on the continent of Europe but had also a considerable overseas empire, both in the east and in the New World of the west. However, in the course of the eighteenth century it was destined to lose out, in one war after another, to Britain.

In terms of the population, territory and natural wealth within its historical boundaries, France still remained far ahead of Britain. Its language, the *lingua franca*, had long been a rival to Latin in science, commerce and diplomacy and the phrase had been used to connote any language widely accepted for use outside the domain of native speakers.[9] (Somewhat ironically, by the end of the twentieth century the French had had to accept that in this sense, English had become the world's 'lingua franca'.)

However great the ascendancy of France had once been, it hardly justified the claim made by a French diplomat, Louis-Guillaume Otto, in 1799 that *La révolution industrielle est commencée en France*.[10] The reality was quite different. There were many adverse factors making it unlikely that such a revolution would start in France. Above all the legacy of its greatest king, Louis XIV, who reigned from 1643 to 1715, was a nation ill-suited to a modern industrial age, and whose system of government the two succeeding kings, Louis XV (1715–74) and Louis XVI (1774–93) were never minded to reform in any way that would rectify the grievances of a vast, impoverished, mainly rural population. Land, rather than commerce of industry, was seen as the essential source of wealth. What is more, ownership of land – as a result of long established systems of tenure – was organized so as to constrain a vast mass of subsistence farmers to provide an income for a small governing class. This in turn supported an absolute monarchy whose character was summed up by Louis XIV with the famous words, *l'état, c'est moi* – an approach to monarchy which, in England, had in 1649 cost King Charles II his head. The Glorious Revolution of 1689, which in England led a new king, William III, to recognize the role of Parliament in governing the nation, had no equivalent in France, and when revolution finally came a hundred years later, the country suffered a series of convulsions that almost completely destroyed the old order.

The ordering of French society, as described above, inevitably encouraged the growth of luxury industries, benefiting not only noblemen tied to the conspicuous consumption expected by the court at Versailles, together with a small but wealthy bourgeoisie, but also boosting a lucrative, if limited, export market in which consumers were ready to pay for the quality, taste and elegance characteristic of French court life.[11] Because the manufacture of luxury goods that met such criteria depended on labour, which was cheap and abundant in France,[12] and at the same time offered few economies of scale, it inhibited investment in capital goods that in England were of the essence of the Industrial Revolution.

A typical case was that of the French silk industry, established centuries earlier in Lyon and the surrounding countryside, which was rivalled in Europe only by that of Italy. In particular, the Jacquard loom, developed in the first decade of the nineteenth century, which made it possible for one man to weave, automatically, complicated patterns of silk,[13] was technologically extremely sophisticated.[14] In quite another field, the heavy chemicals industry owed much to the inventions made by two Frenchmen, Berthollet and Leblanc, in the 1780s.

France, together with much of the rest of the continent of Europe, adopted the British model of industrialization, already recognizable at the end of the eighteenth century. The traditional economy receded into the background, and although not stagnant, developed slowly, with relatively small increases in productivity and capital–labour ratios. It comprised agriculture, together with construction, cottage industries and many other occupations, such as those of bakers, millers, tailors, shoe makers, hatters, blacksmiths, tanners and other craftsmen – all operating on a small scale to satisfy the demands of local, rather than national markets. All this was overshadowed by the modern 'industrial' economy, comprising cotton, iron smelting and refining, engineering and heavy chemicals, mining, some parts of transportation, and some consumer goods such as pottery and paper. Here also, modernization was far from complete, so that dualism still existed within, as well as between the various products recognized as characteristic of the modern economy.[15]

The traditional economy had always counted for more in France than it ever did in England and in one way or another the same was true of every other country in Europe. The question to be asked is what steps were taken, and on whose initiative, to catch up with England?

As to France, a widely travelled American army officer noted, as late as 1807, that apart from Paris, 'there are absolutely no interior towns like Norwich, Manchester and Birmingham'[16] – a choice of cities that incidentally reflects how far the Industrial Revolution had reached in England. In 1801, the population of Paris, with more than half a million inhabitants, was greater than that of the six next largest cities – Marseille, Lyon, Bordeaux, Rouen, Nantes and Lille – combined.[17] Paris, for all its sophistication, was far from representing the country as a whole. The great majority of the population, who lived in the vast and little known countryside, belonged to an earlier stage of civilization than the remarkably small number of people who played an important part in eighteenth and nineteenth century French history. Ignorance and illiteracy were the price paid for their isolation from the centre; a widely dispersed population was just as difficult to educate as it was to govern.[18]

For all their backwardness, some regions, in terms of economic development and integration into a national economy, were far ahead of the country at large. In addition to the areas surrounding the larger cities, the valleys of the great rivers, the Seine, Loire, Gironde and Rhône attracted new investment, as did the coast of the English Channel from the Belgian frontier to Normandy's Cherbourg peninsula, and the whole boundary area adjacent to Belgium and what is now Germany. It was no accident that the north-eastern half of France was the scene of most growth and industrial change.[19]

During the nineteenth century, the economic potential of both the French province of Alsace, west of the Rhine, and of the German Grand Duchy of Baden east of the river, was greatly enhanced by vast engineering works, which made the river navigable by much larger ships, while at the same time eliminating continual changes of course that had for centuries played havoc with local geography.[20] (The United States' greatest river system, that of the Mississippi, was tamed in much the same way.) It was no accident that the new German empire, as it emerged after victory in the Franco-Prussian war of 1870, claimed Alsace – by then a 'dynamic and important district'[21] – as part of the spoils of victory.

The French industrial revolution, at almost every stage, owed much to Britain, and although the British government in turn did its best to ensure that its lead was not lost to France, British artisans still sold their skills to French industrialists, who at the same time imported British machinery and engaged unashamedly in industrial espionage – as often as not with the collusion of disgruntled British entrepreneurs. This was particularly true of the early days at the end of the eighteenth century. For instance, James Milne of Lancashire, helped by his sons, supplied seventeen French textile firms with carding, roving, drawing or spinning machines while others such as William Wilkinson helped set up modern factories for cannon founding and other iron based operations.[22] Almost all innovations came from England, but once a new industry was set up, the French government lost little time in protecting it with high tariff walls.[23] In such 'modern' industries the workforce was mainly locally recruited; the role of British workers and foremen was to train, not to replace it.[24]

The French were superior to the British in pure science, and with such institutions as the Ecoles des Arts et Métiers were far ahead in providing institutionalized training in industrial technology. All this was reflected in a number of achievements in such fields as industrial chemistry – with many important inventions even before the end of the eighteenth century.[25] Given the political situation this was little help to France, so that, for instance, the paper making machine invented by L. Robert in 1798 was perfected and first used in England.[26] The lot of Barthelemy Thimonnier, who in 1830 became a pioneer inventor of a sewing machine, was in the end even more desperate. Although within ten years his factory contained eighty machines sewing uniforms for the French Army, his industrial career came to an end when this was destroyed by rioting tailors afraid of losing their livelihood. This left the way open to Americans to reinvent the sewing-machine, of whom much the best known, Isaac Singer, became a millionaire manufacturer a generation later.

Critically, also, the French were nowhere when it came to iron and steel, so that 'puddlers'[27] were prominent among skilled British immigrants.[28] Although iron founding at Le Creusot had started at least as early as the sixteenth century, a modern industry, designed to meet the requirements of the French navy, was set up in 1782 with the name *Fonderie royale de Montcenis*, following a survey ordered by King Louis XVI. This required the construction of *hauts fourneaux et autres usines à la manière anglaise*. However, it was only well after the end of the Napoleonic wars that two brothers, Joseph-Eugène and Adolphe Schneider, transformed the *fonderie* (no longer '*royale*') into the leading French centre for iron, steel, and above all armaments. It also produced the first French steam locomotive, taken into service in 1832 on the railway linking Lyon with St Etienne, the city where Le Creusot was located.

A major reason for the time lag vis-à-vis Britain was that France – like the United States – was slow to discover and exploit its reserves of coal, while at the same time it had both abundant water power and extensive forests where wood could be cut for charcoal. (On the continent, quite generally, both factors encouraged the dispersal of industry through the countryside.[29]) With coke as the essential fuel for the advanced technology of the British iron masters, it is no wonder that when the challenge came from Europe, it was – as related later in this chapter – from Belgium with its comparable resources in coal and iron. At a much later stage, the relatively high costs of coal meant that French industry led the way in adopting efficient and economical high pressure steam engines, while Britain was still content to work with the legacy of James Watt's atmospheric engines.[30]

As in the United States, the abundance of water power greatly helped the development of the textile industry – and here Frenchmen were among the leading innovators with such inventions to their credit as Benoit Fourneyron's prototype water turbine.[31] After 1815 the local manufacture of spinning machinery in factories with low labour costs meant that homespun cotton lost out entirely to that produced by new water-powered mills.[32] In due course the same was true of both linen – where Lille, using machinery smuggled from Britain, became the leading centre[33] – and wool. Weaving was a quite different case, as it was in Britain, with 'putting-out' encouraged by cheap labour in the countryside. For some time Alsace was the only province where power-weaving was economical.[34]

It was not until the 1850s that the French industrial revolution could claim a firm base, reflected in 1851 by the prize-winning French exhibits at the Great Exhibition in London. This could be seen in a whole new industry based on the new coalmines of Nord and Pas-de-Calais – the only part of France where the diversity of industry rivalled that of England[35] – but even then charcoal held its own in most other parts of France. In the first half of the nineteenth century, industrial growth was mainly to be found in the labour-intensive consumer sector, based on the manufacture of such products as soap, candles, glass, paper, ceramics and beet sugar. In the Lyon silk industry, the continued dependence of artisanal technology was no bar to prosperity – after all, the Jacquard loom, which represented state of the art technology, was still hand operated – but this was a special case.[36]

For all the considerable growth of French industry, the statistical indicators measuring both its productivity and sales were, even as late as 1860, hardly more than a fifth of the level achieved by Britain – and this level depended on a home market protected by high tariffs. That Britain was ahead of all competitors explains this discrepancy. More serious still was the fact that per capita income in France was 30 per cent less than in Britain,[37] without this even providing the advantage of lower production costs.[38] At the same time, France – in contrast to Britain and Germany with near zero population growth – was not an expanding market, which meant that there was little redeployment of resources to urban industry from rural agriculture.[39]

Although by the 1860s France could be counted an industrial power, it had yet to become an industrial nation.[40] This was due to a number of specific factors. The iron and steel industry suffered from a lack of cheap coking coal, which in turn restricted progress in engineering – exacerbated by a secular shortage of skilled labour, the slow pace of both railway construction and the diffusion of the steam engine. More generally, French industry was caught in a vicious circle. The narrowness of the market restricted growth, and this in turn held back modernization. There was also little scope for employment to shift from the traditional to the modern sector.[41] In many respects, therefore, France resembled more the countries of southern Europe – Spain, Italy, Austria-Hungary – than the successful and happier industrial nations of

the North: Britain, Belgium, Germany and the Scandinavian countries. Both economically and geographically,
France belonged to both North and South,[42] as can be
seen by its subsequent history. It is not for nothing that
the manufacturing centre of today's European aircraft
industry is in the southern French city of Toulouse.

Small Countries of Europe

With many different factors, relating to both time and
space, determining the emergence of modern industry in
nineteenth-century Europe, its history is inevitably one
of special cases. An examination of three countries in
particular – Belgium, the Netherlands and Switzerland –
shows the range of factors that counted in different
contexts.

Belgium distinguished itself for being in the vanguard,
both in exploiting its own resources and in adapting
processes already established beyond its frontiers in
Britain. Where Belgium was always an essentially modern country, the same was no longer true of the
Netherlands, its northern neighbour. There, although
the time in which the country had played a dominant
role on the international stage had long passed, government policy was focused on the restoration of the old
order until well into the nineteenth century – a process
in which industrialization played no more than a
subsidiary role. Even though the new kingdom of the
Netherlands, as established in the nineteenth century,
was never going to restore the glory of the seventeenth
century; tradition still tied its hands. The same, to some
extent, was true of Switzerland, but in this case there was
no history of long lasting international involvement.

With the addition of new, mainly French-speaking cantons as a result of the Congress of Vienna of 1815, the newly enlarged Swiss confederation joined the industrial revolution by adapting its traditional craft industries, such as watch making. Even so, it continued to deal with the outside world at arm's length, as it always had.

Taking the average percentage increase in gross national product in the period 1830–1910, yields a good measure of what Belgium, the Netherlands and Switzerland achieved in the European industrial revolution. For Belgium, the figure is between 1.2 and 1.4; for the Netherlands, below 1.0; and for Switzerland, higher than 1.4.[43] The contrast between Belgium and the Netherlands is particularly remarkable for showing how much government policy influenced industrial progress.

Belgium indeed confronts the historian of the industrial revolution with its greatest European success story. Although the name derives from the tribe of the Belgae which occupied that part of Europe in Roman times, the country itself is, and always was, essentially modern – even in the days before 1830 when it was always part of some greater empire. In late renaissance times the 'Low Country' provinces of Flanders and Brabant, home to the most advanced economy in the dukedom of Burgundy, to which they belonged, challenged the great Italian city states – with which they had close ties. With local industry based mainly on wool imported from England, there were even closer commercial links across the North Sea. The wealth of this part of the Netherlands – still to be seen in such cities as Bruges and Ghent – was proverbial, so much so that the Burgundian lifestyle that it reflected connoted the enjoyment of life, good food and extravagant spectacle. After many changes and upheavals in the political fortunes of the Netherlands, this inheritance led Belgium to become the most industrialized state in Europe after becoming an independent state in 1831.

The time was extremely propitious. Throughout almost the whole of the eighteenth century the southern Netherlands – as a result of the Treaty of Utrecht of 1713 – was part of the Austrian empire, where previously it had been subject to Spain for more than 150 years. (The northern Netherlands had been recognized internationally as an independent republic, following the Treaty of Westphalia of 1648.) The government in Vienna had every reason to encourage economic development, so that new canals and roads were built, and the seaport of Ostend – critically important with access to Antwerp blocked by the Dutch – expanded. At the same time the extensive, if heterogeneous, Austrian empire offered new prospects for transcontinental trade.[44] Local enterprise soon responded to the favourable economic climate, so that as early as 1720 a Newcomen atmospheric steam engine was installed in a coalmine near Liège[45] – a key innovation in what would prove to be an immensely successful coal and iron industry. At the same time agriculture was transformed, as it was elsewhere in northern Europe, with the adoption of the nutritious and easy to cultivate potato as the mainstay of peasant agriculture, while on the commercial side there was a considerable increase in the production of grain for brewing, and of flax for linen. The result was that an increasing number of cottagers concentrated on the industrial production of linen (which fetched a high price) while buying cheap potatoes for their own consumption – both aspects of an essentially modern microeconomy.

Things changed once more for the better – at least in the short term – when, at an early stage in the Napoleonic wars, Austria lost the southern Netherlands to France in 1797. This had two immediate advantages: first, France offered a vast new national market, while second, it provided protection against British competition in local markets. The new economic climate was particularly favourable to two new areas of growth, Verviers–Liège and Mons–Charleroi in French-speaking Wallonia. What is more, in 1798–9, Napoleon reopened the River Scheldt (which the Dutch had closed since 1585), making possible the recovery of Antwerp, which in early renaissance times had been the most important port in northern Europe.[46]

Somewhat paradoxically, in 1798 a British immigrant, William Cockerill, combined with a local entrepreneur, Jean-François Simonis, to build five mechanized spinning mills in Verviers, establishing an industrial dynasty that would lead the way in developing the coal and iron industry of Liège, a much larger town some 30 kilometres to the west. The Cockerills went on to be first on the continent of Europe to build a modern blast furnace, locomotives, iron ships and iron rails.[47] Once Belgium became independent in 1831, their achievement led, in the course of time, to new coalmines and plants involved in every stage of industrial metallurgy – with the River Meuse,[48] as it crossed the country from east to west, providing the location of much of the new development.

By the eighteenth century, the construction of canal
links to Flanders and France had led to the development
of the coalmining region of the Borinage, close to Mons,
in the west of Wallonia, and even after the defeat of
Napoleon at Waterloo – not far to the north – in 1815,
French industry continued as an important consumer.
Not far from Mons, local entrepreneurs in Charleroi –
where the Austrians had encouraged the development of
the local cottage industry of nail making (in competition
with that of Liège) – established what would become a
major centre of iron ore smelting, with engineers from
England introducing the newest technology.[49] In 1831
they opened the first continental blast furnace, overtak-
ing Cockerill in Liège. Although this was the year in
which Belgium became independent of the Netherlands,
the Dutch, under King Willem I, had already built canals
connecting the Mons–Charleroi region, via Brussels,
with Antwerp, which then went on to become a centre
of ship building and ship repair as well as the processing
of imported colonial goods and grains, including raw
materials for the Walloon industries.[50]

In the 1830s Belgium strengthened its competitive
position enormously by being in the vanguard of public
railway construction: the line from Brussels[51] to
Mechelen opened in 1835 was the first in continental
Europe to carry passengers. This added greatly to the
market potential of Wallonia, which enjoyed a pro-
nounced technological lead over France and Germany
combined with the advantage of being geographically
much closer than England to continental industrial
markets. It is no wonder then that Belgium developed
the densest rail network of any country in the world, to

supplement what was already a first class system of inland waterways. All this was helped by the development of a banking system concentrating on the needs of basic and capital goods industries.[52] This was accompanied by almost complete failure to develop consumer banking directed to the needs of the population at large, who, for such a rich country, remained relatively impoverished until well into the twentieth century. Inevitably then, industrial unrest was a constant factor in Belgian social history, as it was in the neighbouring regions of France.[53] Only after the end of the Second World War, by which time the days were numbered for the heavy industry of Wallonia, did the people at large begin to rediscover their traditional Burgundian lifestyle. Belgium – or the original provinces now comprised in it – was always essentially modern, and prosperous, by the standards of any day and age. In the vanguard of the European industrial revolution, Belgium was, in a sense, only fulfilling its destiny.

The question then arises, if Belgium, why not the Netherlands? By the end of the seventeenth century the Dutch republic, with a colonial empire extending across every known continent, was famed – and sometimes feared – for its power and prosperity. Even though the colonial economy steadily lost ground in the course of the eighteenth century,[54] the Dutch republic could claim almost to its end to be more highly developed, urbanized, learned and rich than any other country in the world.[55] While subordination to France had worked in favour of the southern Netherlands during the twenty-odd years (1795–1815) of the Napoleonic Wars, the Dutch in the north, dependent economically on their worldwide maritime links, had to contend with Britain's domination of the world's oceans. When, after the end of the wars, the Dutch colonial empire was restored on terms dictated by the British, priority in both government and business was given to the development of its economy – which had, after all, been the main source of Dutch wealth in the seventeenth century.

For the Dutch colonial economy, the key lesson of the eighteenth century was that investment should concentrate on planting tropical export crops such as coffee, sugar, indigo and tobacco. The question was what means should be adopted to achieve the best results. The answer – as imposed in 1830 on Java, much the richest island in the Dutch East Indies – was the so-called 'Culture System', under which millions of peasant cultivators were forced to work on land planted with one of the export staples, while subsistence cultivation, however essential for their own livelihood, was completely marginalized. For the local population this meant 'agricultural involution', a term introduced by the twentieth-century American anthropologist Clifford Geertz[56] to describe rural, and characteristically tropical economies, in which increased labour inputs of a local subject population contribute next to nothing to its own wealth or economic development. However, the system brought enormous profits to the Nederlandsche Handels-Maatschappij (NHM),[57] a trading house founded with government support in 1824 with the express purpose of exploiting the wealth of Java, for which it was, needless to say, granted a trade monopoly.

As a result, industry and investment in the Netherlands concentrated on the needs of the NHM, so that

Amsterdam acquired modern sugar refineries, which were the first in the country to use steam power on a large scale, and shipyards with a monopoly in constructing the ships chartered by the NHM. In Java itself, discrimination against cotton cloth from Lancashire opened the way to the expansion and modernization of the Dutch textile industry in Twente, a frontier region close to Germany. All in all, the demands of the colonies for its products dominated the growth of Dutch industry in the first half of the nineteenth century, with little advance, if any, of the standard of living of the Dutch population as a whole.[58]

The result of putting 'all one's eggs in one basket' was a fragmented and one-sided economic structure, which was vulnerable to any downturn in demand from Java, such as occurred in 1842–3, while at the same time little was done to develop the essential transport infrastructure in the Netherlands. The first railway, opened in 1845,[59] came ten years after Belgium's first line, and little was done to develop the system until the 1860s.

By this time the Dutch had begun to realize that they were lagging behind, so that the second half of the nineteenth century witnessed the development of a balanced industrial structure, with far less reliance on the exploitation of a colonial empire – and the ruinous Culture System was abandoned in 1870.[60] The writing on the wall had been there for any who cared to read it:[61] in the final quarter of the nineteenth century Indonesia was no longer a source of profits but of losses, for which the Dutch state consistently disclaimed responsibility.[62] The new order brought with it a serious decline in Dutch shipping and ship building. The opening of the Suez

Canal in 1869 made it imperative for the shipyards to build steamers, rather than sailing ships, at a time when the Dutch banking system – with Dutch investors preferring state funds and foreign investments[63] – was unable to provide the necessary finance.

The Netherlands, however wealthy, was also a relatively small country. In the nineteenth century, its small population, particularly in relation to that of Britain, increasingly counted against it. As a result, its prosperity still depended on agriculture, and not on trade and industry. Circumstances favoured farmers; free trade made export to Britain, their chief customer, easier. Demand for their products was followed by an increase in sales; prices rose as communications steadily improved. Few saw any need for agrarian reform, and Dutch prosperity was largely based on a conservative agriculture that had failed to innovate. Significantly, a Belgian radical, de Laveleye, noticed in 1865, 'that the Netherlands had been unwittingly transformed from a commercial into an agrarian nation'.[64] There are other factors relevant to the relatively unimpressive achievements of the Dutch industrial revolution[65] – though it is to be noted how much was achieved in the last quarter of the nineteenth century.[66] In a chapter relating to Europe as a whole, I have deliberately chosen to emphasize two factors which are distinctively Dutch: first, colonial economic exploitation; and second, traditional agriculture.

Although any attempt to recount the history of the Swiss confederation before the year 1798 – when the French Emperor Napoleon first took the stage – is bound to involve any number of special local instances, it must still be recognized that these provide the historical background to the Swiss industrial revolution. The Congress of Vienna of 1815, which established 'modern' Switzerland, did little to threaten the economic freedom of its twenty-odd cantons. Restrictions were imposed locally, so that there were about as many trade regulations, customs systems, monies, weights and measures as there were cantons[67] – not, one would think, a sound basis for an industrial revolution. Nonetheless the lesson of history is that Switzerland, next to Belgium, was in the forefront.

Needless to say the economy was fragmented, so that any particular segment had its own geographical – or in political terms, cantonal – base. Linen was to be found in the present cantons of Aargau and St Gallen, and silk in Basel and Zürich. Then, in the second half of the eighteenth century, these, and many other cantons, were seized by the so-called *Baumwollwut*, or cotton mania, which infected all branches of textile production – spinning, weaving, cloth printing and embroidery[68] – making use of already existing skills and the technology of a long established cottage industry. Of the 140,000 persons employed in the industry in 1800, some 100,000 worked in cotton, which shows just how successful the *Baumwollwut* had been. The figures show the remarkable size of the labour force in a country with a population of only two or three million.

The good times were not to last. From 1785 Swiss weavers, complaining of a bottleneck in the local supply chain, began to work with imported machine-spun English yarn, on such a scale that by the end of the century the number of hand-spinners had declined by nearly a half. The industry was plainly ready for restructuring based on a much increased scale of operations, made possible only by the introduction of new machinery. This took place in Zürich in the generation following the Congress of Vienna, but even so the new large mills never accounted for as much as 40 per cent of the whole production.

Inevitably the result was a decline both in production and the number of those employed, so that in 1865 these numbered only 65,000, with comparable if smaller numbers being employed in the traditional silk, linen and wool sectors.[69] Such figures led Swiss entrepreneurs to specialize in niche sectors, such as the production of high quality goods. In this context the most distinctive case was that of watch making; concentrated in the mainly French-speaking Jura regions of north-west Switzerland. There, in 1850, a million watches, (two thirds of the entire world production) were made,[70] in any number of small ateliers – some only carrying out a single stage in the manufacturing process.

In Switzerland as a whole it was only in 1880 that the number of those employed in factories became higher than the number working in cottage industries. By this time Switzerland was on the threshold of making a major contribution to the European communications infrastructure, with the St Gotthard rail tunnel – where construction started in 1872 – finally opening for traffic, ten years later, in 1882.[71]

A final point to be made, is that by the nineteenth century, Switzerland had long relied on international trade supporting local money based economies – because even in foodstuffs the country was not self-supporting.

Not for nothing had European armies relied for centuries on Swiss mercenaries, who, unlike many soldiers recruited locally, actually got paid in hard cash. This was well recognized outside Switzerland – *Point d'argent, point de Suisses.*[72] But that was the old times; in the period 1800–1850 textiles and watch making exported some 90 per cent of their production, and of this three quarters went outside Europe – mainly to the United States.[73] Proportionately Switzerland, as an exporting nation, was ahead of Britain, but as also in Britain, about half the export earnings were needed to pay for the import of raw materials. For all the popular image of Switzerland as a land of remote and inaccessible villages in long Alpine valleys, its people, wherever they lived, were always involved in the outside world – just think of the way Hannibal crossed the Alps more than 2,000 years ago. When it comes to head-counting rather than scenery, Switzerland has proved itself to be a remarkably urban civilization.

Germany and Italy

Somewhat late in the day, Germany became the great success story of the industrial revolution in Europe, while Italy's story was largely one of failure. Although many of the German and Italian principalities were represented at London's Great Exhibition in 1851, it would be another twenty years before Germany and Italy, as unified states, were part of the map of Europe. By this time it was clear enough how industrialization was developing in both countries – with Germany so far ahead of Italy that its success was a great concern to both Britain and France. In 1871 the success of Germany culminated in victory in the Franco-Prussian war, as a result of which France lost Alsace and Lorraine; its two most advanced industrial provinces. Italy, on the other hand, was nowhere; indeed, in 1860 it had lost Nice and Savoy to France.

Germany – defined in terms of its frontiers at the time of unification in 1870 – consisted mainly of a vast expanse of relatively low-lying land left over by the last ice age – which ended some 10,000 years ago.[74] The fact that to the south it was mainly bounded by successive chains of mountains from the Alps to the Carpathians, and to the north by the North Sea to the west of Denmark, and by the Baltic to the east, meant that its great rivers, the Rhine,[75] Weser, Elbe, Oder and Vistula[76] – to name the most important – also flowed north, each one of them with tributaries defining a vast drainage basin, extending both east and west to countries outside Germany, such as Poland[77] and France.[78] The nature of the countryside, combined with the seasonal changes in weather – which included heavy snowfalls in the winter months – meant that the levels of all these rivers, and their rate of flow, varied greatly according to the time of year and, over the longer term, from one year to another.[79] The channels through which these rivers flowed were constantly changing; in the process leaving new land, often in the form of islands, open for settlement, while at the same time old land was lost to erosion. In terms of physical geography, Germany, then, was comparable to the Mississippi catchment area of North America, although the river system of the latter had only one outlet to the sea; in terms of human geography, however, the cases were quite different.

It need hardly be said that the north German system of natural waterways posed considerable problems to navigation – although the general direction of flow had certain advantages, such as allowing logs to be floated downstream from the upland forests of both south Germany and the lands beyond its frontiers. By the nineteenth century this vast area had been home to European civilization for centuries, exemplified by such great inland cities as Leipzig and Cologne, or seaports such as Hamburg and Danzig. For their survival, man-made defences against flooding were essential, though not always adequate (as seen in the twenty-first century in the devastating floods along the Elbe and its tributaries that occurred in August 2002). In earlier times, where great cities might just afford such defences, any number of villages – unable to do so – simply disappeared. It is no wonder that the expenditure on public works was largely devoted to the control of water.

Historically, such programmes that were adopted were essentially local. In part this was the result of the political fragmentation of Germany, which left taxpayers reluctant to fund projects extending outside their own frontiers, but economically also, large-scale works were simply beyond the resources of any state. The picture began to change when, in 1740, Frederick II became King of Prussia and Elector of Brandenburg.[80] In consolidating and extending his realm, he had the will and the means to bring some order to its waterways, and his legacy, on his death in 1786, was a transformed communications infrastructure of north-central Germany. What is more, the good work he did was continued after his death, to extend to new lands added

to the kingdom of Prussia. Then, in the first half of the
nineteenth century, what had been achieved in Prussia
led further to a vast and successful long term project to
tame the Rhine, largely by turning sections of the river
into canals. Between Basel and Worms its length was
shortened from 220 to 170 miles, with any number of
cuts and 150 miles of main dykes; some 2,200 islands
simply disappeared.[81]

For geographical reasons, the improvements to the
natural inland waterway system, while including the
construction of a number of east–west canals, were never
going to provide Germany with adequate transport links
running in the same direction. While in the early
nineteenth century this deficiency was made good by the
construction of new roads, the most far-reaching transformation came with the building of railways with traffic
hauled by steam locomotives.[82] A short line was opened
in Bavaria in 1835, followed by the first long distance
line from Leipzig in Saxony in 1837 to reach Dresden,
120 kilometres away, in 1839. By this time Prussia had
completed a short line from Berlin to Potsdam in 1838.
New lines followed rapidly, so that there were 2,000
kilometres of rail in 1845, and 8,000 in 1855. All this was
critically important because railways were the driving
force behind the industrial breakthrough in Germany.[83]
In particular their construction encouraged the rapid
growth of the coal, iron and steel industries – for all of
which Germany, in contrast to France, had more than
sufficient natural resources of its own. These 'backward'
linkages were the essence of the German industrial
revolution; railways reduced very substantially the time
needed for the shift from the older charcoal technology

to more efficient coke smelting and refining methods. At the same time, new industrial enterprises were based on such recent organizational forms as the joint stock company.[84]

By the end of the second half of the nineteenth century, large-scale business enterprise dominated Germany's industrial economy.[85] This was reflected not so much in the companies comprising the railway networks, which tended to be fragmented – partly as a result of the way Germany was divided up into separate principalities – but in such dominant enterprises in heavy industry as are associated with the familiar names of Krupp and Siemens. Both of these giant concerns – as they emerged in Prussia in the nineteenth century – are worth looking at in the context of Germany's industrial revolution.

In the city of Essen, on the River Ruhr, a tributary of the Rhine, the Krupp family had been armament manufacturers since the late sixteenth century. Some 200 years later, the business came into the hands of the widow of a great-great-grandson of its founder, who expanded it by acquiring a mill, shares in four coalmines, and in 1800 an iron forge located on a stream near Essen. In 1807 the widow Krupp, by appointing her nineteen-year-old grandson Friedrich to manage the forge, set him off on a career that would transform the business. After her death in 1810, Friedrich, recklessly intent on winning a prize of 4,000 francs offered by Napoleon to anyone on the continent who could replicate a secret British process for producing crucible steel, founded the Krupp Gusstahlfabrik ('cast steel works'), whose only source of power was a waterwheel, and went on to produce his first smelted steel in 1816 – too late to win the prize, but in good time for him to become a founder of the German steel industry – although, when he died in 1826 he did not consider this ambition adequately fulfilled.

Success, however, did come in the end, when in 1841 Friedrich's son, Alfred, invented the spoon roller. This brought in enough money to enlarge the mill so that it could produce cast steel blocks. In 1847 it made its first cannon of cast steel, to be followed by a six pound (2.7 kg) cannon, together with a flawless solid ingot of steel weighing 2,000 pounds (907 kg) – more than twice as much as any previously cast. Exhibited in London in 1851 they proved to be an engineering sensation. Alfred Krupp never looked back as Europe's leading manufacturer of heavy armaments, and when he died in 1887 he was employing 20,200 men in his Essen mills, and more than 50,000 elsewhere.

Seeing himself as a model employer, Alfred Krupp constructed special 'colonies' for employees and their families – with parks, schools and recreation grounds – while the widows' and orphans' and other benefit schemes provided insurance in case of illness or death. A control freak when it came to his workers' lives, he demanded loyalty oaths, required written permission from a foreman to use the toilet, and forbade any involvement in national politics. All this fitted in with his wish to have 'a man come and start a counter-revolution' against Jews, socialists and liberals – a role he occasionally considered taking on himself.[86] For all that, the German industrial revolution would not have been the same without Krupp's vast armaments industry. In 1887 Alfred died, and in the new era that then started under his son Friedrich Alfred the firm manufactured, among many other things, Hiram Maxim's new machine gun and Rudolf Diesel's new engine.

Another great German industrial dynasty was that founded by Werner von Siemens, who – although born in 1816 as one of fourteen children of a rent collector in the kingdom of Hanover – made his career in Berlin, the capital of the much more dynamic kingdom of Prussia. Werner von Siemens' first business success was as an inventor and manufacturer in the field of the electric telegraph, pioneered by the American Samuel Morse.[87] In 1848 his company, Telegraphen-Bauanstalt von Siemens & Halske,[88] built Europe's first long distance telegraph line, linking Berlin with Frankfurt-am-Main, some 500 kilometres away. This was just the beginning of an international business empire, which in 1867 opened the first telegraph link between London and Calcutta. Not only in telegraphy, but also in the mechanical generation of electric currents, Werner von Siemens profited from his collaboration with the English inventor Charles Wheatstone – who in turn had worked with Michael Faraday, one of the greatest scientists of the day. With such good British connections, it is not all that surprising that Werner's brother, Wilhelm (1823–83), chose, at the age of twenty – to set up in England. There he branched out from the core electricity based business into the realm of iron and steel, and in the course of the 1850s, his regenerative open-hearth furnace – along with Bessemer's 'converter' – revolutionized steel production.

Siemens' industrial empire, like that of Krupp, was noted for its progressive employment practices, which included a standard nine hour working day and old-age pensions for retired employees – innovations in social welfare which in their day were revolutionary,[89] although they reflected a business philosophy that was largely self-serving. Also like Krupp, Siemens' operations in Germany – which during the Second World War employed 'slave labour'[90] – were seriously compromised during the Nazi era. (The British side, founded by Wilhelm, who later changed his name to Sir William Siemens, worked for the allied war effort.)

As the histories of Krupp and Siemens illustrate, the industrial revolution, if relatively late in coming to Germany, is notable for the capacity of its entrepreneurs to organize on a large scale in close collaboration with the state. This was principally the legacy of the renowned nineteenth-century chancellor, Prince Otto von Bismarck, whose basic philosophy was that investment by employers in model labour conditions would pay off by keeping labour unrest at bay. The price to be paid for this high cost approach was in the advantages it gave to foreign competitors. This was particularly true of the Netherlands, first in the textile sector, located along the German frontier, and then later in such fields as electric lighting, in which Philips' low cost operation in Eindhoven[91] – a site chosen specifically for its cheap labour[92] – competed successfully with Siemens.[93]

Italy, in the context of the industrial revolution, is something of a paradox. Although like Germany it did not become a single unitary state until the second half of the nineteenth century, the process was quite different in that it involved a successful revolution, originating in the kingdom of Piedmont (which then included Sardinia and much of French Savoy) and directed to overthrowing existing regimes in regions such as Tuscany and Sicily, together with the states (such as Umbria) directly ruled from the Vatican, and others, such as Lombardy and Veneto, which were governed by Austria. The line-up, such as it was in the early 1860s when the revolution led by Garibaldi conquered the whole of Italy, was in any case quite recent, and as in Belgium, largely the product of the Congress of Vienna in 1815.

In Italy, the origins of industry could be traced even further back, to a period in which Italian cities, in key sectors such as silk (with Bologna at the head) and armaments (led by Venice), were known across Europe for their advanced manufacturing methods. All this was supported, in the Po valley, by a transport infrastructure of navigation canals which had its origins in the thirteenth century[94] – as did many of the industries that it served. In their day they were the most advanced in Europe, if not the world; both in scale and mechanization. By the sixteenth century the water-powered silk mills of Bologna, some three storeys high, employed dozens of workers (many of them children), and with production totally mechanized, manufactured silk thread of the highest quality.

Where Bologna led the way, others followed, so that by the end of the eighteenth century it had been overtaken by many other centres, headed by the Venetian republic and Piedmont, both with an annual production of silk thread measured in millions of pounds.[95] In the silk mill at Racconigi in Piedmont, John Lombe acquired the technical know-how to enable him to build his own mill in Derby in 1720, where he is often credited with introducing the first factory system in

England,[96] half a century ahead of Arkwright's cotton mills.

But all this was too good to last. John Lombe was not alone in appropriating Italian know-how: in eighteenth-century France, the city of Lyon, by doing the same and improving upon Italian technology, came to dominate the international silk cloth trade – a process greatly helped by Paris becoming the centre of the world of fashion. Although the silk itself still came from Bologna, the loss to Italy was irretrievable. Furthermore, the relative decline in advanced technology, measured against what was being achieved in other parts of Europe, was also the fate of other traditional Italian industries, such as the glass, soap and dyes for which Venice was once famous. It is difficult to believe now that this was once the largest industrial city in Europe.[97]

With the Industrial Revolution Italy, simply failed to keep up with the times. There was little government support for industry, while poverty, both urban and rural, restricted domestic demand. Too many influential people valued just those aspects of Italy – such as its climate, air, sun and landscape – that still appeal to tourists today, rather than encouraging innovation in the manufacturing economy. Small-scale craft industries, still known under the generic name *artisanale*, blocked factory production in many sectors such as clothing and footwear. Railways, in particular, made little progress outside Piedmont – so much so that when unification came in 1860, the papal states, to which most of central Italy belonged, had less than 120 miles of track, and no outside links at all, whether north or south. This was largely the legacy of the reactionary and ultramontane

Pope Gregory XVI (1831–46), who preferred to invest state funds in imposing buildings and museums. (The joke was told after his death that he would have arrived in heaven more quickly if had allowed railways to be built.[98])

This then, was the picture of the economic stagnation from which Italy as a whole began to escape at the end of the nineteenth century. By this time the state had to contend with a long-term annual rate of growth in gross domestic product of less than 0.6 per cent,[99] a level equal to that of Spain and Portugal, Serbia and Bulgaria – all countries with nothing like the industrial achievements of Italy in earlier centuries. The state consistently protected traditional occupations – whose numerous adherents still retain considerable political power – while at the same time expanding the government bureaucracy to such a size that millions, with equal weight at the ballot box, still depend upon it for their livelihood. Even today, when it comes to industry, Italy is still making up for lost time.

10

ELECTRICITY AND CHEMISTRY

The Realm of Science
In the course of the Industrial Revolution, the application of scientific discoveries relating to both electricity and chemistry became increasingly essential. Until the end of the eighteenth century, practical men in the vanguard of the Industrial Revolution, such as James Watt and Richard Arkwright, if they knew anything of the remarkable advances in both these sciences associated with such names as Franklin[1] and Cavendish,[2] Priestley[3] and Lavoisier,[4] had little scope for applying such knowledge. There were links between the two sides, so that Watt and his business partner, Matthew Boulton, knew Joseph Priestley (the first to discover oxygen),[5] a fellow member of Birmingham's Lunar Society,[6] but the accumulated wisdom of the Society's members was only marginally relevant to such practical matters as the development of steam power. Even so, the discovery of

atmospheric pressure in the first half of the seventeenth century, by the Italian scientist Evangelista Torricelli[7] (1608–47), was essential to the design of Newcomen's working steam engine.

Electricity

Although the potential contribution of scientific discovery to industry was beginning to be recognized even before the end of the eighteenth century, there were still few practical applications. Then in 1800 the Italian Alessandro Volta (1745–1827) made a remarkable new discovery; his 'electrochemical battery' was the first source ever of continuous current electricity. But it was not until the 1830s that there was any practical application of the 'Voltaic pile' – the basic unit of any battery. On the other hand, the laboratory process, known now as 'electrolysis', would have been impossible without it.

Leading figures in the world of science such as, notably, Humphry Davy in Britain and Jöns Jacob Berzelius in Sweden, lost little time in adopting the Voltaic pile in the laboratory. In chemistry, this led to remarkable new discoveries, but it could not do the same for electricity. The reason for this failure was simple; the potential of an electric current to have useful applications apart from electrolysis depended on essential discoveries only made in the 1820s. Michael Faraday, a leading figure in this area, started his life in science as assistant to Humphry Davy, and went on to become one of greatest scientists of the nineteenth century. However, Davy, although best known for his work as a chemist, discovered the electric arc in 1810 before he knew Faraday. This was the result of connecting the electrodes of a giant Voltaic cell to two carbon rods, between which – when separated by a small distance – a brilliant arc of light appeared. Once initiated, its power could be strengthened by increasing the distance between the two rods. One witness to this remarkable phenomenon reported,

> a most brilliant ascending arch of light, broad and conical in form at the middle. When any substance was introduced into this arch, it instantly became ignited; platina melted as readily in it as in the flame of a common candle; quartz, the sapphire, magnesium, lime all entered into fusion . . . The light which was so intense as to resemble that of the sun, produced a discharge of heated air of nearly three inches in length, and of dazzling splendour.[8]

Until the invention of the incandescent light bulb in 1879,[9] such arcs produced the only possible electric lighting, but the problems involved in manufacture and installation meant that they were only useful for special, and sometimes spectacular, purposes. Apart from lighting, the intense heat at the heart of the light discharge made the electric arc ideal for welding metals, but this industrial use dates from the 1880s.

However useful the electric arc proved to be, it contributed little to the development of either science or technology outside its own specialist field of operation. Historically, progress in human understanding of electricity was made in another realm, largely developed as a result of the remarkable success of Michael Faraday and other scientists, from the 1820s onwards; in establishing and exploiting the links between electricity and magnetism. Faraday's first step was to invent the solenoid,[10] which was no more than a long length of wire wound around a core, like a thread around a bobbin. The solenoid, when activated by an electric current passed through the wire, acted like a magnet. Producing the reverse effect, that is, the use of a magnet to produce an electric current, proved to be much more difficult, but finally, on 29 August 1831, Faraday's induction ring experiment produced results that would change the course of history. In the following year, 1832, further experiments showed that the electricity Faraday had produced by induction had the same chemical, magnetic and other effects as that produced by Voltaic cells or any other method.[11]

Faraday's discoveries in electromagnetism led to two important practical instruments, both developed with the help of his colleague, Charles Wheatstone (1802–75). The first of these was the electric telegraph, whose basis was a circuit, of indefinite length, linking two stations and carrying an electric current determining, according to its direction, two possible positions of a compass needle. By the end of the 1830s this system had been adapted by Wheatstone and others to send elementary signals, with meanings agreed in advance, over any distance up to a limit determined by such physical factors as the electrical resistance of the wire used in the circuit.[12]

It only needed the genius of the American inventor, Samuel Morse, to invent a code, based on the two 'activated' positions of the compass needle, which enabled a written message to be communicated from one station to another. Although the first patent application for the 'Morse code' was filed in 1837, it was only in 1844 that it was used for the first time over a telegraph line along the tracks of the Baltimore & Ohio Railroad linking Baltimore with Washington, to send the historic first message, 'what hath God wrought'.[13] This was the beginning of a communications revolution that, within a decade or two, would make the world a very small place.

The second instrument, derived from Faraday's discoveries in the 1820s, was the electric motor and generator. Although Faraday produced a prototype electro-motor as early as 1822[14] and – with his induction ring experiment[15] – a prototype generator in 1831, the key industrial breakthrough came about as a result of Wheatstone and Werner von Siemens inventing the self-exciting generator, in the course of the 1860s. The key to this invention was that the magnetic field essential for producing electricity by induction was itself created by current tapped from the generator.

Not only is this still the standard model to be found in any power station – whatever its source of mechanical power – but, even more important, feeding current into the generator effectively converts it into an electric motor providing rotatory power. In other words, the process of applying mechanical power to rotate the shaft in order to generate electricity, can be reversed in such a way that an electric current can be used to provide mechanical power. As this process took practical form at the end of the 1860s, its industrial potential was almost unlimited. The range of electric power supply was far beyond that of steam – so much so that by the second half of the twentieth century, the main use of steam power worldwide[16] was to generate electricity; for another, electricity, by its nature, could be transmitted over extremely long distances, particularly after Westinghouse developed the technology of alternating current during the 1870s.

The Chemical Revolution

Although, by the mid-nineteenth century, there was no gainsaying the contribution of chemistry to the manufacture of producer and consumer goods, history tends to downplay its role in the Industrial Revolution.[17] Yet the level of production of industrial goods – and above all of textiles – on the basis of traditional technology had, by the end of the eighteenth century, reached a critical threshold. However essential such purely mechanical processes as spinning and weaving were to the production of textiles, they were nonetheless intermediate steps in the manufacturing process. Traditional technology dictated the use of human urine to remove the grease from raw wool before it could be spun, or of sour milk to bleach cotton or linen cloth after it had been woven. Both processes depended on chemical reactions for which alternatives would have to be found if production was to take place on the scale of new textile mills.

In the eighteenth century, one essential industrial chemical, alum, was produced by a manufacturing process. It was used by textile manufacturers as a mordant, which once applied to cloth, fulfilled the essential function of fixing natural dyes. Alum is a crystalline compound of aluminium and potassium; occurring naturally as kalinite, its use in the textile industry dated back to a time long before chemistry had reached the point of being able to identify the separate elements comprised in it.

If, originally, textile manufacture defined the most important market for chemicals, quite early in the nineteenth century glass, paper and soap became large-scale industrial consumers – and here they were not alone. Scale is important, because it provided, almost from the earliest days of the manufacture of chemicals, the rationale for its organization as a 'heavy industry'. As to the production of consumer goods, next to nothing was achieved before the first quarter of the nineteenth century. Then, even before the end of the Napoleonic wars in 1815, gas lighting and phosphorus matches had begun to lead the way as domestic consumer products of industrial chemistry.[18] Products such as photographic materials and synthetic pharmaceuticals followed a generation later.

Another key aspect of the chemical revolution was its close ties to scientific discovery, rather than to technological innovation, as can be seen from an article relating to bleaching, a key process in textile production, published by the Manchester chemist Thomas Henry in 1785:

Bleaching is a chemical operation. The end of it is to extract the oily parts of the yarn or cloth, whereby it is rendered more fit for acquiring a greater degree of whiteness, and absorbing the particles of any colouring material to which it may be exposed.

The materials for this process are the creatures of chemistry, and some degree of chemical knowledge is required to operate and judge of their goodness. Quicklime is prepared by a chemical process. Pot-ash is a product of the same art; to which vitriolic, and all other acids owe their existence.[19]

Although industrial applications were relatively few, chemistry was making remarkable progress in the second half of the eighteenth century. In 1754 Joseph Black identified carbon dioxide (which he called 'fixed air') as a separate gas; in 1766 Henry Cavendish isolated hydrogen and in 1774 Joseph Priestley did the same for oxygen, so opening the way, in 1783, for Antoine Lavoisier in France to cause these two elements to react by heating them, to produce water.

All this was just the beginning; the century between these discoveries and Dimitry Mendeleyev's, of the periodic table in 1869, witnessed a revolution in the world of chemistry. This brought an end to a world in which the chemical processes used by industry, particularly in the field of textiles (which was the main concern of Henry's article), had developed mainly by a long process of trial and error. The great French chemist Antoine Lavoisier (1743–94) observed – as he began to research the properties of air – that such knowledge as existed already was, 'composed of absolutely incoherent ideas and unproven assumptions . . . with no method of instruction and . . . untouched by the logic of science'.[20] Indeed, textile manufacturers who had long used cow dung to eliminate excess mordant residues in the process of dyeing, were not concerned as to why such application actually worked; allowing for a somewhat inapt metaphor, the proof of the pudding was in the eating.

Even so, the need to rely on cows did constitute something of a bottleneck. What is more, phosphorus, the active ingredient in cow dung, was only present in very small quantities. It was not until 1775 that a German chemist, C.W. Scheele (1742–86), found a remedy by discovering that bone ash could be used as the basis for producing pure phosphorus.[21] However, this required the use of sulphuric acid, which had only recently become available in commercial quantities. This in turn, followed from its extraordinary usefulness in any number of new industrial processes, to the extent that Justus von Liebig, a renowned German chemist, wrote in 1843, 'We may fairly judge the commercial prosperity of a country from the amount of sulphuric acid it consumes.'

Sulphuric acid, historically, was produced by distilling green vitriol[22] – a natural product of the oxidation of pyrites; a compound of iron and sulphur found in England mainly on the Isle of Sheppey.[23] Distillation of a solution of green vitriol in water separated out the iron to produce a powerful acid appropriately labelled 'oil of vitriol'. Once this became an industrial process, the end product proved to be – like alum[24] – extremely effective as a mordant essential in the finishing processes of the textile trade.[25] In fact, green vitriol, which the oil replaced, was used as a mordant as early as 1576. The problem was that some ten parts of green vitriol were needed to produce one part of oil. It would have helped little to produce the oil close to natural deposits of green vitriol, since the state of the roads in the early eighteenth century made its corrosive strength over any distance extremely hazardous.[26]

The way was open for a better and more economical manufacturing process. Intuitively this should have exploited natural deposits of pure sulphur – such as were to be found in certain parts of the Continent but rarely in Britain – but sulphur alone does not yield sulphuric acid, even though the chemical formula, H_2SO_4, suggests that this was no more than a compound of sulphur with water and oxygen (whose true nature, in any case, was unknown in the early eighteenth century). Once again, the solution was to work with a compound of another metal, potassium, identified in 1807 by Sir Humphry Davy as a separate element.[27] It was sufficient that a compound, nitre (now known also as potassium nitrate, KNO_3), occurred in substantial and accessible natural deposits.

This then was the basis of an alternative method of manufacturing sulphuric acid, developed on the Continent and introduced by Joshua Ward and John White into Britain from France in 1733, in time to start commercial production in 1736.[28] This operation produced sulphuric acid in such volume (in glass vessels of some forty to fifty gallons capacity) as to enable it to be sold at the same price per pound (1s.6d to 2s.6d) as had previously been paid for an ounce. All that was wrong was the location of production, first in Twickenham and then, after 1740, in Richmond, which had the double disadvantage of being far from the main markets in the Midlands, while upmarket Thameside residents complained of noxious smells – a foretaste of the environmental costs of heavy chemical manufacture.

In any case, entirely new markets were beckoning. As a scarce and expensive commodity, sulphuric acid had mainly been used by pharmacists to produce such medicaments as Glauber's *sal mirabile*[29] – much in demand as a laxative. When it became available at a mere fraction of the original price, industry found any number of uses for it. In response, then, to market factors, a second and much larger production operation was set up at the heart of industrial Britain, in Birmingham, by John Roebuck and Samuel Garbett, as an adjunct to their metal refinery at Steelhouse Lane. This was a turning point in eighteenth century economic history.[30] One important innovation in the Birmingham operation was the substitution of lead for glass in the vessels in which the sulphuric acid was made. This made production possible on a much larger scale, housed in structures comparable to the largest buildings of the day; chemical factories, rather than cathedrals, became the characteristic feature of many an urban skyline.[31]

The result was lower prices, more varied industrial applications and new factories built to serve developing markets. One of the most important of these, in which John Roebuck was also involved, was at Prestonpans on the Firth of Forth just east of Edinburgh. The sulphuric acid produced there was mainly used to replace sour milk in the bleaching of linen, whose production, in the eighteenth century, was Scotland's most important industry.[32] Given that, except for coal, the raw materials required at Prestonpans were not available locally, they had to be imported by sea. Sulphur came from Sicily and the nitre from the East India Company's sales in London.[33] A substantial part of the production was also exported by sea, to such destinations as Dunkirk, Rotterdam, Hamburg and Copenhagen, where – just as in Scotland – local textile industries were the main end-users.

By the end of the eighteenth century, the use of sulphuric acid in bleaching was, however, being superseded as the result of the discovery of a new chemical element, chlorine, by C.W. Scheele, in 1774 – a year before he discovered how to extract phosphorus from bone ash. Chlorine's usefulness as a bleach (realized in the first instance by the French chemist, C.L. Berthollet) became known to James Watt in England in 1786. By the end of the eighteenth century a Scotsman, Charles Tennant, had founded a vast new industry, with its own substantial works at St Rollox, in Glasgow. This manufactured a chlorine based bleaching powder,[34] which ideally suited the demands of a rapidly expanding textile industry.[35] The scale of its contribution was to lead St Rollox to become the largest chemical works in Europe.

For all the many purposes for which sulphuric acid could profitably be used, the greatest demand came from the manufacture of an even more useful range of industrial chemicals, known generically as 'soda'. This new industry depended upon a process invented by Nicholas Leblanc, a French chemist, by which sodium carbonate (also known as 'soda ash'), the most common form of soda, was produced by combining sulphuric acid with common salt. Leblanc's invention came at a propitious time for France, for during twenty-odd years of war with Britain – which ended only with the battle of Waterloo in 1815 – the country's own resources in natural alkalis were hardly sufficient as a source of soda produced by traditional methods. The problem was solved by mass production of sulphuric acid by Leblanc's process.

Where force of circumstance had led France to establish a national synthetic alkali industry, even as late as 1820 British industry still depended on natural raw materials – so that thousands of kelp gatherers, kept busy along the shores of Scotland, effectively maintained an obsolete and inefficient technology.[36] Plainly this situation could not last, and during the 1820s, a Liverpool entrepreneur, James Muspratt, built and put into operation an acid chamber, 120 feet long and 20 feet wide, to produce sulphuric acid by the Leblanc process.[37] Another factory was built on the same scale in St Helens. These locations in Lancashire were extremely well chosen; the steadily increasing concentration of British production of both soap and glass in the same area guaranteed a substantial market, whose demands production based on natural alkalis could never have satisfied. Where Muspratt led the way, others were bound to follow in such new industrial areas as the Midlands and Tyneside. It was the death knell for Scottish kelp gatherers.

The manufacture of soap was particularly significant, as it relied on caustic soda,[38] an industrial chemical, produced by treating soda with quicklime.[39] From early in the nineteenth century this had not only transformed the manufacture of soap – and, derivatively, of the detergents which largely supplanted the bleaches used in the manufacture of textiles[40] – but also greatly extended the variety of linen rags[41] that could be used to make paper.

The new 'soap' technology depended on the discovery, in 1813, by the French chemist M.E. Chevreul (1786–1889), that one of the constituents of animal fats is glycerine, a chemical compound that occurs in all living organisms. If such fats are treated with caustic soda, the glycerine is separated out and the residue is soap, which in chemical terms is therefore, a salt of a fatty acid.[42] Quicklime in turn is produced by heating limestone in a dedicated lime kiln, and quite apart from its usefulness in producing caustic soda,[43] becomes – with the addition of water and heating in a process known as 'slaking' – a product useful for the manufacture of whitewash, bleaching powder and glass.

These are good examples of the way that industrial chemistry was becoming a science based industry. The essential first step was the introduction of the Leblanc process for producing soda. Although, when applied on an industrial scale, it proved to have many drawbacks, both economic and environmental,[44] it still held its own for some seventy-odd years. Its use only came to an end in 1861 after the Belgian chemist Ernest Solvay (1838–1922) patented a quite different, and much more advanced process, based on ammonia. By this time the invention of the first synthetic dyestuff in 1856 by William Perkin[45] signalled the beginning of a new era in industrial chemistry.

Nonetheless, during the first half of the nineteenth century, the production of alkali still dominated the chemical industry,[46] with its key chemical, sulphuric acid, and its key product, soda. It was not – at least by today's standards – an efficient science based industry. Even the largest firms were without research and development departments, although entrepreneurs were ready enough to adopt new technology, often at the risk of having to contest expensive patent claims. In doing so they changed the face of their country, and this is true not only of Britain, but of other countries such as France, Belgium, Germany, and above all the United States, in the vanguard of the Industrial Revolution.

Although the chemical industry, compared to textiles, coal, iron and steel, or railways, employed relatively few people – in Britain only 40,000 as late as 1880[47] – this reflected neither its importance to the rest of the nation's industry, nor its impact on the landscape and the life of its people. This was noted and condemned by many contemporary observers such as Robert Blatchford, who described St Helens in Lancashire – at the heart of industrial chemistry – as,[48]

> a sordid ugly town. The sky is a low-hanging roof of smeary smoke. The atmosphere is a blend of railway tunnel, hospital ward, gas works and open sewer. The features of the place are chimneys, furnaces, steam jets, smoke clouds and coal mines. The products are pills, coal, glass, chemicals, cripples, millionaires[49] and paupers.

Parallel to the development of the alkali trade to meet the demands of the textile industry, the destructive distillation of coal, driven by the demand for coke to be used in iron furnaces, also led to the manufacture of a remarkable range of new products. The first by-product of coke to become significant in the British economy was coal tar, a substitute for the pitch essential to shipbuilding at a time when ships were built of wood. Even before the eighteenth century, British forests were unable to satisfy the demands of British shipbuilders. North European nations, led by Sweden, had a monopoly on the supply of pitch and combined to maintain high prices. Britain, confronted by this cabal, turned to its North American colonies for an alternative supply, but although the raw material was abundant on the other side of the Atlantic, the colonists exacted a high price for responding to the needs of the mother country – so much so that between 1719 and 1779 some £1,250,000 was paid for American pitch. This sum was noted as a considerable 'waste of treasure' in a 1785 *Memorandum concerning the Progress, and the Uses of the Discovery of Extracting Tar from Coal*, which effectively proposed a way to free British shipbuilding from its dependence on imported pitch. The question was, who was going to grasp the nettle and engage in the commercial separation of tar from coal?

The man who took up the challenge was an impoverished Scottish nobleman, the ninth Earl of Dundonald, who, noting the sea coal resources of his entailed and indebted estate of Culross Abbey, conceived of the idea of converting them into tar as a means of retrieving the family fortunes. The earl, while serving as a young naval office on the west coast of Africa, had noted the harm done to ships' bottoms by worms, and from his chemical knowledge he reasoned that an extract from pit coal in the form of tar might be a good counter measure.[50] Putting his ideas into practice, Dundonald founded the British Tar Company in 1782, and with extra funding raised from three other Englishmen he also hoped to forestall an importunate creditor called Cuthbert. In principle the venture was well founded. This, at least, was the judgement of Scotland's leading chemist, Joseph Black (1728–99),[51] who commented that Dundonald's process was[52] 'easy and cheap in execution ... and produces excellent tar for the bottom of ships'.

For a number of reasons Dundonald's investment in coal tar never enjoyed the success it deserved. The British Admiralty, the most important prospective client, let him down by switching to copper sheathing for protecting the bottoms of ships, a practice then adopted by other ship owners. At the same time, for those who chose to apply Dundonald's tar, it was so much better than the pitch it replaced that ships did not require such frequent repair.[53] To a degree therefore, Dundonald was undermined by his own success, but then he was also, in the words of his son, neither[54] 'by habit [nor] inclination "a man of business". Many who were so knew how to profit by his inventions without the trouble of discovery, whilst their originator was occupied in developing new practical facts to be turned to their advantage and his consequent loss.' One of these streetwise entrepreneurs was Dundonald's own second cousin, J. Loudon Macadam, who became famous for the 'tar Macadam'[55] used in the construction of roads.

Among the other technologies that interested Dundonald were the conversion of sea salt to soda, the manufacture of alum as a mordant for silk and calico printers, the manufacture of iron and the production of sugar. But it was left to others to profit from them, as is shown by the *Prospectus of Index to Lord Dundonald's Intended Publication*, published in 1799, in which he complained of 'the most cruel and oppressive usage from individuals and neglect on the part of the government'. One missed chance above all shows Dundonald for the sort of man he was; quoting his son once more,[56]

having noticed the inflammable nature of a vapour arising during the distillation of tar, by way of experiment, [he] fitted a gun-barrel to the eduction pipe leading from the condenser. On applying fire to the muzzle, a vivid light blared forth across the waters of the Firth, becoming, as was afterwards ascertained, distinctly visible on the opposite shore.

Historically this may have been the first ever demonstration of coal gas as a source of light, but Dundonald failed to exploit its potential – another chance missed.

William Murdock, an employee of Boulton and Watt in Birmingham where Dundonald was an occasional visitor, did realize the potential of coal gas. Sent by the firm to represent it in Cornwall in 1792 and helped by a local physician, he devised the means for using it to light his house. Since this involved conducting the gas through some seventy feet of metal tubes, Murdock had in fact laid the foundations for providing gas as a mains service. He went on to improve his apparatus, which by 1798 was ready to light the inside of the main building of his employers' Soho Foundry. Then, in 1802, to the astonishment of the local population, he lit the outside as well to celebrate the peace with France secured by the Treaty of Amiens.[57]

This display was something of a pre-emptive strike, for in 1801 a Frenchman, Philippe Lebon, had already used gas to light his house and garden in Paris. Following the public display of 1802, Boulton and Watt proceeded to develop gas lighting for factories, theatres and other large buildings, each with its own plant. In 1805 the company installed gas lighting in the Manchester cotton mills of Phillips and Lee, thus paving the way for textile manufacture to continue around the clock – until then a practice only to be found in mining and iron founding. Murdock was soon able to demonstrate that the increase in productivity more than justified the cost of installing and running the gas plant. Little thought was given to the social consequences of an industry operating twenty-four hours a day. In 1806 the Lyceum Theatre in Glasgow installed gas lighting, further demonstrating its vast range. By the second decade of the nineteenth century, the advantages of conversion to gas lighting had almost completely won over the captains of British industry.

For all their success with industry, Boulton and Watt gave little thought to providing a public gas supply, even though their own experience had made clear the advantages of lighting houses with gas. At the same time British scientists cast doubts on any such project, while its main supporter, Frederic Albert Winsor (from Moravia in the Austrian empire), was regarded as something of a crank. Even so, he persevered in London in the face of considerable local opposition and in 1809 was granted a patent for the scheme he proposed for the metropolis; in 1812 he received a charter for his new Gas, Light and Coke Company.

A year later, the company poached a native Mancunian, Samuel Clegg, from Boulton and Watt, and by doing so secured the services of an outstanding engineer whose skills brought constant improvements to the service offered. Gas lighting spread rapidly across Britain, providing lighting at a fraction of the cost of the oil lamps and candles it replaced, and the same was true outside Britain, with Baltimore, for instance, the first American city (in 1816) to install it. With gaslit streets, cities became much safer at night, while increasingly literate populations could devote evening hours to reading. Although at the end of the nineteenth century, electric lighting took over from gas, the mains gas supply remained important for cooking and heating[58] – although here natural gas gradually took over from coal gas in the course of the twentieth century. At all events, the mains supply pioneered by London's Gas, Light and Coke Company led the way in establishing a principle of provision of services to domestic and industrial users from a distant centre, which is one of the most important legacies of the Industrial Revolution.

Almost as important as the mains supply of gas were the by-products of its manufacture. The coke resulting from the destructive distillation of coal had a ready market in the steadily expanding iron and steel industry. Although coal gas was originally a by-product of tar, the spectacular growth of mains gas in the first half of the nineteenth century reversed their relative importance. Once tar became the by-product there were doubts about its usefulness to industry. These were dispelled first by J. Loudon Macadam's discovery that it could combine with road stone grit to make a first-class top surface for roads, and then by that of William Perkin, and others, that it provided the essential base for artificial dyes.[59]

Quite apart from coke and tar, the manufacture of coal gas produced other useful industrial chemicals such as naphtha and ammonia. The first industrial use of naphtha was discovered in 1823 by Charles Macintosh,[60] a manufacturing chemist in Glasgow who succeeded in finding a way to use what otherwise was no more than a waste product of the Glasgow gasworks. Macintosh discovered that naphtha could be used to dissolve rubber into a form which could be used for making double-textured waterproof cloth. His commercial success was the result of a partnership with Hugh and Joseph Birley, owners of a successful Manchester cotton mill, on whose premises a new plant for making the waterproof cloth was set up. This was the start of a business that would go on to produce the mackintosh (note the change in spelling), which by the end of the nineteenth century had become the modern world's leading raincoat.

Ammonia was a quite different case; a simple compound of nitrogen, its usefulness derived from being extremely soluble in water. Like soda and sulphuric acid, it is a major product of industrial chemistry, with a range of uses which includes explosives and fertilizers. The Haber process by which it is now produced was only developed in 1908; before then the destructive distillation of coal provided a major source of supply.

In the second quarter of the nineteenth century the manufacture of synthetic fertilizers developed to become a major component of the chemical industry. Although this process was in part led by the demands of British farmers intent upon increasing productivity – both to satisfy the needs of a steadily increasing urban population and to compete with overseas agriculture at a time when tariffs could no longer protect them – it depended also on an increase in scientific understanding largely attributable to the German chemist Justus Liebig (1803–73).

Liebig, generally acknowledged to be the father of organic chemistry, became an extraordinary professor at the University of Giessen (now named after him) at the age of twenty-three. There he was the first to establish a university based research laboratory, where his own work was largely directed towards meeting the needs of agriculture and medicine. As the first of its kind, the laboratory inevitably attracted foreign researchers; among them were the two sons, Sheridan and Edmund, of James Muspratt. This immediately provided Liebig with a link not only with England, but also with the exploitation of science by industry. In the course of six visits to England in the period 1837–55 he observed, critically, both current agricultural practice and the failure to use local resources for improving productivity.

Liebig was particularly struck by the way fields were covered with lime, making them look 'as if they were covered with snow'.[61] In its way this was good applied science, for the alkali base of lime was effective in counteracting the local acidity of soil. Lime was cheap and abundant, but acidity was not the only factor that reduced productivity. Although Liebig's theory that plants obtained essential minerals from the soil and nitrogen from ammonia in the atmosphere[62] was sub-stantially correct, he still had to discover which minerals were actually taken from the soil – for without such knowledge there would be no systematic way of replacing them with synthetic products of the chemical industry.

The British fertilizer industry emerged when Mus-pratt's two sons, applying the knowledge gained from Liebig, began the manufacture of 'various formulations of plant ashes, gypsum, calcined bones, silicate of potash, phosphates of magnesium and ammonia, as well as common salt'.[63] These were fused together by roasting in a furnace, a process calculated to make them less soluble (so as not to be washed away with every rainfall) but which had the disadvantage of making it more difficult for growing plants to absorb them. British farmers began to see Liebig as 'a Pope believed to be not only infallible, but beyond the reach of criticism'.[64]

British entrepreneurs, nonetheless, sought to improve upon Liebig's methods, and in doing pioneered the use of superphosphates, which became the world's leading synthetic fertilizer. Although the first factory, at Deptford, was opened by J.B. Lawes in 1841, the industrial breakthrough came when Packard & Company's works opened at Bramford in 1854. Whereas at Deptford the fertilizer was produced by treating bones with sulphuric acid, at Bramford these were replaced by coprolites; a substitution earlier recommended by Liebig after he had observed vast natural deposits along the banks of the Severn.[65] The switch to this fossilized dung of dinosaurs established an industry that became the largest industrial user of sulphuric acid – to be supplied in concentrations not previously achieved by the industry.

Liebig's essential insight was that the need of living organisms for phosphorus could be satisfied, historically, by compounds known generically as 'phosphates' that were naturally present in soil. The term 'superphosphate' was adopted by industry to describe, generically, the result of extracting such compounds, in which the use of coprolites was an intermediate stage. Alternative sources of natural phosphate proved to be more economical, so that in 1857 Lawes began to import apatite from Norway, followed by others in the industry who imported raw materials from Belgium (1870s), the United States (1880s) and North Africa (1890s).[66] Nevertheless the superphosphate industry, as established by Lawes in the 1840s, remained a British monopoly almost to the end of the nineteenth century.[67]

Although phosphate derivatives dominated fertilizer production, both nitrates and potashes were also important. As to the former, Liebig's principle that the atmosphere was an adequate source of supply was no more than a half-truth. Not only are nitrate compounds to be found in minerals, but their contribution to plant nutrition is far from negligible. One step further leads to the principle that nitrate based fertilizers can increase agricultural productivity. This was known – implicitly at least – by Native Americans in Peru long before the Spanish conquest, when they used guano as fertilizer. Guano, composed of seabird droppings, is not only the richest known natural source of nitrates, but also contains phosphates. In the early nineteenth century vast deposits were discovered on islands off the coast of Peru, where the complete absence of human settlement was more than made up for by the presence of millions of cliff nesting seabirds. In a part of the world where rain almost never fell, the guano had accumulated over the centuries to a considerable depth.

The German explorer Wilhelm von Humboldt brought the first sample to Europe in 1804. In 1840 it began to be imported into Britain, which – after negotiating a monopoly with the Peruvian government – became the world's leading supplier. By the time exploitation had peaked in 1870, it was well known that the remarkable and indeed valuable properties of guano were mainly the result of exceptionally high concentrations of nitrates.

Although the Gas, Light and Coke Company had already produced ammonium sulphate as a by-product, its adoption as a fertilizer was slow. With the natural reserves of guano diminishing after 1870, ammonium sulphate came into its own, so that between 1879 and 1889 production increased from 40,000 to 117,000 tons. By this time the natural reserves of guano were almost exhausted. A comparable story can be told for fertilizers based on other sulphates and potash – and here German manufacturers played an important part in the early development of the industry from their own local resources.

Finally, as the nineteenth century approached its mid-point, the chemical industry began to expand so as to incorporate two new fields of development; the first was the use of electrolysis for the production of metals on a commercial scale; the second the manufacture of new types of explosive to replace gunpowder. Electrolysis, although applied by Humphry Davy and others of his generation as a key laboratory process from the beginning of the nineteenth century, only became possible on a scale of interest to industry after the German chemist Robert Bunsen (1811–99) developed, at mid-century, a new zinc-carbon battery. Where Davy was able to demonstrate that alum had a metallic base, which Friedrich Wöhler, in 1827, was able to isolate in its pure form, now known as aluminium, Bunsen – although his battery was no more than a Voltaic cell of unprecedented scale – produced not only aluminium (1852), but also magnesium (1851) and chromium (1852).

For aluminium this was no more than a step on the way to an industrial breakthrough; this only came with the development of the Hall-Héroult process, which – being dependent on high voltage direct current electricity such as could only be produced by a power station

– was only adopted by the mining industry at the end of the nineteenth century. While magnesium is commonly produced from the electrolysis of brine, the process is much simpler with no need for power on a scale comparable to that required by industrial aluminium. Industrial chrome is produced directly from the ore, without electrolysis playing any part.

Until the second half of the nineteenth century gunpowder, already known about for hundreds of years (if not longer in China where it originated), was the only explosive available either to the construction industry or for use with armaments. Compounded of readily access-ible raw materials, its usefulness can be measured by the fact that in 1843 some 18,500 lbs were used for blasting the cliffs at Dover as part of the construction of the South Eastern Railway.[68] Although the ingredients were cheap enough, the product itself was not very effective.

There was clearly room for an alternative, and in 1846 two applied scientists, C.F. Schönbein in Switzerland and A. Sobrero in Italy, both working with a mixture of nitric and sulphuric acids, provided it. The former, applying the mixture to cotton, produced guncotton (aka nitrocellulose), and the latter, applying it to glycerine, produced nitroglycerine. Both of these new substances proved to be highly explosive, so much so that the early industrial production of guncotton (from 1847 by John Hall & Son in England) and of nitroglycerine (from 1863 by the Nobel brothers in Sweden) was bedevilled by accidental explosions and consequent loss of life.[69]

Plainly, if there was to be a way forward, and government restrictions were to be overcome, both products had to be stabilized, and after further research and development this is just what happened. After 1863, following the discovery of a new process that allowed guncotton to be manufactured safely, the restrictions on production in Britain were removed, and the same happened with nitroglycerine in Sweden in 1864, following Alfred Nobel's discovery that it could be stabilized with an earth known as *kieselguhr*. With the resulting product, which he called 'dynamite', and two others that followed in 1875 and 1889, Alfred Nobel went on to become one of the world's richest men, now known above all for the prizes named after him.

11

GLOBALIZATION: RAW MATERIALS, MARKETS AND LOCAL MANUFACTURE

Industrialization Comes of Age

Globalization was an inevitable result of the Industrial Revolution. Such familiar trials of the twenty-first century world as excessive carbon emissions, with the threat of irreversible, if not catastrophic, global warming, are the price paid now for the process of industrialization that started in England in the eighteenth century. As demonstrated by the conference at Copenhagen at the end of 2009, deciding on the measures essential for reducing this threat and, just as critically, the extent of the responsibility of each individual state, whether rich or poor, for adopting them, is a major concern of international politics. This means, in particular, that nations such as India and China, which in the nineteenth century were unashamedly exploited in the interests of European and American imperialism, must accept a much higher price for membership of the club of industrial powers than was ever paid by its original members in Europe and North America.

In the period of forty-five years between 1869, the year in which the Suez canal was opened, and 1914, in which the First World War started – and incidentally the Panama canal was opened – the Industrial Revolution went global. In 1869 the world created by the 'classic' Industrial Revolution was in a sense 'mature'. Looking first at Britain, this meant that while the number of those living in cities, and employed in factories, was still increasing, the worst excesses of the Industrial Revolution were being mitigated. Working hours were limited by law, particularly for women and children; state education was beginning to establish a literate adult population, which, with the voting rights granted by Disraeli's Reform Act of 1867, acquired a voice that was heard at Westminster. Mains services for providing safe clean water, the disposal of sewage or the supply of gas for lighting – with London in the vanguard – made urban life healthier and much more agreeable, and a comprehensive national network of railways of unprecedented safety, speed and comfort enabled even the working classes to see something of the country outside their home towns – so that, for example, with mills in Lancashire closing for Wakes Week, the hands could enjoy the charms of the seaside at Blackpool. Business, realizing the potential of the working classes as a consumer society and their ability to organize such institutions as trade unions, adopted new and progressive employment policies – at least in some sectors of the economy. In the twentieth century, this process culminated in Henry Ford's principle of 'every worker with a car in front of his own house'. Such progressive employers were not to be found everywhere. In extractive industries such as mining, particularly in developing countries, the only improvement of conditions of employment was that which was prescribed by legislation.

At this late stage in the Industrial Revolution, comparable conditions to those described above were to be found in the other emerging industrial powers in Europe and North America. Some, such as Germany, were ahead in literacy and amenities for workers in industry, but Britain, judged in terms of national wealth, was more prosperous overall. The United States, although still recovering from the trauma of the Civil War, was becoming a nation self-sufficient to a degree that no European power could rival. The opportunities for individual economic advancement were almost unlimited – at least as they were reported in Europe – so that millions of immigrants from southern and eastern Europe found new homes across the Atlantic. Once in the United States many found employment in the industries of what is now the American rust belt. Although their success meant a substantial loss of American markets for European manufacturers, this could be made good by their exploiting the world outside Europe and North America – continuing, on an unprecedentedly large scale, a process that went back to the earliest days of European overseas imperialism.

The Scramble for Africa

In the period 1869–1914, Britain, France, the Netherlands, Spain and Portugal – the five nations of Europe whose colonial empires had their origins in the sixteenth century – were joined by three new rivals, Belgium, Germany and Italy, none of which had existed as an independent state at the beginning of the nineteenth century. The rivalry was played out mainly in Africa, where, until the end of the eighteenth century, the commercial interest of the established imperial powers was focused on the slave trade – the source of much of the capital that financed the earliest stages of the Industrial Revolution. The trade involved no more than a few precarious coastal outposts[1] for the Europeans engaged in it, and with few exceptions the trade in Africans from inland, destined for slavery in the New World, was itself organized by Africans.[2] This type of commerce, in any case, left the rest of Africa's very considerable natural wealth untouched.

One reason for this was the utterly inhospitable nature of a continent with few natural harbours or navigable rivers, coastlines where the hinterland, if not desert or semi-desert, was likely to be impenetrable forest, and plagues of insects such as the anopheles mosquito, which carried malaria – all too often fatal – or the tsetse fly, whose bite was fatal to horses which might otherwise have been used as beasts of burden, and cattle.[3] Even to those engaged in the slave trade, the coasts of Africa were known as 'the white man's grave'; the interior of the continent promised to be no more salubrious. What is more, apart from legend, there was little reason to believe in hidden wealth waiting to be discovered – although, even before the end of the nineteenth century, this certainly proved to be the case.

The interior of Africa had attracted explorers long before the nineteenth century. Most were bent on tracing the courses of the continent's few great rivers: the Blue and the White Nile, the Niger, the Congo and the Zambezi. Typically these explorers – many of whom failed to return alive – were evangelical Christians, serving God rather than Mammon, intent on subverting the demographic base of the slave trade far from the coasts from which captives were shipped to New World plantations. If – granted that both Britain and America abolished the slave trade in 1807 – their cause had already been largely won, the Dutch and Portuguese remained involved, and as David Livingstone (1813–73) discovered later in the nineteenth century, so also were Arabs in east and central Africa.

Africa proved to be not quite as inimical to exploitation and settlement as was commonly believed. In the early 1840s, a British expedition travelled by steamship up the Niger, from the delta in the Gulf of Benin, to continue some hundred of miles up the Benue, its most important tributary. By constantly taking quinine (a medicinal extract of the bark of chinchona trees from South America), the Europeans avoided malaria, or at least mitigated its effects. The interior of Africa was becoming much safer and more accessible. With the increasing use of ocean-going steamships, the same was true of its coastlines where European ships in earlier times had come merely to pick up slaves.

To the European powers at the end of the 1860s, the economic potential of inland Africa was reckoned to be such as to make its territory worth adding to their colonial empires – or, in the case of King Leopold II of Belgium, to his private estate. The 'scramble for Africa' was set in motion by Leopold in 1876, who, with the co-operation of the leading African explorers and the support of several European governments, set up the International African Association for the promotion of African exploration and colonization.[4] A year later, in 1877, King Leopold employed Henry Morton Stanley – at that time world-famous as an African explorer[5] – to explore the vast Congo river system. Stanley, in the course of his explorations, acquired vast territories in the Congo basin by means of treaties agreed with a number of native chiefs, who had little idea of what their purpose was, nor, in many cases, any right to dispose of the land subject to them. In this way Leopold acquired an estate seventy times larger than Belgium.

King Leopold then organized a new International Association of the Congo[6] to become the single owner of all the land ceded to Stanley by local chiefs. What is more, skilful Belgian diplomacy in Washington led the US government, on 22 April 1884, to recognize the International Association of the Congo as a sovereign independent state, to be known as the Congo Free State.[7] (It helped no doubt that Stanley was an American citizen.)

Europe lost little time in following America, with Austro-Hungary, France, Germany, the United Kingdom, Italy, the Netherlands, Portugal, Russia, Spain, and Sweden all recognizing the Congo Free State before the end of the year. If history had stopped at this point, one small European state, or rather its king, would have extended his realm to include a new political entity comprising the whole of the basin of a major river system. King Leopold had prudently claimed that he acted from the noblest of motives – the complete opposite of the truth – and would willingly support similar enterprises undertaken by other European powers.

This invitation to join the party – which was particularly welcome to the French, who wished to claim vast territories north of the Congo river – led Prince Otto von Bismarck, the German Chancellor, to convene a Great Power conference in Berlin, which opened at the end of 1884. The future of Africa would be determined by the established colonial powers with competing claims to African land. This meant France, Portugal, the United Kingdom and, needless to say, the host state, Germany. Other great powers, such as Russia, Austro-Hungary and the United States, with no such claims, also attended as 'onlookers',[8] together with a number of smaller states, such as Denmark, Sweden, Norway, the Netherlands and notably Belgium. With no invitation given to his International Association of the Congo, King Leopold had reason to be concerned that the recognition achieved earlier in the year by Belgian diplomacy might count for nothing. As events ran their course, it became clear that he should not have worried. With little enthusiasm, both Britain and France ensured that the Belgian king, at the end of the day, should have his way.

The British government, for historical reasons, was at first inclined to support a Portuguese claim to the Congo. The French, on the other hand, with an eye to the land north of the Congo river, favoured Belgium, which promised not only unqualified support for French claims, but also a reversion on its own claims south of the river in the event that it could not find the financial resources needed to exploit them.[9] King Leopold astutely encouraged German interest in South West Africa (the present state of Namibia) and undermined the British government on the home front by reminding the people of Portugal's poor record of colonial slavery – which Britain had abolished some fifty years earlier – and assuring the business community that Britain would be granted the same 'most favoured nation' status as Portugal was ready to offer. Even so, the British Foreign Office was rightly sceptical about what King Leopold had in mind. The king, however, had made the same offer to Germany,[10] who had agreed to it. (Its value in 1885 was extremely problematic given that the Congo, at this stage in history, had little apparent economic potential.) Bismarck in turn put the British under pressure by suggesting that the refusal of King Leopold's offer might lead to serious problems with the French in West Africa. Unwilling to risk conflict with France, Britain accepted it.[11]

King Leopold's diplomacy was crowned by success; the Berlin conference, on 5 February 1885, recognized him as sole owner of the Congo. France, in turn, was able to retain all the territory it had claimed; Portugal, even more in what then became the colony of Angola; and the way was open for Germany to take over and exploit South West Africa. All in all, the area effectively divided up at the conference between Belgium, France, Germany and Portugal was not far short of five million square kilometres, with a population counted, according to estimates made by Stanley, in tens of millions. The interests of the Africans themselves counted for nothing.

Britain, although strongly represented at Berlin, gained little from the conference. Geography determined that the European colonies, recognized at Berlin, were only to be exploited from the Atlantic coast of Africa. In the late nineteenth century Britain's involvement in Africa was mainly based on access from the Mediterranean, down the two branches of the Nile. It was also involved in the East Coast, through the old Arab trading ports of Mombasa and Zanzibar, and the Cape Colony in the far south. In addition, at the end of the Berlin conference, Britain still retained four West African colonies: the Gambia, Sierra Leone, the Gold Coast[12] and Nigeria.

Exploitation of natural resources and international rivalry explain why King Leopold, and the European governments that followed the same path, committed themselves to Africa. In the king's case *folie de grandeur* played a major part; succeeding, in 1865, as the crowned head of a kingdom, which although only founded in 1830 soon established a position in the vanguard of the European industrial revolution, he was only too ready to go one better than the two countries with which he was most involved: the Netherlands and the United Kingdom. As to the former, Belgium had to accept that the state from which it had, with some difficulty, gained independence in 1830[13] still had a vast colonial empire, mainly in the East Indies. That this empire – which went back to the beginning of the seventeenth century – revived after the end of the Napoleonic Wars, was largely the result of British policy following the Congress of

Vienna in 1815. The main British concern was then, as it had been since the seventeenth century, to keep France at bay. Here the Dutch presence in the East Indies, and also that of Spain in the Philippines – reflecting another aspect of British diplomacy – played a useful role. (It is worth noting that King Leopold, before venturing into the Congo, had offered to buy the Philippines; Spain refused to sell.)

Even more than the Netherlands, Britain as an imperial power was exemplary for the policy of King Leopold. For one thing Prince Albert had been his first cousin. For another, British capital had played an important part in the Belgian industrial revolution, and Belgian industry paid the taxes which gave the state treasury funds that it in turn made available to the king for his African adventure. Even though, at the opening of the conference in Berlin in 1884, Britain made clear that it would rather see Portugal than Belgium in the Congo, the recognition of King Leopold's dominion proved to be perfectly acceptable; after all, Belgium was still preferable to either France or Germany.

Although the Berlin conference led to no formal agreement of frontiers in Africa, it effectively established mutual recognition of the African territories claimed by the states represented. It was not immediately clear to any of these newly recognized colonial powers how best to make their new colonies profitable. Their usefulness as markets for manufactured products from the metropolitan powers depended on having something to offer in exchange. Historical precedent was little help, since until the beginning of the nineteenth century African exports had consisted mainly of captives destined for slavery in the New World. By the end of the century any such prospect was anathema. Equatorial Africa was, however, a major source of ivory, and this, from the earliest days of King Leopold's Congo, was a valuable export product.

At the same time the range of raw materials required by industry had become much wider, and included rubber, for which the essential natural base, latex, was only to be harvested from trees growing wild in the tropics. Of these the most important, worldwide, was the *hevea brasiliensis* from the Amazon valley, but the *funtumia elastica* from the Congo came next. In those forest areas where the trees grew, Belgian overseers ruthlessly exploited local African labour in harvesting the latex they produced. The regime, as harsh and cruel as anything enforced in the plantations of the New World, was so widely condemned internationally that in the end Leopold had to transfer his African empire to the Belgian state – but this had to wait until 1908. Ending the king's regime was largely the achievement of E.D. Morel, a Liverpool shipping agent who, while examining the commercial documents of the Congo Free State, noted that while vast quantities of rubber and ivory were being exported, all that was sent back in exchange was rifles and chains. This evidence was enough to lead him to devote his life to destroying the labour regime enforced in the Congo. When success finally came, the harvesting of latex had long been unprofitable; the Congo never really competed with the Amazon – which was one reason why the labour regime there had to be so harsh – and when, at the end of the nineteenth century, rubber became a plantation crop, cultivation in Africa was concentrated along the west coast, mainly in Liberia. The leading producers, worldwide, were by this time Malaya and Sumatra.

However, the Berlin conference was something of a sideshow for Britain. From the perspective of London, after the opening of the Suez canal in 1869, British control of Africa was anchored at two extremes of the continent, Egypt and the Cape Colony. Egypt, although in principle part of the Turkish Ottoman Empire, was subject to a local ruler, known as the 'Khedive'. The terms on which Britain and France negotiated the right to build and operate the Suez canal made it clear to the Khedives that it was London and Paris, not Istanbul, that called the shots. If in principle the economy of the country they ruled should have benefitted from the canal, which provided substantial new opportunities both for local enterprise and the labour market, their government was chaotic and relied for finance on oppressive taxes raised from millions of peasants cultivating the rich agricultural land in the Nile delta and along the upper Nile above Cairo. In the end, a peasant revolt made clear that the Khedives could not measure up to British standards of law and order, and in 1882 British troops occupied Egypt, where they would remain for another seventy years.[14] They came with all the paraphernalia of a modern industrial power: railways were constructed and steamboats plied the Nile. With the American cotton belt devastated by the Civil War, Egypt, together with India – now, via the Suez canal, much more accessible – became major suppliers of cotton to Lancashire.

In the climate of the day Britain was not going to hold back in Egypt; the discovery, in 1862, by the British explorer John Speke of the source of the White Nile, in the vast Lake Victoria, was a challenge to open up the whole course of the river. The process involved a number of epic incidents in late Victorian history, which, in September 1898, culminated in the battle of Omdurman in the Sudan. The victory won there by the British over the forces of a local Islamic charismatic leader, known as the 'Mahdi', effectively added the whole catchment area of the White Nile and its tributaries to the empire.

In the context of European power politics, the British objective was, however, to forestall France, which, seven weeks after Omdurman, prudently abandoned its claim to this part to Africa. In effect, globalization had won the day; railways, steamboats and the electric telegraph – all part of the legacy of the Industrial Revolution – made it next to impossible for the French to effectively contest the British presence.

At the same time Britain was involved in a somewhat different game at the other end of Africa. In the two hundred-odd years since the Dutch East Indies Company, in 1653, had established Cape Town as a victualling post for its ships on the way to the Far East, a small colony had developed in the hinterland on land well suited both for temperate agriculture and an agreeable lifestyle. As the population steadily increased, there was always new land to cultivate, and as the settled area increased the Dutch farmers were less concerned to supply ships calling in at Cape Town than they were to ensure their own subsistence. With the annexation of the Cape Colony after the Napoleonic Wars, the British government encouraged its own citizens to make their home in South Africa. The result was twofold; first, the

Cape, together with Natal some hundreds of miles away on the south-east coast of the continent, became home to thousands of British settlers; second, a substantial number, though by no means all, of the original Dutch settler families preferred to move inland.

Eventually, and after a number of bloody confrontations with native African principalities – such as notably that of the Zulus – this 'great trek' led these so-called *voortrekkers* to settle a vast area of open country, which they called simply the *veld*, where few others, African or European, would contest their occupation of the land. Here in 1852 they established the independent republic of the Transvaal, north of the sluggish Vaal river, and in 1854 that of the Orange Free State, to the south of it. There, if they had their way, they would simply be lost to history.

This idyll was never going to last. In 1867 a twenty-carat diamond[15] was discovered on the banks of the Vaal. Passing from one hand to another, it was first recognized as such by a British doctor in Grahamstown, hundreds of miles away on the coast, to end up being sold for £500 to Sir Philip Wodehouse, governor of the Cape Colony. By this time there was no turning back the hoards of prospectors who, coming down from the Cape, crossed hundreds of miles of semi-desert to reach the township of Kimberley that had sprung up, almost overnight, to become the centre of the whole diamond mining operation.

The scale of the migration can be judged from the fact that by 1871, Kimberley had a population of 37,000, several times that of the whole of the Orange Free State to which it strictly belonged.[16] Cape Town took the matter in hand by proclaiming a new colony, Griqualand West – named after the local African tribe – and appointing a lieutenant-governor, Richard Southey. Protests – from the Griquas, the government of the Free State and even from that of a self-proclaimed 'diggers' republic', with an ex-able-bodied seaman as its president[17] – went unheeded.

By 1873 four diamond mines: Kimberley, De Beers, Bultfontein and Dutoitspan, had been established, each with hundreds of 31 by 31 foot claims being worked by individual entrepreneurs, employing in turn African labourers who saved their meagre pay mainly to buy guns, of which 18,000 had already been imported into Griqualand West – another new market, incidentally, for Britain's small arms industry.

This was a repeat of the Wild West scenario of the California Gold Rush of 1849, and as in California it could not last. The days of the independent diggers were numbered, and by 1880 new companies, financed from London, began to take over. The greatest of these, De Beers Consolidated Mines Ltd, established by Cecil Rhodes in 1888, is still in business.

By this time large-scale mining operations, often carried out underground, depended on imported power-driven equipment, including, as so often with mining, pumps to extract unwanted water. After 1886, almost everything needed by the Kimberley mines could be brought up from the Cape by rail. South African diamond mining had become an industrial operation, with a global market. It was, however, almost completely dependent on imported equipment. Moreover it was no longer a local enterprise: in 1906 the high court in

London ruled, in favour of the Inland Revenue, that De Beers, although registered in Kimberley, was a business resident in the United Kingdom.[18]

Diamond mining was no more than the first step on the road to exploiting the mineral wealth of Southern Africa. The discovery of outcrops of gold in the Transvaal in the mid-1880s set off a mining fever at a level far above that experienced by Kimberley's diamond miners. Profitable exploitation depended on finding a way to separate the gold from the quartz in which it was embedded, but in 1886 this problem was solved by a wealthy Transvaal farmer, Fred Struben, who first reduced the ore to powder with a five stamp battery – imported, it hardly need be said, from England – and then separated the gold by running it in a stream of water over copper plates coated with mercury;[19] a refining process long used by South American mines. Applying this process, in February 1886, Struben was able to deliver sixty-one ounces of gold to the Standard Bank in Pretoria, the capital city of the republic.

It helped the Rand – as the gold mining area of Transvaal came to be known – that fortunes were still being made from diamonds, some 300 miles to the south-west in Kimberley, for two reasons. The first, purely psychological, was that South Africa, in popular estimation, connoted wealth underground. The second was that the wealth accumulated by the great diamond-mining companies was available for new investment. By 1889 investment on the London Stock Exchange in gold mining on the Rand had reached a level higher than that ever attained by diamond shares.[20] Nonetheless, gold mining on the Rand soon ran into problems far graver than any encountered in the Kimberley diamond mines.

Some of these, particularly on the technological side, were soon resolved. As new mines were opened the reef proved to consist not so much of quartz as of pyritic ore, from which gold could no longer be separated by Struben's mercury process. But then two chemists from Edinburgh had already shown, in 1887, how suspension of the crushed ore in a cyanide solution could achieve separation up to a level of 96 per cent pure gold – a breakthrough so valuable that it vastly extended the reserves of payable ore.[21] The cyanide process, after first being used in 1890, led to a even higher level of investment in the Rand. Inevitably, with every new mine there was a demand for labour, which, if un-skilled, could only be met by Africans, and if skilled, by Europeans – a class taken to include local Dutch-speaking farmers whose families had been in Africa for generations.

The recruitment of both classes of labour was bound to create problems. One main reason for the original Dutch settlers choosing to make their homes in the Transvaal was that there were very few Africans present:[22] the land was up for grabs. This meant that African labour for the mines had to be recruited from hundreds of miles away, in areas such as Zululand and the Transkei close to the east coast, where the presence of large numbers of Africans had always inhibited Dutch settlement. To attract labour from so far away, the mine owners not only competed among themselves in offering ever higher wages, but also called on European traders in the border areas to extend cash credit to Africans, which could only be paid off by working in the mines – a classic case of debt slavery.

In a situation intolerable for the mining companies, in which recruitment costs were double the wage bill, the rival companies joined together in 1889 to establish the Chamber of Mines, whose remit – to reduce labour costs and standardize working conditions for African mine workers – was largely achieved by 1897. The labour shortage was further relieved by the adoption of a policy of recruiting outside South Africa – for which purpose, in due course, the Witwatersrand Native Labour Association was set up – while Cecil Rhodes, premier of the Cape Colony and a major investor in both diamonds and gold, helped by imposing a tax on Africans that forced them to look for work in the money economy.[23] That all these measures would combine to bring vast numbers of Africans to an area entirely unknown to their ancestors, where their livelihood would depend on employment on terms that were never freely negotiated, was of no concern to those who imposed these terms. On the contrary, it meant that the labour policy of the Chamber of Mines had achieved its purpose. By the turn of the century nearly 100,000 Africans were employed on the Rand.[24]

The arrival of hundreds, if not thousands of Europeans, many from outside Africa, created other problems. If less numerous than the Africans, the Europeans were certainly a more heterogeneous population, and had in common only the desire to share – in one capacity or another – in the newly created wealth of the Rand. In the Wild West scenario of the Rand mining towns the government of a republic of farmers, with less than 10,000 citizens, was in no way capable of enforcing law and order. A few of the farmers, by virtue of owning land with an outcrop of gold, became rich men. Others, though not that many, still found opportunities to improve their fortunes by taking advantage of the new mining economy. After negotiations with the Portuguese government, a new railway was constructed in the early 1890s linking the Transvaal to the sea at Delagoa Bay in the Portuguese colony of Mozambique.[25] This was a sound investment, on purely economic terms, since the line was hundreds of miles shorter than the rail link to Cape Town via Kimberley. The Cape Colony did not welcome the consequent loss of revenue.

The government of the Transvaal had its own share in the mining economy in the form of a monopoly right to supply dynamite – an essential commodity for the industry[26] – to say nothing of the benefit it gained from being able to tax the mines at a punitive level. Even so it still represented only its own citizens, of which the great majority, seeing their country being taken over by newly arrived settlers (known as *uitlanders*[27]), were far from happy about the way things were going. For the Dutch-speaking farmers – or 'boers' – on the veld, gold mining on the Rand meant globalization in an entirely un-welcome form, with the prospect that they would become second class citizens in their own country. The *uitlanders*, on the other hand, would not take long to discover the principle of 'No Taxation without Repre-sentation'. But then, as Paul Kruger, the Transvaal President, said, 'If we grant them the franchise, we might as well pull down the flag.'[28]

The impasse could not last, and the result was the bitterly fought Boer War, in which the Transvaal, allied with the Orange Free State, fought the British for three years (1899–1902). Although, at that time, no one saw it in such terms, the war was fought about globalization. The question at issue was whether the Dutch republics were ready to become part of the global economy, as the British insisted. The war was finally settled, in 1909, on terms that established a new Union of South Africa, incorporating, as provinces, both the two former British colonies and the two former Dutch republics: this then joined Canada, Australia and New Zealand as a self-governing dominion under the British Crown.

Although in the twentieth century, mining – not only of gold and diamonds – continued to be the dominant sector of the South African economy, industry, which first developed to meet the needs of the mines, extended to meet the demands of other sectors, such as agriculture, and of individual consumers. The chemical industry, which had a solid base in the mining sector, extended to produce fertilizers and other agricultural chemicals, and then such standard products as paints and dyes for the economy as a whole. As with mining, much of the capital and know-how came from Britain. The obvious potential of a mass consumer market – in which the needs of the African majority population counted for relatively little – led in time to such local industries as the manufacture of clothing and food processing: this followed the common pattern of secondary industrial development in the world outside Europe and North America.

South America and Asia

In the globalization of the industrial revolution South Africa must be seen as a special case. In the greater part of the world outside Europe and North America, the impact of the revolution was mainly to be seen in the construction of a transport infrastructure designed to provide access to local mineral resources or to agriculture (including ranching) producing for the export market. More specifically, in the second half of the nineteenth century this meant the construction of railways connecting seaports with mining centres – as indeed took place in South Africa. A classic, and indeed earlier example of this process is to be found in the railways of South America, particularly those linking coastal harbours with inland mines that produced copper and nitrates in Chile, copper and silver in Peru and silver and tin in Bolivia.[29]

Not only steam locomotives, but also steamboats, belonged to British exports. Of these one of the earliest, the *Yavari*, crossed the oceans from the Hull shipyard where it was laid down in 1862 to end up at the Peruvian port of Mollendo. There it was dismantled, to be sent by train to Puno on Lake Titicaca, 12,500 feet above sea level, to be reassembled with its firebox converted to burn llama dung. Its standard route crossed the lake to Guaqui in Bolivia, where it linked up with the railway to the capital city, La Paz, some sixty miles away.

The history of railways in nineteenth-century Argentina,[30] as a classic instance of British interests exploiting the economic potential of an entire country provides another instance of the dependency model introduced in chapter six.[31] British investment in Argentine agriculture opened the way to Britain importing wheat and cattle, sugar, coffee and wine in exchange for manufactured capital and consumer goods produced by

British industry. With almost every part of the country home to one or other of the different sectors of the agricultural economy, its exploitation required the construction and operation of an extensive railway network. This was achieved mainly by British entrepreneurs who worked hard to win the support of successive Argentine governments, which often had to choose between meeting the conflicting demands of the City of London and those of its own electorate – a choice as often as not favouring London rather than the Argentine voters.

One man who tried hard to please the people, President Miguel Juárez, brought about financial chaos by reckless government spending during his administration, so losing his country's entire gold reserves, while his cronies lost the last of their foreign credit. Blaming the British-owned railways for economic disaster did not save him. Forced out of office in 1890, his successors changed direction – so much so that President Julio Roca (1898–1904) praised the British for rescuing the country from a grave financial crisis, recognizing, at the same time, 'a new and wonderful testimony of the benefits given to the country by British capital and enterprise'.[32]

The British were rewarded accordingly. For an extension of the British-owned Great Southern Railway, which the Argentine government supported for strategic reasons, it granted the company a sixteen million peso handout, all the land required for the permanent way, and a forty year exemption from import duties on all equipment needed for construction and operation.[33]

Although by the end of the nineteenth century the continuing expansion of the Argentine railway network had led to the emergence of a considerable urban middle class, with the vast capital city of Buenos Aires as its main stronghold – with the Argentine economy ranking fourteenth in terms of wealth worldwide. This proved, in the twentieth century, to be a house built on sand. By mid-century one failed government after another blamed British and American economic imperialism for a legacy of distorted capital development, and looked for solutions in measures, such as nationalization of the railways, which were no longer appropriate for solving Argentina's economic problems.

The answer, according to the Argentine economist, Raúl Prebisch, was to be found in the principles of 'structuralism' and 'inward development',[34] which involved developing a strong domestic market for local manufactures, that at the same time would be able to compete in world markets. Where in Argentina the populist leader Juan Perón blocked the application of Prebisch's policies in the critical decade of the 1950s – and terminated his appointment as chairman of the central bank – South Korea, and other Asian tiger economies, successfully adopted them in the second half of the twentieth century. But then, in the nineteenth century, British capital – except in the occasional odd case such as tin mining in Malaya – had avoided these countries.

When the Industrial Revolution did finally come to Argentina, with foreign direct investment represented, for example, by European and American automobile manufacturers setting up local production lines, there was hardly any export market, and the domestic market was too poor for sales at a European or American level.

The economic rationale of all this railway construction was to provide raw materials for Britain's industry and, to a lesser degree, agriculture. Although running and maintaining railways is impossible without some local industrial activity, it can hardly be said that Britain's railways brought the Industrial Revolution to the developing world. On the contrary, the process had two essential purposes: the first was gaining access to essential raw materials, and the second, the opening of new markets for British industry. There was never any other intention.

This general principle, implicit in British economic strategy in Argentina, applied equally to almost the entire developing world outside Europe and North America – most of which, by the end of the nineteenth century, was economically, if not politically, subordinate to nations in these two continents. This was even true of China – the world's most populous country – as a result of the extraterritorial rights granted to foreign powers in the so-called 'treaty ports' in the course of the nineteenth century.

However, India and Japan are two cases worth special consideration. In India, industrialization started with the construction of railways in the days, before 1857, when the East India Company was still responsible for government. The opening of the first line in 1853, which led inland from Bombay, was described as, 'a triumph to which, in comparison, all our victories in the east seem tame and commonplace. The opening of the Great Indian Peninsular Railway will be remembered by the natives of India when the battlefields of Plassey, Assaye, Meanee and Goojerat have become the landmarks of history.'[35]

Calcutta, next to Bombay, the most important port in India, had a special reason for constructing a railway. With the number of steamships steadily increasing, the

Raneegunge coalmines, thirty miles inland from the city, had a promising new market which could best be supplied by rail. The new East India Railway opened its line from Calcutta in 1855. Although the rails and the locomotives were imported from England, the ship transporting carriages from England sank in the Hooghly River. To make good this loss, John Hodgson, the railway's chief locomotive engineer, successfully made new carriages in the railway's own workshops. This was not only a triumph of British resourcefulness, but also laid the foundation of a new local industry. Even so, Indian railways continued to import the heaviest material, such as the steel girders for the long bridges over the Ganges and Brahmaputra rivers, from Britain.[36]

At every stage India was far ahead of the rest of the developing world in the construction of railways. Even in 1900, when both China and Japan had constructed thousands of miles of railway, India still accounted for 65 per cent of all the railway mileage in Asia. Although there were by this time railways in almost every part of the sub-continent, the fact that the lines had developed haphazardly, with a number of different gauges, meant that there was no single national network. This only came after independence was granted to India and Pakistan in 1947. Even so, the railways, long before the end of the nineteenth century, had become part of the life of tens, if not hundreds of millions of Indians, of whom the majority – with little money to spend beyond the cost of the cheapest tickets – had to tolerate what, in a petition to the Viceroy in 1866, was described as 'dire evil and slavery' imposed on third class passengers.[37] Moreover, hours spent waiting for trains could be an additional hardship; 'Many a poor Native's illness of death is traceable to sufferings at a Railway Station.'

The sufferings of travellers were small in comparison with those of the labourers who actually built the lines. This was often the result of the challenge of appallingly difficult topography. Of the tens of thousands who worked on the construction of the spectacular line from Bombay, inland across a range of hills known as the Bhore Ghat, a third died from accidents and sickness.[38] Yet the prospect of paid employment was so attractive that there was never a shortage of labour, just as on trains, there was never a shortage of passengers. In the everyday life of the mass of Indians the railways were unrivalled as a unifying force.

With tens of thousands of miles of line, hundreds of thousands of employees, and tens of millions of passengers, the railways – even before the end of the nineteenth century – clearly represented a force that could be mobilized in the service of industry. If the British government in India valued railways mainly for their strategic usefulness in deploying a large army in any part of the country where local unrest threatened law and order, this was not a view shared by millions of ordinary passengers. To many of these passengers, in a country which was profligate with labour at a time when its plantation economy, particularly in tea, was rapidly expanding, trains were indispensable – and not only to those who were seasonal workers. Other passengers travelled to the seaports to find a passage to indentured labour on plantations overseas, whether in the Dutch islands of the East Indies, the coastal areas of South Africa[39] or the Caribbean.

The success of the railways, and the market which they represented, was bound, sooner or later, to inspire local industrial enterprise. More than any other, a single family, that of the Tatas of Bombay, accepted the challenge. The founder of the dynasty, Jamsetji Nusserwanji Tata, was born in 1839 into a Parsee trading family, which, by coming to terms with the British presence in India, had become wealthy in the cotton trade. After travelling widely as a young man, he became convinced that an Indian cotton mill, if located close to the plantation area of western India, could compete successfully with Lancashire. In 1874, he founded the Central India Spinning, Weaving and Manufacturing Company. Following the devastation of the cotton plantations of the American south during the Civil War, the time was well chosen for exploiting Indian-grown cotton.

Although Tata's company opened the Empress mill in Nagpur in 1877, on the same day that Queen Victoria was declared Empress of India, Tata himself was devoted to the cause of an independent India. As a founder member of the Indian National Congress, his main concern was for industrialization. Here he saw the cotton industry, in which he was indisputably the leading entrepreneur, as no more than the first stage in the process. As in Britain in the eighteenth century, iron and coal were equally important. Tata, as a man of the times in the late nineteenth century also set his sights on hydroelectric power – but here he was ahead of his time.[40]

From British and American experience, Tata knew that the best location for the new industry would be on a river close to substantial natural deposits of both coal and iron. Although surveys of the coal producing areas of north-east India started in the 1880s, little could be achieved until the British government of India introduced a more liberalized mineral concession policy in 1899. This led Tata to call on American specialists, who began surveying in 1903. Although he died in 1904, his two sons, Dorabji and Ratanji, who were his business successors, continued the survey, and in 1907 rich iron ore deposits were found at the confluence of two rivers in the dense jungle of the state of Bihar. This became the site of a factory and township named Jamshedpur, where a new enterprise was set up, the Tata Iron and Steel Company, to be financed entirely by Indian investors. Within eight weeks of the offer being made the whole issue of 23.2 million rupees in shares was subscribed by some 8,000 local investors, with the Tatas retaining 11 per cent of the stock for themselves. In spite of enormous problems in clearing the site and finding coal of a uniform quality, the venture was a success – a process helped by the outbreak of the First World War in 1914, which soon produced a contract for the export of 1,500 miles of steel rails to Mesopotamia. After the First World War, the Tata companies had their ups and downs, but there is no doubt that they played a major part in bringing the Industrial Revolution to what is now the second most populous country in the world.

Japan, even more than India, had its own successful Industrial Revolution in the years leading up to the First World War. Although both in Asia, the two countries could hardly be more dissimilar. Japan, an island state, with essentially one single language and a remarkably uniform culture, maintained itself, until the year 1854, in almost complete isolation from the outside world except for China. The only contact with Europe was through a Dutch trading post on a very small island, known as Deshima, just offshore from the seaport of Nagasaki, which was about as far as it could possibly be from the effective seat of government in Edo. (Only in 1868 did this city, after changing its name to Tokyo, become the official capital of Japan.) The primary remit of Dutch on Deshima island, was to satisfy the demands of the court in Edo for European goods and exotic plants and animals. In this way those who ruled Japan gained a glimpse of what was manufactured in Europe, and a rudimentary acquaintance with western science, which they called *rangaku*.[41]

In the year 1853, an American naval squadron, commanded by Commodore Matthew C. Perry USN, and consisting of four iron clad steam-powered warships, anchored in Edo bay. Perry's mission was to deliver a letter from the American President, requesting that Japan's port be opened to foreign trade. He returned the following year, with a much larger force, to receive the reply. When it came, this allowed for foreign consuls to be appointed and supplies to be delivered to visiting ships. As a matter of principle the Japanese also had to agree to better treatment, and eventual repatriation, of the crews of western merchantmen occasionally shipwrecked off the coast of Japan.[42] These were concessions to overwhelming *force majeure*. Perry's firepower, to say nothing of the seaworthiness of his ships, went far beyond anything the Japanese could conceive of from their well recorded history. At the same time, the Japanese were confronted with the Industrial Revolution at its most advanced stage: everything on Perry's ships was 'state of the art'.

A continuing state of crisis in mid-nineteenth century Japan made it difficult for the government in Edo to work out any realistic long term policy to deal with the powers that Perry's mission represented. It was plain that the concessions made in 1854 were no more than a holding action. One immediate reaction, true to the character of the Japanese, was to invest heavily in armaments, especially in steamships purchased through the foreign merchants at Nagasaki.[43] Elite companies of soldiers were equipped with rifles imported from the West and trained. While diplomats and students were sent abroad, largely to gather intelligence about the western world, western ships were still subject to harassment by the Japanese military, even though the western powers did not hesitate to retaliate when shore batteries opened fire.

The greatest threat came from the coasts of the province of Choshu, which overlooked the narrow Shimonoseki strait, separating the main island of Honshû from Kyûshû, where Nagasaki was to be found. In 1863, French warships, retaliating for attacks on merchantmen, fired on the Choshu batteries, and a year later four of the western powers combined to send a force ashore to dismantle them completely. In spite of rearmament, Japan was not going to keep the western powers at bay.

Helped by intrigue on the part of the foreign consuls, a coalition of provincial leaders, opposed to the government in Edo, signed an agreement to open the key port of Hyogo[44] in Osaka bay, some 500 kilometres to the west, to foreign trade on 1 January 1868. This proved to be a declaration of war. With the foreign fleets assembled in Osaka bay, the forces opposed to the government defeated it first in Osaka in January – leaving the medieval castle in flames – and then, on 3 May, in Edo. This was the end of a regime established in 1600.

An entirely new form of government was created, with, as its nominal head, the last in a long line of 'emperors'[45] that, throughout the whole period of government from Edo, had lived in seclusion in the ancient capital city of Kyoto. This was a fourteen-year-old boy, known to history as the Emperor Meiji (1867–1912), who had succeeded to the 'Chrysanthemum Throne' on the death of his father, the Emperor Kômei, in 1867. By a process somewhat misleadingly known to history as the 'Meiji Restoration', he became the head of a state which, from its earliest days, was intent on becoming an active and powerful participant in the world economy. Modernization, along western lines, was the name of the game.

In 1869 the new Council of State – the effective power behind the Emperor – decided to introduce railways into Japan, a country whose topography little favoured their construction. Nonetheless, railways were built, with the first line, eighteen miles long, linking Tokyo with Yokohama, being opened in 1872. The locomotives burnt wood, as they had in the early days of American railways, with the result that property along the lines was all too often set on fire. Narrow gauge lines with poor quality rails meant that travel was slow and uncomfortable, while operation was often unprofitable as the result of high construction costs. In the 1870s, the Japanese military had often complained that money was better spent on armaments, but by the 1890s they wanted railways for strategic reasons. By this time Japan was fighting, and winning, its own foreign wars against Russia and China, in the latter case with the benefit of overwhelmingly superior modern armaments. Armament manufacture, both for land and sea, had become a major sector of the economy. But the question remains, how was all this achieved by a country whose industry and technology, only a half century earlier, was almost medieval?

As shown by the events leading up to the opening of the port of Hyogo, its hinterland – along with Japan's second city, Osaka, and its ancient capital, Kyoto – had, long before the end of the Edo era, become something of an economic powerhouse. Local entrepreneurs controlled a network of trade in rice, textiles and sake, extending to the remotest corners of Japan. Four of the great trading houses not only welcomed the Meiji restoration (which they had doubtless helped bring about) but survived to become vast business conglomerates, known as *zaibatsu*. Of these, two, Mitsui and Sumitomo, are now well known multinational corporations. With the opening of Japan to foreign trade and investment, the *zaibatsu* lost little time in expanding their trading operations to include banking, manufacturing and shipping.[46] In this process, with the initial advantage of a huge integrated domestic market, the *zaibatsu* – unashamedly borrowing 'western know-how' with the help of locally employed western engineers[47] and managers – created a modern industrial economy within a generation.

None of this would have been possible without foreign exchange: Japan, although self-sufficient in coal, had few of the natural resources essential for its own industrial revolution, nor, in the earlier stages, the ability to manufacture its own steamships, locomotives and textile machinery. Its one advantage was a steadily growing, homogeneous, well educated population that – as was the case in Europe – could be mobilized to work in factories, regardless of the cost in human terms (which in Japan proved to be just as high as it ever was in Europe).

The key to the finance of Japan's industrial revolution, in the forty-odd years leading up to the First World War (in which Japan was one of the allied powers), was the production and export of silk. Historically silk was the product of cottage industry located in rural areas favourable to the planting of mulberry bushes. The essential industrial process was to reel the silk contained in the cocoons produced as an essential stage in the lifecycle of the silkworms fed on mulberry leaves. This was a task for female labour, committed to untangling and reeling some hundreds of metres of silk extracted from a cocoon no larger than a walnut. Once the cocoon was ready for this process, any delay longer than a day or two in reeling the silk led to unacceptable deterioration. The result, in an era when transport over land relied on pack animals, was vertical integration of the silk industry in any village that cultivated mulberry bushes.[48] This defined an industry constituted out of hundreds of small units, with little scope for economies of scale.

By the 1890s Japan had developed the technology for reeling silk on a much larger scale that was ever possible in the traditional cottage industry. At the same time the government realized that the technology could only be applied if silk was shipped by rail to new factories incorporating it. With private capital little interested in such a project, the new Chûô line, providing a second link inland between Tokyo and the port of Nagoya, was constructed as a state project. Its route was chosen to provide access to major areas of mulberry cultivation at the smallest possible cost.[49] Such areas, freed from the necessity to reel silk locally, were able to increase production several times over, while areas not along the line of the railway lost out. Nonetheless, the overall gain in production was so substantial that the export of silk became Japan's major earner of foreign exchange.

The industry, with the advantage of the new technology, became concentrated in factories – many of them in Tokyo – where hundreds of girls, housed in dormitories, worked long, poorly remunerated hours, reeling silk. Conditions were no better than those in the Lancashire cotton mills described by Engels some fifty years earlier. What is more, there was little improvement in the years before 1941, when Japan's air attack on the American fleet in Pearl Harbor brought it into the Second World War – losing it, incidentally, almost its entire export market in silk. By this time Japanese industry, particularly that part of it devoted to the manufacture of armaments, had overcome its late start in the Industrial Revolution.

1914

Just as the Great Exhibition of 1851 provided the opportunity to take stock of what the Industrial Revolution had achieved by that year, so too did the cataclysmic war that broke out in August 1914 make clear the achievements of the years since 1851. As seen by contemporary historians, this second phase is a sequel to the revolution, rather than part of it. One point is now clear enough, in any case; Britain was losing its lead. The United States and Germany, followed (even before the end of the nineteenth century) by India and Japan, were key actors on the world industrial stage, to say nothing of France, the Austrian empire and even Russia. All these states were combatants in what proved to be, by the time it ended in 1918, the most devastating war in history, and the first ever to be fought in almost every corner of the world.

By now the modern world was coming to terms with industrial processes, mains services, construction methods, new media for communication and transport and science based medical care, almost completely unknown in 1851 – to say nothing of innovations in the consumer economy. An exhaustive list in any of these realms is far beyond the scope of this chapter, but it is worth noting how large-scale production of steel and aluminium added a new dimension to the materials available to industry. How the central generation of electricity and the invention of the electric light bulb created a new mains service for transport, manufacturing and domestic users. How the use of concrete coupled with elevators powered by electric motors enabled the construction of buildings of unprecedented height. How the refinement of petrochemicals made possible first the automobile, and then, within scarcely a decade, the aeroplane, at the same time as the first electric locomotives appeared on railways – particular on new urban lines built underground. How the telephone and, scarcely a generation later, wireless, transformed communications and the mass media. How the preservation of food was transformed by refrigeration. How, in medicine, diagnosis and treatment were transformed with new instruments, such as those that could measure blood pressure, and new drugs, such as those that enabled immunization against ills ranging from hydrophobia to yellow fever – the list goes on and on.

The great war of 1914–18 not only increased the pace at which almost everything came into use; with constant improvements on original designs, but also provided the occasion for new weapons, such as tanks and poison gas, to be tried out for the first time, or for already existing weapons, such as submarines, to be used on an unprecedented scale. In the years that followed the war all this was taken for granted, even by the generation that could well remember the days when there were neither telephones, electric light, nor motor cars; with industry and transport still running on steam, and streets, factories and homes lit by gas.

NOTES

Chapter 1

1. R. Pearson, Thackeray and *Punch* at the Great Exhibition: authority and ambivalence in verbal and visual caricatures, in L. Purbrick (ed.), *The Great Exhibition of 1851: New interdisciplinary essays*, Manchester University Press, 2001, pp. 179–205, p. 185.
2. J.A. Auerbach, *The Great Exhibition of 1851: A Nation on Display*, New Haven: Yale University Press, 1999, p. 140.
3. F. Crouzet, 'France', in M. Teich and R. Porter (eds), *The Industrial Revolution in National Context: Europe and the USA*, Cambridge University Press, 1996, pp. 36–63, p. 45; this could be the earliest recorded use of the term ever.
4. F. Engels, *The Condition of the Working Class in England*, Oxford University Press, 1993, p. 15.
5. Y. Ffrench, *The Great Exhibition: 1851*, London: Harvill Press, 1950, p. 10.
6. J.A. Auerbach, *The Great Exhibition of 1851: A Nation on Display*, New Haven: Yale University Press, 1999, p. 18.

7. Ibid., p. 29.
8. Ibid., p. 57.
9. Ibid., p. 62.
10. Ibid., pp. 78–9.
11. Ibid., p. 88.
12. Ffrench, *The Great Exhibition*, pp. 276–7.
13. Ibid., p. 243.
14. Ibid., p. 130.
15. C. MacLeod, *Heroes of Invention: Technology, Liberalism and British Identity 1750–1914*, Cambridge University Press, 2007, pp. 213–14; Ffrench, *The Great Exhibition*, p. 215.
16. Auerbach, *The Great Exhibition of 1851*, p. 55.
17. Ffrench, *The Great Exhibition*, p. 213.
18. Ibid., p. 248.
19. See MacLeod, *Heroes of Invention*, Chapter 5, 'Watt, inventor of the Industrial Revolution'.
20. Auerbach, *The Great Exhibition of 1851*, p. 32.
21. This was proclaimed in 1848, only to come to an end in 1852, when Louis Napoleon, supported by a massive popular vote, proclaimed a new French empire (which would last until France's defeat in war with Prussia in 1871 followed by the establishment of the Third Republic).
22. J. Saville, *1848: The British State and the Chartist Movement*, Cambridge University Press, 1987, p. 120; Auerbach, *The Great Exhibition of 1851*, p. 129.
23. Argentina, Bolivia, Chile, Colombia, Costa Rica, Ecuador, Guatemala, Honduras, Mexico, Paraguay, Peru, El Salvador, Uruguay and Venezuela.
24. Slavery in Brazil only ended in 1888.
25. T. Crump, *A Brief History of the Age of Steam: The Power that Drove the Industrial Revolution*, London: Constable & Robinson, 2007, p. 223.

26. Auerbach, *The Great Exhibition of 1851*, p. 180.
27. Crump, *Brief History of the Age of Steam*, p. 113.
28. E.H. Kossman, *The Low Countries 1780–1940*, Oxford: Clarendon Press, 1978, p. 163.
29. Ibid., p. 183.
30. R. Hughes, *The Fatal Shore*, London: Vintage Press, 1987, p. 557.
31. New South Wales, Queensland, South Australia, Tasmania and Victoria.
32. Ibid., p. 563.
33. M. King, *The Penguin History of New Zealand*, Auckland: Penguin Books, 2003, p. 157.
34. Auerbach, *The Great Exhibition of 1851*, p. 101.
35. Cook himself never returned home; he was murdered in Hawaii on 14 February 1779. George Vancouver, his second in command, brought the ships back to England.
36. London had a Penny Post as early as 1680: see S. Pincus, *1688: The First Modern Revolution*, New Haven: Yale University Press, 2009, p. 72.
37. This was at the heart of industrial France, where St Etienne and Lyons were linked by the country's first railway.

Chapter 2

1. T. Crump, *A Brief History of Science*, London: Constable & Robinson, 2001, p. 146.
2. L.T.C. Rolt, *Thomas Newcomen: The Prehistory of the Steam Engine*, London: Macdonald, 1963, p. 34.
3. The right to 'captain' was very dubious: ibid., p. 35.
4. Ibid., p. 39.
5. Ibid., p. 41.
6. Ibid., p. 44.
7. Ibid., p. 68.
8. e.g. the engraving by Henry Beighton referred to on p. 29.

9. Rolt, *Thomas Newcomen*, p. 119.

10. H.W. Dickinson, *James Watt: Craftsman and Engineer*, New York: Augustus M. Kelley, 1967, p. 18.

11. Ibid., p. 16. There is no precise English equivalent to the Scottish bailie, who was both a magistrate and an alderman.

12. Ibid., p. 19.

13. The University was then home to Adam Smith (1723–90), the founder of the science of political economy.

14. From an advertisement in the *Glasgow Journal*, 1 December 1763.

15. The name derives from a local pottery, recently set up to produce earthenware based on that of Dutch city of Delft.

16. Dickinson, *James Watt: Craftsman and Engineer*, p. 43.

17. R.H. Campbell, 'John Roebuck', *Oxford Dictionary of National Biography*, online edition, 2009, p. 3.

18. Dickinson, *James Watt: Craftsman and Engineer*, p. 51.

19. Ibid., p. 52.

20. Ibid., p. 79.

21. Ibid., p. 87.

22. Campbell, 'John Roebuck', p. 3.

23. Dickinson, *James Watt: Craftsman and Engineer*, p. 92.

24. Ibid., p. 99.

25. R.S. Fitton, *The Arkwrights: Spinners of Fortune*, Manchester University Press, 1989, p. 109.

26. Ibid., p. 138.

27. Ibid., p. 140.

28. Dickinson, *James Watt: Craftsman and Engineer*, p. 124.

29. Ibid., p. 126.

30. Ibid., pp. 127–8.

31. Ibid., p. 129.

32. Ibid., p. 148.

33. Ibid., p. 150.

34. Ibid., p. 151.

35. Well known for his answer to King Louis XVIII when asked whether he believed in God, 'I have no need of that hypothesis'.
36. Dickinson, *James Watt: Craftsman and Engineer*, p. 145.
37. 1 horsepower = 745.7 watts.
38. Dickinson, *James Watt: Craftsman and Engineer*, p. 166.

Chapter 3

1. Over the years 1848–52 the lake was finally drained by three steam-powered pumps. The biggest, known as the 'Cruquius', was driven by the largest Watt design reciprocal steam engine ever built; it is now a museum. Although the reclaimed land was originally intended for agriculture, some 15 per cent now comprises Schiphol International Airport.
2. For the maximum dimensions for wooden sailing ships, see *Oxford Companion to Ships and the Sea*, Oxford University Press, 2006, pp. 486–7, 520.
3. Ibid., p. 33: *France II*, the largest sailing ship ever built, had a gross register displacement of 5806 tons: at 500,000 tons capacity modern tankers and container ships are a hundred times larger: ibid., pp. 575 and 131.
4. E.A. Wrigley, 'A Simple Model of London's Importance in a Changing English Society and Economy 1650–1750', in P. Abrams and E.A. Wrigley (eds), *Towns in Societies: Essays in Economic History and Historical Sociology*, Cambridge University Press, 1978, pp. 215–44, p. 231.
5. T.S. Reynolds, *Stronger than a Hundred Men: A History of the Vertical Water Wheel*, Baltimore: Johns Hopkins University Press, 1983, p. 4.
6. Ibid., p. 5.
7. D. Larkin, *Mill: The History and Future of Naturally Powered Buildings*, New York: Universe Publishing, 2000, p. 6.

8. After 223 years, the company became insolvent in 1982 and was later acquired by the Franke Corporation.

9. See the picture in Larkin, *Mill*, p. 44.

10. A sluice is appropriate where a weir has been constructed; a race is where this flow of water is left uncontrolled – the choice depends on local topography. At Sutter's mill in California, digging the race for a new saw mill led in January 1848 to the first critical discovery of gold in the California 'gold rush'.

11. R.C. Walter and D.J. Merritts, 'Natural Streams and the Legacy of Water-powered Mills', *Science*, vol. 319, pp. 299–304, p. 300.

12. Varying from 2.5 to 3.7 metres: ibid., p. 301.

13. Ibid., p. 302.

14. This was just in time because after 1750 the practice was forbidden by a British statute: see C. Hill, *Reformation to Industrial Revolution*, London: Pelican, 1969, p. 235. The law, however, was widely disregarded – as so many others were in the North American colonies.

15. P. Laslett, *The World We Have lost*, London: Methuen, 1965, p. 16.

16. B. Freese, *Coal: A Human History*, London: Penguin, 2004, p. 6.

17. T. Crump, *A Brief History of the Age of Steam: The Power that Drove the Industrial Revolution*, London: Constable & Robinson, 2007, p. 149, Map 4.

18. Coal's fumes, particularly smoke and sulphur compounds, disqualified it from many applications, including cooking and iron smelting. In 1603, Sir Henry Platt suggested that coal might be charred in a manner analogous to the way charcoal is produced from wood. This process was not put into practice until 1642, when coke was used for roasting malt in Derbyshire. Coal cannot be used in brewing because its sulphurous fumes would impart a foul taste to the beer.

19. See Crump, *A Brief History of the Age of Steam*, pp. 21–5.

20. P. Deane, *The First Industrial Revolution*, Cambridge University Press, 1965, p. 101.

21. Ibid., p. 104.

22. Such as is now recorded at the site of the Lonaconing Iron Foundry, now a Maryland state historical site: see also chapter 8, page 209.

23. Before the eighteenth century, British casts were a compound including loam or clay, with casting in sand only adopted after a visit by Abraham Darby to the Dutch Republic in 1704, where he observed the process: see T.S. Ashton, *Iron and Steel in the Industrial Revolution*, New York: Augustus M. Kelley, 1968, p. 27.

24. Deane, *The First Industrial Revolution*, p. 104.

25. N. Cox, 'Abraham Darby I', *Oxford Dictionary of National Biography*, online edition, Oxford University Press, 2009.

26. B. Trinder, 'Abraham Darby II', *Oxford Dictionary of National Biography*, online edition, Oxford University Press, 2009.

27. Ibid., p. 2.

28. This is now open to visitors.

29. Joseph Fry, a Bristol Quaker, was one of the earliest suppliers of chocolate to a national market.

30. Trinder, 'Abraham Darby II', p. 1.

31. Deane, *The First Industrial Revolution*, p. 105.

32. In 1800 Sweden produced 10 per cent of the world's iron: see Ashton, *Iron and Steel in the Industrial Revolution*, p. 98.

33. Ashton, *Iron and Steel in the Industrial Revolution*, p. 88.

34. Ibid.

35. Ibid., p. 89.

36. Ibid., p. 90.

37. Quoted from *A Brief State of the Facts* written by a friend of Cort and cited in Ashton, *Iron and Steel in the Industrial Revolution*, p. 92.

38. Ibid., p. 95.
39. Ibid., p. 55.
40. This means a temperature of some 1600°C.
41. Ibid., p. 58.
42. Ibid., pp. 58–9.

Chapter 4

1. The present law courts in the Strand opened nearly a hundred years later.
2. R.S. Fitton, *The Arkwrights: Spinners of Fortune*, Manchester University Press, 1989, p. 96.
3. The present Court of Appeal was created by the Judicature Act of 1873.
4. Fitton, *The Arkwrights*, p. 202.
5. Father of the future Prime Minister.
6. E. Gaskell, *North and South*, London: Vintage Books, 2007, p. 100.
7. Ibid., p. 104.
8. P. Deane, *The First Industrial Revolution*, Cambridge University Press, 1965, p. 85.
9. W. W. Rostow, *The Stages of Economic Growth*, Cambridge University Press, 1960, cited in Deane, *The First Industrial Revolution*, p. 84.
10. E.J. Hobsbawm, 'The Machine Breakers', *Past and Present*, Vol. 1, 1952, pp. 257–70.
11. The first recorded production of fustian was in Bolton in 1601: see Fitton, *The Arkwrights*, p. 10; silk and worsted could also be substituted for cotton.
12. Fitton, *The Arkwrights*, p. 7.
13. Ibid., p. 9.
14. Ibid., p. 10.
15. Ibid., p. 99.
16. But mistakenly, according to http://www.cottontimes.co.uk/hargreaveso.htm.

17. Deane, *The First Industrial Revolution*, p. 86.
18. Ibid., p. 87.
19. S.D. Chapman, 'Robert Peel', in *Oxford Dictionary of National Biography*, online edition, 2009, p. 21.
20. Fitton, *The Arkwrights*, p. 14.
21. A tributary of Nottingham's Trent.
22. Fitton, *The Arkwrights*, p. 28.
23. Letter in Arkwright family archives, cited Fitton, *The Arkwrights*, p. 51.
24. Ibid., p. 114.
25. D.A. Farnie, 'Samuel Crompton', *Oxford Dictionary of National Biography*, online edition, 2009, p. 4, but according to S.D. Chapman, Robert Peel applied steel power to mule spinning as early as 1789: see 'Robert Peel' in ibid., p. 1.
26. W.J. Bernstein, *A Splendid Exchange: How Trade Shaped the World*, New York: Atlantic Monthly Press, 2008, p. 278.
27. Deane, *The First Industrial Revolution*, p. 93; see also Bernstein, *A Splendid Exchange*, p. 137.
28. Chapman, *The Cotton Industry*, p. 43.
29. Ibid.
30. Admitted as the eighteenth State of the Union in 1812.
31. The highest production levels are now in north-west Texas.
32. Fitton, *The Arkwrights*, p. 64.
33. Ibid., p. 65.
34. Ibid., p. 69.
35. T.S. Reynolds, *Stronger than a Hundred Men: A History of the Vertical Water Wheel*, Baltimore: Johns Hopkins University Press, 1983, p. 327, Table 6.2, p. 327.
36. Reynolds, *Stronger than a Hundred Men*, p. 328 (see also chapter 2).
37. Chapman, *The Cotton Industry*, p. 19, Table 1.

38. Ibid., p. 20, Table 2.
39. Ibid., p. 22.
40. Ibid., p. 25.
41. Ibid., p. 26.
42. Ibid., pp. 33 and 34, Tables 5 and 6.
43. A. Randall, *Before the Luddites; Custom, community and machinery in the English woollen industry 1776–1809*, Cambridge University Press, 1991, p.76.
44. Ibid., p. 79.
45. Ibid., p. 85.
46. W.B. Crump, *The Leeds Woollen Industry, 1780–1820*, Leeds: Thoresby Society, 1931, pp. 8–9.
47. P. Hudson, *The Genesis of Industrial Capital: A Study of the West Riding Wool Textile Industry c.1750–1850*, Cambridge University Press, 1986, p. 32.
48. Ibid., p. 33.
49. Ibid., p. 43.
50. Priestly, U., 'Norwich stuffs, 1600–1700', in N.B. Harte (ed.), *The New Draperies in the Low Countries and England*, Oxford University Press, 1997, pp. 275–88, p. 277.
51. See B.A. Holderness, 'The reception and distribution of the new draperies in England', in Harte (ed.), *The New Draperies in the Low Countries and England*, pp. 217–44, Map 4.
52. Allen, R.C., *The British Revolution in Global Perspective*, Cambridge University Press, 2009, pp. 19, 109; Martin, L., 'The rise of the new draperies in Norwich, 1550–1622', in N.B. Harte (ed.), *The New Draperies in the Low Countries and England*, Oxford University Press, 1997, pp. 245–74, p. 264.
53. Priestley, 'The rise of the new draperies in Norwich, 1550–1622', p. 285.
54. C. Hill, *Reformation to Industrial Revolution*, London: Pelican, 1969, p. 173.

55. Fitton, *The Arkwrights*, p. 141.

56. Hudson, *The Genesis of Industrial Capital*, p. 44.

57. Hill, *Reformation to Industrial Revolution*, p. 175.

58. R.G. Wilson, 'Benjamin Gott', *Oxford Dictionary of National Biography*, online edition, 2009, p. 1.

59. Crump, *The Leeds Woollen Industry*, pp. 24–5.

60. The largest of these, at Armley, Leeds, is now a museum.

61. Reynolds, *Stronger than a Hundred Men: A History of the Vertical Water Wheel*, p. 326.

62. Ibid., p. 327; see also Wikipedia for ramie (or China grass),one of the strongest natural fibres. It exhibits even greater strength when wet. Ramie fibre is known especially for its ability to hold shape, reduce wrinkling, and introduce a silky lustre to the fabric appearance. It is not as durable as other fibres, and so is usually used as a blend with other fibres such as cotton or wool. It is similar to flax in absorbency, density and microscopic appearance. However, it will not dye as well as cotton. Because of its high molecular crystallinity, ramie is stiff and brittle and will break if folded repeatedly in the same place; it lacks resiliency and is low in elasticity and elongation potential.

Chapter 5

1. S. Pincus, *1688: The First Modern Revolution*, New Haven: Yale University Press, 2009, p. 73.

2. Ibid., pp. 84–5.

3. Ibid., p. 74.

4. J. Uglow, *The Lunar Men: The Friends who made the Future, 1730–1810*, London, Faber, 2003, p. 18.

5. Ibid., p. 19.

6. L. Namier, *The Structure of Politics at the Accession of George III*, 2nd edn, London: Macmillan, 1957, pp. 102–104.

7. R. Quinault, 'The Industrial Revolution and parliamentary reform', in P. O'Brien and R. Quinault (eds), *The Industrial Revolution and British Society*, Cambridge University Press, 1993, pp. 183–202, p. 193.

8. Quoted in Uglow, *The Lunar Men*, p. 49.

9. Pincus, *1688: The First Modern Revolution*, p. 65.

10. Uglow, *The Lunar Men*, p. 59.

11. For the importance of the North American market, see Pincus, *1688: The First Modern Revolution*, p. 86.

12. Uglow, *The Lunar Men*, pp. 167–8.

13. Pincus, *1688: The First Modern Revolution*, p. 79.

14. Ibid., pp. 264–5.

15. A. D. Gilbert, 'Religion and stability in early industrial England', in O'Brien and Quinault (eds), *The Industrial Revolution and British Society*, pp. 79–99, p. 83.

16. *Reflections on the Revolution in France*, cited in W. Hague, *William Pitt the Younger*, London: Harper-Collins, 2004, p. 288.

17. Uglow, *The Lunar Men*, p. 441.

18. Hague, *William Pitt the Younger*, p. 290.

19. Ibid., Chapter 16, 'The Cautious Crusader'.

20. J. Tann, 'Matthew Boulton', *Oxford Dictionary of National Biography*, online edition, 2009, p. 1.

21. Ibid., p. 4.

22. Ibid., p. 4.

23. Uglow, *The Lunar Men*, p. 18.

24. D. Symons, 'Matthew Boulton and the Royal Mint', in M. Dick (ed.), *Matthew Boulton: a Revolutionary Player*, Studley: Brewin Books, 2009, pp. 170–84, p. 175.

25. Ibid., p. 183.

26. Ibid., p. 314.

27. In the late eighteenth century Haviland porcelain from Limoges became very important.

28. A. Clow and N.L. Clow, *The Chemical Revolution: A Contribution to Social Technology*, London: Batchworth Press, 1952, p. 314.
29. A.J.L. Winchester, 'William Cookworthy', *Oxford Dictionary of National Biography*, online edition, 2009, p. 1.
30. Ibid.
31. J. De Vries, *The Industrious Revolution: Consumer Behavior and the Household Economy, 1650 to the Present*, Cambridge University Press, 2008, p. 132; Uglow, *The Lunar Men*, p. 49.
32. Clow and Clow, *The Chemical Revolution*, p. 307.
33. Ibid., p. 309.
34. C. Hill, *Reformation to Industrial Revolution*, London: Pelican, 1969, p. 242.
35. Ibid.; p. 319 cites the Willow Pattern as the classic case.

Chapter 6

1. For a recent confirmation of the situation as described by Defoe, see S. Pincus, *1688: The First Modern Revolution*, New Haven: Yale University Press, 2009.
2. C.W. Chalklin, *The Provincial Towns of Georgian England: A Study of the Building Process 1740–1820*, London: Edward Arnold, 1974, p. 25.
3. P.S. Atiyah, *The Rise and Fall of Freedom of Contract*, Oxford University Press, 1979, p. 13.
4. Ibid., p. 24.
5. B.H. Slicher, *The Agrarian History of Western Europe, A.D. 500–1850*, London: Edward Arnold, 1963, p. 112.
6. Ibid., p. 113.
7. The best known name here is that of Charles ('Turnip') Townshend (1674–1738).
8. Ibid., p. 278.
9. D. Defoe, *A Tour Through the Whole Island of Great Britain*, London: J.M. Dent & Sons, 1974, p. 79 describes the scale and technique of such traditional occupations.

10. Quoted in J. Canyon (ed.), *Oxford Companion to British History*, Oxford University Press, 1997, p. 154.

11. Defoe, *A Tour through the Whole Island of Great Britain*, p. 78.

12. C. Hill, *Reformation to Industrial Revolution*, London: Pelican, 1969, p. 250.

13. J. De Vries, *The Industrious Revolution: Consumer Behavior and the Household Economy, 1650 to the Present*, Cambridge University Press, 2008, p. 94.

14. Ibid., p. 102.

15. Ibid., p. 96.

16. Ibid., p. 94; Pincus, *1688: The First Modern Revolution*, p. 86.

17. De Vries, *The Industrious Revolution*, p. 100.

18. Ibid., p. 127.

19. Ibid., p. 143.

20. As in Essex Street, Buckingham Street and the Adelphi.

21. De Vries, *The Industrious Revolution*, p. 151; for exact figures, see W.J. Bernstein, *A Splendid Exchange: How Trade Shaped the World*, New York: Atlantic Monthly Press, 2008, p. 265.

22. The oldest British shop, dating from the sixteenth century, is in Thirsk in Yorkshire.

23. Defoe, *A Tour through the Whole Island of Great Britain*, pp. 80–81.

24. See Chalklin, *The Provincial Towns of Georgian England*, p. 52.

25. See 'turnpikes' in *Oxford Companion to British History*, pp. 936–7 and Pincus, *1688: The First Modern Revolution*, p. 70.

26. The original model was the Amsterdamse Wisselbank founded in 1609: T. Crump, *The Phenomenon of Money*, London: Routledge, 1980, p. 157.

27. P.G.M. Dickson, *The Financial Revolution in England, 1688–1756*, London: Macmillan, 1967, p. 470.

28. Ibid., p. 198.

29. Quoted in Crump, *The Phenomenon of Money*, p. 219.

30. Pincus, *1688: The First Modern Revolution*, p. 74.

31. See page 143.

32. Bernstein, *A Splendid Exchange*, pp. 265–6.

33. De Vries, *The Industrious Revolution*, p. 114.

34. Henry Ford, known for his cars, was the pioneer manufacturer who first applied this principle on a large scale.

35. B. Disraeli, *Sybil or the Two Nations*, London: Wordsworth Classics, 1995, p. 12.

36. L. Namier, *The Structure of Politics at the Accession of George III*, 2nd edn, London: Macmillan, 1957, p. 57.

37. See F.M.L. Thompson, *Gentrification and the Enterprise Culture: Britain 1780–1980*, Oxford University Press, 2001, Chapter 2, 'Aristocrats as Entrepreneurs' and Chapter 3, 'Entrepreneurs as Aristocrats'.

38. Disraeli, *Sybil or the Two Nations*, p. 18.

39. C. Dickens, *Hard Times*, London: Wordsworth Classics, 1995.

40. C. Brontë, *Shirley*, London: Wordsworth Classics, 1993.

41. E. Gaskell, *North and South*, London: Vintage Books, 2007.

42. D.C. Coleman, 'Growth and Decay during the Industrial Revolution: the Case of East Anglia', in *Scandinavian Economic History Review*, vol. 10, pp. 115–127, p. 127.

43. Lorenzo Dow, *Reflections on the Love of God*, quoted in the *Penguin Dictionary of Quotations*, London, 1960, pp. 144–5.

44. E. Richards, 'Margins of the Industrial Revolution', in P. O'Brien and R. Quinault (eds), *The Industrial Revolution and British Society*, Cambridge University Press, 1993, pp. 203–28, p. 220.

45. This is the present site of the city of Winnipeg.

46. J. Morris, *Pax Britannica: The Climax of an Empire*, London: Penguin, 1968, pp. 126–7.

47. Ibid., pp. 354–6.

48. E.J. Hobsbawm, *Industry and Empire: An Economic History of Britain since 1750*, London: Weidenfeld & Nicolson, 1968, p. 73.

49. Ibid., p. 70.

50. F. Engels, *The Condition of the Working Class in England*, Oxford University Press, 1993.

51. D. McLellan, Introduction to Engels, *The Condition of the Working Class in England*, pp. ix–xx, p. xvi.

52. Engels, *The Condition of the Working Class in England*, p. 13.

53. Ibid., p. 57.

54. Ibid., p. 41.

55. Dickens, *Hard Times*, pp. 49–50.

56. Ibid., p. 50.

57. Second edition 1803.

58. M.D. George, *London Life in the Eighteenth Century*, London: Penguin, 1966, p. 124.

59. Richards, 'Margins of the Industrial Revolution', in O'Brien and Quinault, *The Industrial Revolution and British Society*, pp. 203–28, pp. 214–15.

60. To be seen in the Van Gogh Museum in Amsterdam; the oil light illuminating the scene was a late nineteenth-century innovation.

61. As witness the achievements of the Kennedy dynasty in the United States.

62. It also provides the leitmotiv for Gaskell, *North and South*.

63. C. Brontë, *Shirley*, p. 13.

64. Ibid., p. 41.

65. Ibid., p. 127.

66. R. Quinault, 'The Industrial Revolution and parliamentary reform', in O'Brien and Quinault (eds), *The Industrial Revolution and British Society*, pp. 183–202, p. 194.
67. T. Crump, *A Brief History of the Age of Steam: The Power that Drove the Industrial Revolution*, Constable & Robinson, 2007, p. 188.
68. Krupp and Siemens are the best-known names: see also chapter 9.
69. The name in full is 'Verenigde Oostindische Compagnie', meaning United East Indian Company.
70. Today the East Indies mainly consists of the independent Republic of Indonesia.
71. The standard text is A.G. Frank, *Capitalism and underdevelopment in Latin America: historical studies of Chile and Brazil*, London: Penguin, 1971.
72. J. Walvin, *Making the Black Atlantic: Britain and the African Diaspora*, London: Cassell, 2000, p. 22.
73. Ibid., p. 29.
74. Ibid., p. 51.
75. Ibid.
76. Ibid., p. 54.
77. Pincus, *1688: The First Modern Revolution*, p. 85.
78. In the third Lincoln–Douglas debate of 1858.
79. T. Crump, *Abraham Lincoln's World: How Riverboats, Railroads and Republicans Transformed America*, London: Continuum, 2009, pp. 97–8.
80. Ibid., p. 165.
81. See now H.B. Stowe, *Uncle Tom's Cabin or Life among the Lowly*, New York: Limited Editions Club, 1938.

Chapter 7

1. The propeller was not developed until the 1830s: T. Crump, *A Brief History of the Age of Steam: The Power that Drove the Industrial Revolution*, London: Constable & Robinson, 2007, pp. 292, 296–7.

2. *Gibbons* v. *Ogden*, 22 US 1 (1824).

3. The middle stretch of the Grand Trunk Canal, linking the Trent and Mersey rivers systems, could only accommodate boats with a beam no greater than seven feet, if they were to be able to pass each other: this established the narrow boat standard that is still in force: see Crump, *A Brief History of the Age of Steam*, p. 103.

4. This is a small eastern tributary which joins the Mississippi in Illinois, just south of the Wisconsin state line.

5. Oliver Evans, a western pioneer, had seen the advantages of high pressure engines for steamboats as early as 1785 (according to his own account) but the steamboat he launched in 1803 was a failure; he had more success introducing high pressure engines for industrial use in the west: L.C. Hunter, *Steamboats on the Western Rivers: An Economic and Technological History*, Cambridge, Mass.: Harvard University Press, 1949, p.7.

6. F. Donovan, *River Boats of America*, New York: Thomas E. Crowell Company, 1966, p. 52.

7. Ibid., p. 62.

8. Ibid., p. 87.

9. Ibid., p. 184.

10. It was not critical that the altitude of Lake Erie was marginally lower, and that of Superior, higher, by a wider margin. The latter is now accessed from Lake Huron by locks at Sault Ste Marie, with Canada on one side and the United States on the other.

11. There were also occasional problems with ice on the Ohio and the Upper Mississippi.

12. T. Hahn, *The Chesapeake & Ohio Canal: Pathway to the Nation's Capital*, Metuchen, New Jersey: The Scarecrow Press, 1984, p. 1.

13. Cited in ibid., p. 28.

14. For a map see ibid., p. 149.

15. Ibid., p. 54; M.J.T. Lewis, *Early Wooden Railways*, London: Routledge & Kegan Paul, 1970, p. 205.

16. See Crump, *A Brief History of the Age of Steam*, p. 34. This system is still the most efficient in special cases, such as funicular railways.

17. A plateway – an alternative to a railway – consisted of flat plates, some 6 to 7 inches wide, supported longitudinally on wooden sleepers. The wagons or 'trams' that ran on it were specially constructed for this type of track, which was favoured by many mine owners and ironmasters throughout Britain. For a full description see J.E. Vance, *Capturing the Horizon: the Historical Geography of Transportation*, New York: Harper & Row, 1986, p. 187.

18. Although he did produce a locomotive named *Catch Me Who Can* for an exhibition in London in 1808, where it ran around a circular track .

19. After the Prussian Field Marshal, whose forces were to play a key role in 1815, alongside those of the Duke of Wellington, in defeating Napoleon at Waterloo.

20. Quoted L.T.C. Rolt, *George and Robert Stephenson: The Railway Revolution*, London: Longmans, 1960, p. 57.

21. Ibid., p. 37.

22. This was close to the River Wear but at a point where it was *no longer suitable for coal traffic.*

23. Cited in Rolt, *George and Robert Stephenson*, p. 63.

24. Ibid., p. 164.

25. Ibid., p. 175.

26. Within a year the Stephensons delivered a new advanced locomotive, the *Samson*, which on its test run hauled a train of eighty tons up the Whiston incline: Crump, *A Brief History of the Age of Steam*, p. 161.

27. Ibid, p. 89.

Chapter 8

1. A. Taylor, *American Colonies: The Settling of North America 1700–80*, New York: Penguin, 2001, p. 311.
2. Ibid.
3. H.S. Klein, *A Population History of the United States*, Cambridge University Press, 2004, p. 60.
4. The exact figures are to be found in S.H.H. Carrington, 'The American Revolution and the British West Indies Economy', in B.L. Solow and S.L. Engerman (eds), *British Capitalism and Caribbean Slavery: The Legacy of Eric Williams*, Cambridge University Press, 1987, pp. 135–62, p. 135.
5. Taylor, *American Colonies*, p. 306.
6. Klein, *A Population History of the United States*, p. 59: the ancestors of Abraham Lincoln were among the many who were part of this process.
7. Taylor, *American Colonies*, p. 307.
8. F.J. Deyrup, *Arms makers of the Connecticut Valley: A Regional Study of the Economic Development of the Small Arms Industry, 1798–1870*, York, PA: G. Shumway, 1970, p. 34.
9. P. Deane, *The First Industrial Revolution*, Cambridge University Press, 1965, p. 87.
10. A cotton gin powered in this way can still be seen – although it no longer operates – at the Frogmore Plantation in Louisiana.
11. T. Crump, *Abraham Lincoln's World: How Riverboats, Railroads and Republicans Transformed America*, London: Continuum, 2009, p. 174 and F. Douglass, *On Slavery and the Civil War*, Mineola NY: Dover Publications, 2003, p. 31.
12. D. North, 'Industrialization in the United States', in M. Postan and H.J. Habakkuk (eds), *The Cambridge Economic History of Europe*, vol. VI, Part II, pp. 673–705, p. 674.

13. Any visitor to Cairo, Illinois, where the two rivers join, will note how much more water is carried by the Ohio.

14. Note also the Alabama river, which reaches the Gulf of Mexico at Mobile.

15. Klein, *A Population History of the United States*, p. 59.

16. B. Freese, *Coal: A Human History*, London: Penguin, 2004, p. 113.

17. Cited in ibid., p. 114; this proved to be quite otherwise, after a fire started in the Lehigh mine in 1859 continued to burn for eighty-two years.

18. T.S. Reynolds, *Stronger than a Hundred Men: A History of the Vertical Water Wheel*, Baltimore: Johns Hopkins University Press, 1983, Chapter 2.

19. Ibid., p. 9.

20. Ibid., p. 267.

21. R.C. Walter and D.J. Merritts, 'Natural Streams and the Legacy of Water-powered Mills', *Science*, vol. 319, pp. 299–304, p. 300.

22. See chapter 3, note 10.

23. Production at its peak, required one acre of woodland per day.

24. Freese, *Coal: A Human History*, p. 106.

25. Ibid., p. 107.

26. In 1832, out of 249 American factories outside Pittsburgh, only four were powered by steam: see ibid., p. 110.

27. North, 'Industrialization in the United States', in Postan and Habakkuk (eds), *The Cambridge Economic History of Europe*, p. 687.

28. Klein, *A Population History of the United States*, Graphs 3.1 and 3.2, on p. 74.

29. Freese, *Coal: A Human History* op. cit., p. 112.

30. Which defines the entire eastern boundary of Pennsylvania.

31. See also chapter 3.

32. Freese, *Coal: A Human History*, p. 122.
33. Ibid., p. 125.
34. Deyrup, *Arms makers of the Connecticut Valley*, p. 3.
35. Ibid., p. 36.
36. Ibid., p. 54.
37. Ibid., p. 44.
38. Ibid., p. 146.
39. Freese, *Coal: A Human History*, p. 119.
40. Deyrup, *Arms makers of the Connecticut Valley*, p. 85.
41. North, 'Industrialization in the United States', in Postan and Habakkuk (eds), *The Cambridge Economic History of Europe*, p. 691.
42. Michael Chevalier, quoted H.J. Habakkuk, H.J., *American and British technology in the nineteenth century: the search for labour-saving inventions*, Cambridge University Press, 1967, p. 4.
43. Ibid., p. 12.
44. Klein, *A Population History of the United States*, graph 3.7 on p. 89.
45. North, 'Industrialization in the United States', in Postan and Habakkuk (eds), *The Cambridge Economic History of Europe*, p. 684.
46. Ibid.
47. Ibid., p. 682.
48. Ibid., p. 683.
49. G.S. Gibb, *The Saco-Lowell Shops, Textile Machinery Building in New England, 1813–1849*, Cambridge University Press, 1950, p. 179.
50. See chapter 4.
51. North, 'Industrialization in the United States', in M. Postan and H.J. Habakkuk (eds), *The Cambridge Economic History of Europe*, p. 679.
52. 'And here's to good old Boston
    The Land of the bean and the cod

Where the Lowells talk only to Cabots
And the Cabots talk only to God.'
Author unknown
53. J.E. Davis, *Frontier Illinois*, Bloomington: Indiana University Press, 1998, p. 202.

Chapter 9

1. F. Crouzet, 'France', in M. Teich and R. Porter (eds), *The Industrial Revolution in National Context: Europe and the USA*, Cambridge University Press, 1996, pp. 36–63, p. 37.
2. Ibid., p. 44.
3. D.S. Landes, *The Unbound Prometheus: Technological Change and Industrial Development in Western Europe from 1750 to the Present*, Cambridge University Press, 2003, p. 146.
4. J.H. Elliott, *Empires of the Atlantic World: Britain and Spain in America 1492–1830*, New Haven: Yale University Press, 2006, p. 404.
5. Landes, *The Unbound Prometheus*, p. 541. This author also notes, however, that 'the period from 1850 to 1873 was Continental industry's coming of age': ibid. p. 193.
6. T. Crump, *A Brief History of the Age of Steam: The Power that Drove the Industrial Revolution*, Constable & Robinson, 2007, p. 81.
7. B. Bathurst, *The Lighthouse Stevensons*, London: Flamingo, 1999, pp. 137–44.
8. For France's early history, note A. Guérard, *France: A Modern History*, Ann Arbor MI: University of Michigan Press, 1959, p. ix.
9. Ibid., p. 13.
10. Crouzet, 'France', in Teich and Porter (eds), *The Industrial Revolution in National Context: Europe and the USA*, p. 45, also cited chapter 1, p. 3 above.

11. Ibid., p. 56.
12. Ibid., p. 48.
13. Ibid., p. 42.
14. Ibid., quoting J. Mokyr, *The Lever of Riches: Technological Creativity and Economic Progress*, Oxford University Press, 1990.
15. J. Mokyr (ed.), *The British Industrial Revolution: An Economic Perspective*, Boulder, CO: Westview Press, 1993, Introduction, p. 11.
16. Cited G. Robb, *The Discovery of France: A Historical Geography from the Revolution to the First World War*, New York: W.W. Norton & Company, 2007, p. 14.
17. Ibid.
18. Ibid., p. 17.
19. Crouzet, 'France', in Teich and Porter (eds), *The Industrial Revolution in National Context: Europe and the USA*, p. 53.
20. Crump, *A Brief History of the Age of Steam*, pp. 104–10.
21. Crouzet, 'France', in Teich and Porter (eds), *The Industrial Revolution in National Context: Europe and the USA*, p. 54.
22. Ibid., p. 38.
23. Ibid., p. 37.
24. Ibid., p. 40.
25. Ibid., p. 42.
26. Ibid.
27. See the definition on page 74.
28. Crouzet, 'France', in Teich and Porter (eds), *The Industrial Revolution in National Context: Europe and the USA*, p. 39.
29. Landes, *The Unbound Prometheus*, p. 188.
30. See chapter 2.
31. Crouzet, 'France', in Teich and Porter (eds), *The Industrial Revolution in National Context: Europe and the USA*, p. 39.

32. Ibid., p. 45.
33. Ibid., p. 47.
34. Ibid., p. 48.
35. Ibid., p. 53.
36. Ibid., p. 55.
37. Ibid., p. 57.
38. Ibid., p. 58.
39. Ibid., p. 52.
40. Ibid., p. 51.
41. Ibid., p. 59.
42. Ibid., p. 60
43. Teich and Porter (eds), *The Industrial Revolution in National Context: Europe and the USA*, p. xxiv. The high Swiss growth rate was equalled only by Denmark and Sweden, but here, in 1830, the industrial base was very low, so there was much ground to be made up.
44. Van der Wee, H., 'The Industrial Revolution in Belgium', in Teich and Porter (eds), *The Industrial Revolution in National Context: Europe and the USA*, pp. 64–77, p. 65.
45. Ibid., p. 66.
46. T. Crump, *The History of the Dutch East Indies Company*, London: Gresham College, Lecture 1, 1 March 2006 (see www.gresham.ac.uk).
47. Van der Wee, 'The Industrial Revolution in Belgium', p. 68.
48. This river rises in eastern France, crosses Belgium from west to east, to reach the North Sea via the Netherlands (where it is known as the Maas) just west of Rotterdam.
49. Van der Wee, 'The Industrial Revolution in Belgium', p. 69.
50. Ibid., p. 71.
51. Brussels South is the oldest railway station in Europe: it is now one of the two European terminals for Eurostar from London – the other is the Paris Gare du Nord.

52. Van der Wee, 'The Industrial Revolution in Belgium', p. 73.

53. E. Zola, *Germinal*, Paris: G. Charpentier, 1885.

54. Crump, *The History of the Dutch East Indies Company*, Lecture 2, 8 March 2006 (see www.gresham.ac.uk).

55. Van der Wee, 'The Industrial Revolution in Belgium', p. 80.

56. C. Geertz, *Agricultural Involution: The Processes of Ecological Change in Indonesia*, Berkeley, CA: University of California Press, 1963.

57. The name in English means 'Dutch trading company'.

58. Van der Wee, 'The Industrial Revolution in Belgium', p. 85.

59. The line, linking Amsterdam and Haarlem, was used in its opening year for a remarkable experiment in the physics of sound, which demonstrated what is now widely known as the 'Doppler effect': see Crump, *A Brief History of the Age of Steam*, pp. 165–6.

60. E.H. Kossman, *The Low Countries 1780–1940*, Oxford: Clarendon Press, 1978, p. 273: in the Dutch West Indian colonies the end of slavery only came in 1863, thirty years later than in the British colonies.

61. H.D. Dekker ('Multatuli'), *Max Havelaar*, Amsterdam: van Gennep, 1860, revealed the harsh realities of their country's colonial rule to the Dutch public. The book's subtitle, in English 'the coffee auctions of the Dutch trading company', describes its historical context. Penguin Classics now publish an English translation.

62. Kossman, *The Low Countries*, p. 272.

63. Ibid., p. 266.

64. Ibid., p. 167.

65. For a comprehensive discussion, see J.L. Van Zanden, 'Industrialization in the Netherlands', in Teich and Porter (eds), *The Industrial Revolution in National Context: Europe and the USA*, pp. 78–94.

66. Note particularly, during the last decade of the nineteenth century, the manufacture of light bulbs in Eindhoven by Philips, a business that in the twentieth century would become a major multinational corporation: A. Teulings, *Philips: Geschiedenis en praktijk van een wereldconcern*, Amsterdam: van Gennep, 1976, pp. 11–14.

67. B. Fritzsche, 'Switzerland', in Teich and Porter (eds), *The Industrial Revolution in National Context: Europe and the USA*, p. 182.

68. Ibid., p. 133.

69. Ibid., p. 135.

70. Ibid., p. 136.

71. Crump, *A Brief History of the Age of Steam*, pp. 195–6; the Simplon Tunnel, which ends in Italy, was an even greater feat of engineering, which was only fully open in 1921.

72. Fritzsche, 'Switzerland', p. 138.

73. Ibid., p. 139.

74. D. Blackbourn, *The Conquest of Nature: Water, Landscape and the Making of Modern Germany*, London: Pimlico, 2007, p. 26.

75. The Rhine actually reaches the sea in the Netherlands.

76. The Vistula is now entirely in Poland.

77. Note that in the period 1798–1918, which included most of the Industrial Revolution – Poland was divided up between Austria, Prussia and Russia.

78. The Moselle, a very long tributary, which joins the Rhine at Coblenz, is mainly in France.

79. See Blackbourn, *The Conquest of Nature*, p. 5.

80. Brandenburg, which had become part of Prussia, had the right to nominate one of the Protestant electors of the Holy Roman Emperor.

81. Crump, *A Brief History of the Age of Steam*, p. 108 and Blackbourn, *The Conquest of Nature*, p. 94.

82. R. Tilly, 'German Industrialization', in Teich and Porter (eds), *The Industrial Revolution in National Context: Europe and the USA*, pp. 95–125, p. 109.

83. Ibid., p. 102.

84. Ibid., p. 106.

85. Ibid., p. 122.

86. According to William Manchester, his great-grandson Alfred would interpret these outbursts as a prophecy fulfilled by the coming of Hitler.

87. Samuel Morse was best known for his invention of the 'Morse' telegraph code; see also chapter 10.

88. Johann Georg Halske (1814–90) was a German engineer chosen by Werner von Siemens as his business partner, who left, after a policy disagreement, in 1867.

89. In the United States Andrew Carnegie became well known for adopting similar policies.

90. In the Second World War, German industry, particularly as related to the manufacture of armaments, was organized under Albert Speer on the basis of forced labour, recruited mainly from German occupied Europe.

91. The first factory in Eindhoven was known as the Philips Gloeilampenfabriek (in English, the Philips Light Bulb Factory).

92. Teulings, *Philips: Geschiedenis en praktijk van een wereldconcern*, p. 14.

93. In particular, Philips, located in the Netherlands, was not burdened by compulsory insurance of its workforce – unlike its German competitors, such as Siemens. After the German invasion in 1940, the Nazi administration of the Netherlands, at the request of German industrialists, imposed comparable insurance on Dutch manufacturers, including Philips. This took the form of *ziekefondsen*, or 'sickness funds', maintained by compulsory contributions to provide basic healthcare for industrial workers and

their families. Such funds had also operated, in certain sectors, on a voluntary basis before the war. The comprehensive cover imposed by the Nazis continued after the war, and only came to an end in 2006, when a new system of compulsory health insurance, covering the whole population, was introduced.

94. C. Poni and G. Mori, 'Italy in the *long durée*: the return of an old first-comer', in Teich and Porter (eds), *The Industrial Revolution in National Context: Europe and the USA*, pp. 149–83, p. 150.

95. Ibid., p. 153.

96. Ibid., p. 155.

97. Ibid., p. 157.

98. Crump, *A Brief History of the Age of Steam*, p. 126.

99. Poni and Mori, 'Italy in the *long durée*: the return of an old first-comer', p. xxiv.

Chapter 10

1. For Franklin's scientific achievements see T. Crump, *A Brief History of Science*, London: Constable & Robinson, 2001, pp. 101–105.

2. Ibid., pp. 293–6.

3. Ibid., pp. 150–52.

4. Ibid., pp. 146–53.

5. The name is due to Lavoisier, the first to discover its true character.

6. See chapter 5, pp. 115–17.

7. Crump, *A Brief History of Science*, pp. 133–4.

8. Cited in ibid., p. 158.

9. By Thomas Edison and Joseph Swan: ibid., pp. 91–2.

10. Although he called it 'helix': Crump, *A Brief History of Science*, p. 112.

11. Ibid., p. 115.

12. T. Crump, *A Brief History of the Age of Steam: The Power that Drove the Industrial Revolution*, London: Constable & Robinson, 2007, p. 171.
13. Ibid., p. 172.
14. Crump, *A Brief History of Science*, p. 114.
15. Ibid., p. 115.
16. This followed the invention and introduction, by C.A. Parsons, of a workable steam turbine during the 1890s: Crump, *A Brief History of the Age of Steam*, pp. 305–7.
17. This has been noted by a number of historians; e.g. D.S. Landes, *The Unbound Prometheus: Technological Change and Industrial Development in Western Europe from 1750 to the Present*, Cambridge University Press, 2003 p. 108.
18. A. Clow and N.L. Clow, *The Chemical Revolution: A Contribution to Social Technology*, London: Batchworth Press, 1952.
19. T. Henry, 'On the Advantages of Literature and Philosophy, and especially on the consistency of Literary, Philosophical and Commercial Pursuits', *Mem. Manchester, Lit. and Phil. Soc.*, Vol. I, 1785, p. 7.
20. Lavoisier, *Oeuvres* (6 cols.), Paris: Imprimerie Impériale, 1862–95, vol. II, p. 7.
21. Ibid., p. 451.
22. Also known as 'copperas'.
23. Clow and Clow, *The Chemical Revolution*, p. 130.
24. Although not necessarily interchangeable with it.
25. Clow and Clow, *The Chemical Revolution*, p. 131.
26. Ibid., p. 133.
27. Represented by the letter 'K' for kali.
28. Clow and Clow, *The Chemical Revolution*, p. 132.
29. Sodium sulphate, $Na_2SO_4.10H_2O$.
30. Clow and Clow, *The Chemical Revolution*, p. 133.
31. D.W.F. Hardie and J. Davidson Pratt, *A History of the Modern British Chemical Industry*, Oxford: Pergamon Press, 1966, p. 17.

32. Clow and Clow, *The Chemical Revolution*, p. 136.

33. Ibid., p. 136.

34. $CaOCl_2$.

35. Clow and Clow, *The Chemical Revolution*, p. 169.

36. Hardie and Davidson Pratt, *A History of the Modern British Chemical Industry*, p. 24.

37. Ibid., p. 26.

38. Sodium hydroxide, NaOH.

39. Calcium oxide, CaO.

40. Clow and Clow, *The Chemical Revolution*, p. 91.

41. This was the only raw material until 1850, but then after this year a wood pulp base was adopted: see ibid., p. 259.

42. Ibid., p. 127.

43. This process is no longer used; instead, caustic soda is produced by the electrolysis of brine, using appropriate diaphragm cells.

44. W.H. Brock, *The Fontana History of Chemistry*, London: Fontana, 1992, p. 287.

45. This is queried by Brock, ibid., p. 300, but see S. Garfield, *Mauve: How one man invented a colour that changed the world*, London: Faber and Faber, 1988.

46. Cited Brock, *The Fontana History of Chemistry*, p. 282.

47. Ibid., p. 283.

48. Ibid., pp. 282–3.

49. St Helens has long been the company town of Pilkington Brothers' glass works, which produces for a worldwide market.

50. Ibid., p. 394.

51. Joseph Black discovered both CO_2 (carbon dioxide) and latent heat.

52. Clow and Clow, *The Chemical Revolution*, p. 409.

53. Ibid., p. 414.

54. Ibid., p. 415.

55. From which the current name, 'tarmac', is derived.
56. Clow and Clow, *The Chemical Revolution*, p. 417.
57. The peace lasted only for three years.
58. The first domestic gas fires were introduced in the 1830s: Clow and Clow, *The Chemical Revolution*, p. 441.
59. Garfield, *Mauve*, chapter 4.
60. Ibid., p. 253.
61. Hardie and Davidson Pratt, *A History of the Modern British Chemical Industry*, p. 49.
62. Ibid., p. 49.
63. Ibid., p. 50.
64. Farmer's Magazine, 1856; cited in Hardie and Davidson Pratt, *A History of the Modern British Chemical Industry*, p. 50.
65. Ibid., p. 49.
66. Ibid., p. 51.
67. Ibid., p. 52.
68. Ibid., p. 53.
69. Ibid., p. 54.

Chapter 11

1. J. Walvin, *Making the Black Atlantic: Britain and the African Diaspora*, London: Cassell, 2000, p. 36.
2. Ibid., p. 37.
3. J. Simmons, 'The Continent and the Explorers', in M. Perham and J. Simmons (eds), *African Discovery: An Anthology of Exploration*, London: Faber & Faber, 1952, pp. 23–33, p. 23.
4. The standard popular text is T. Pakenham, *The Scramble for Africa*, London: Weidenfeld and Nicolson, 1991.
5. Largely as a result of tracking down David Livingstone at Ujiji on the shore of Lake Tanganyika in 1871.
6. Pakenham, *The Scramble for Africa*, p. 161.

7. Ibid., p. 248.
8. Ibid., p. 240.
9. Ibid., p. 241.
10. Ibid., p. 248.
11. Ibid., p. 249.
12. The Gold Coast was ceded by the Netherlands in 1871.
13. The Netherlands withheld recognition until 1839.
14. The full story is told in Pakenham, *The Scramble for Africa*, chapter 8, 'Saving the Khedive'.
15. G. Lanning and M. Mueller, *Africa Undermined: A History of the Mining Companies and the Underdevelopment of Africa*, London: Pelican, 1979, p. 32.
16. Ibid., p. 33.
17. Ibid., p. 35.
18. The court's ruling was met by counsel for De Beers with the words, 'De Beers, de Beers, glorious De Beers/ Registered Kimberley, resident here'.
19. Lanning and Mueller, *Africa Undermined*, p. 43.
20. Ibid., p. 44.
21. Ibid., p. 45.
22. At the beginning of the nineteenth century a vast inland area had been devastated by Tchaka, king of Zululand, where the Dutch *voortrekkers* had first wanted to make their homes. Although in 1837 they won a decisive battle against the Zulus, led by Tchaka's successor, Dingaan, the latter were still present in large numbers, in what, in any case, had become the British colony of Natal. Inland, in the land that was to become the republics of Transvaal and the Orange Free State, they would – until the end of the nineteenth century – be troubled neither by the British nor the Zulus.
23. Lanning and Mueller, *Africa Undermined*, p. 54.
24. Ibid.

25. This was the line of escape of Winston Churchill, after he had become a Boer prisoner of war in 1899.

26. Lanning and Mueller, *Africa Undermined*, p. 123.

27. The local variant of the normal Dutch, *buitenlander*, for 'foreigner'.

28. Lanning and Mueller, *Africa Undermined*, p. 122.

29. T. Crump, *A Brief History of the Age of Steam: The Power that Drove the Industrial Revolution*, London: Constable & Robinson, 2007, pp. 220–4.

30. Ibid., pp. 224–37.

31. See chapter 6, note 71.

32. Crump, *A Brief History of the Age of Steam*, p. 234.

33. Ibid., p. 235.

34. *The Economist*, 5 March 2009.

35. Crump, *A Brief History of the Age of Steam*, p. 212.

36. Ibid., p. 218.

37. Ibid., p. 219.

38. Ibid., p. 218, but compare the employment, in railway construction, of Chinese coolies in the United States and convicts in Russia.

39. Among the passengers to South Africa – though not as an indentured labourer – was a young, and later to be famous, barrister, Mahatma Gandhi.

40. In this field the American Westinghouse Electrical Company led the way in 1886.

41. Literally 'Dutch science'.

42. L.M. Cullen, *A History of Japan, 1582–1941: Internal and External Worlds*, Cambridge University Press, 2003, p. 177.

43. Ibid., p. 190.

44. Hyogo is now known as Kobe.

45. This, the accepted English translation of *Tennô*, fails to convey what the title means to the Japanese.

46. Cullen, *A History of Japan, 1582–1941*, p. 210.

47. R.E. Trevithick, who, as manager of the Kobe railway works, produced the Japanese-made locomotive, was a grandson of Robert Trevithick: see chapter 7, p. 183, and Crump, *A Brief History of the Age of Steam*, p. 282.
48. Ibid., p. 279.
49. Ibid., p. 280.

BIBLIOGRAPHY

Allen, R.C., *The British Revolution in Global Perspective*, Cambridge: Cambridge University Press, 2009.

Ashton, T.S., *Iron and Steel in the Industrial Revolution*, New York: Augustus M. Kelley, 1968.

Atiyah, P.S., *The Rise and Fall of Freedom of Contract*, Oxford: Oxford University Press, 1979.

Auerbach, J.A., *The Great Exhibition of 1851: A Nation on Display*, New Haven: Yale University Press, 1999.

Bathurst, B., *The Lighthouse Stevensons*, London: Flamingo, 1999.

Bernstein, W.J., *A Splendid Exchange: How Trade Shaped the World*, New York: Atlantic Monthly Press, 2008.

Blackbourn, D., *The Conquest of Nature: Water, Landscape and the Making of Modern Germany*, London: Pimlico, 2007.

Brock, W.H., *The Fontana History of Chemistry*, London: Fontana, 1992.

Brontë, C., *Shirley*, London: Wordsworth Classics, 1993.

Campbell, R.H., 'John Roebuck', *Oxford Dictionary of National Biography*, online edition, Oxford University Press, 2009.

Carrington, S.H.H., 'The American Revolution and the British West Indies Economy', in B.L. Solow and S.L. Engerman (eds), *British Capitalism and Caribbean Slavery: The Legacy of Eric Williams*, Cambridge: Cambridge University Press, 1987, pp. 135–62.

Chalklin, C.W., *The Provincial Towns of Georgian England: A Study of the Building Process 1740–1820*, London: Edward Arnold, 1974.

Chapman, S.D., *The Cotton Industry in the Industrial Revolution*, London: Macmillan, 1972.

Chapman, S.D., 'Robert Peel', *Oxford Dictionary of National Biography*, online edition, Oxford University Press, 2009.

Clow, A. and Clow, N.L., *The Chemical Revolution: A Contribution to Social Technology*, London: Batchworth Press, 1952.

Coleman, D.C., 'Growth and Decay during the Industrial Revolution: the Case of East Anglia', in *Scandinavian Economic History Review*, vol. 10.

Cox, N., 'Abraham Darby I', *Oxford Dictionary of National Biography*, online edition, Oxford University Press, 2009.

Crouzet, F., 'France', in M. Teich and R. Porter (eds), *The Industrial Revolution in National Context: Europe and the USA*, Cambridge: Cambridge University Press, 1996, pp. 36–63.

Crump, T., *The Phenomenon of Money*, London: Routledge, 1980.

Crump, T., *A Brief History of Science*, London: Constable & Robinson, 2001.

Crump, T., *The History of the Dutch East Indies Company*, London: Gresham College, 2006

Crump, T., *A Brief History of the Age of Steam: The Power that Drove the Industrial Revolution*, London: Constable & Robinson, 2007.

Crump, T., *Abraham Lincoln's World: How Riverboats, Railroads and Republicans Transformed America*, London: Continuum, 2009.

Crump, W.B., *The Leeds Woollen Industry, 1780–1820*, Leeds: The Thoresby Society, 1931.

Cullen, L.M., *A History of Japan, 1582–1941: Internal and External Worlds*, Cambridge: Cambridge University Press, 2003.

Davis, J.E., *Frontier Illinois*, Bloomington: Indiana University Press, 1998.

Deane, P., *The First Industrial Revolution*, Cambridge: Cambridge University Press, 1965.

Defoe, D., *A Tour through the Whole Island of Great Britain*, London: J.M. Dent & Sons, 1974.

Dekker, H.D. ('Multatuli'), *Max Havelaar of de Koffie-veilingen van de Nederlandsche Handelsmaatschappij*, Amsterdam: van Gennep, 1860.

De Vries, J., *The Industrious Revolution: Consumer Behavior and the Household Economy, 1650 to the Present*, Cambridge: Cambridge University Press, 2008.

Deyrup, F.J., *Arms makers of the Connecticut Valley: A Regional Study of the Economic Development of the Small Arms Industry, 1798–1870*, York, PA: G. Shumway, 1970.

Dickens, C., *Hard Times*, London: Wordsworth Classics, 1995.

Dickinson, H.W., *James Watt: Craftsman and Engineer*, New York: Augustus M. Kelley, 1967.

Dickson, P.G.M., *The Financial Revolution in England, 1688–1756*, London: Macmillan, 1967.

Disraeli, B., *Sybil or the Two Nations*, London: Wordsworth Classics, 1995.

Donovan, F., *River Boats of America*, New York: Thomas E. Crowell Company, 1966, p. 52.

Douglass, F., *On Slavery and the Civil War*, Mineola NY: Dover Publications, 2003.

Elliott, J.H., *Empires of the Atlantic World: Britain and Spain in America 1492–1830*, New Haven: Yale University Press, 2006

Engels, F., *The Condition of the Working Class in England*, Oxford: Oxford University Press, 1993.

Farnie, D.A., 'Samuel Crompton', *Oxford Dictionary of National Biography*, online edition, Oxford University Press, 2009.

Ffrench, Y., *The Great Exhibition: 1851*, London: Harvill Press, 1950.

Fitton, R.S., *The Arkwrights: Spinners of Fortune*, Manchester: Manchester University Press, 1989.

Frank, A.G., *Capitalism and underdevelopment in Latin America: historical studies of Chile and Brazil*, London: Penguin, 1971.

Freese, B., *Coal: A Human History*, London: Penguin, 2004.

Fritzsche, B., 'Switzerland', in M. Teich and R. Porter (eds), *The Industrial Revolution in National Context: Europe and the USA*, Cambridge: Cambridge University Press, 1996, pp. 126–48.

Garfield, S., *Mauve: How one man invented a colour that changed the world*, London: Faber and Faber, 1988.

Gaskell, E., *North and South*, London: Vintage Books, 2007.

Geertz, C., *Agricultural Involution: The Processes of Ecological Change in Indonesia*, Berkeley: University of California Press, 1963.

George, M.D., *London Life in the Eighteenth Century*, London: Penguin, 1966.

Gibb, G.S., *The Saco-Lowell Shops, Textile Machinery Building in New England, 1813–1849*, Cambridge: Cambridge University Press, 1950.

Gilbert, A.D., 'Religion and stability in early industrial England', in P. O'Brien and R. Quinault (eds), *The Industrial Revolution and British Society*, Cambridge: Cambridge University Press, 1993, pp.79–99.

Guérard, A., *France: A Modern History*, Ann Arbor, MI: University of Michigan Press, 1959.

Habakkuk, H.J., *American and British technology in the nineteenth century: the search for labour-saving inventions*, Cambridge: Cambridge University Press, 1967.

Hague, W., *William Pitt The Younger*, London: Harper Perennial, 2005.

Hahn, T., *The Chesapeake & Ohio Canal: Pathway to the Nation's Capital*, Metuchen, NJ: The Scarecrow Press, 1984.

Hardie, D.W.F. and Davidson Pratt, J., *A History of the Modern British Chemical Industry*, Oxford: Pergamon Press, 1966.

Henry, T., 'On the Advantages of Literature and Philosophy, and especially on the consistency of Literary, Philosophical and Commercial Pursuits', *Mem. Manchester, Lit. and Phil. Soc*, Vol. I, 1785.

Hill, C., *Reformation to Industrial Revolution*, London: Pelican, 1969.

Hobsbawm, E.J., 'The Machine Breakers', *Past and Present*, Vol. 1, 1952, pp. 257–70.

Hobsbawm, E.J., *Industry and Empire: An Economic History of Britain since 1750*, London: Weidenfeld and Nicolson, 1968.

Holderness, B.A., 'The reception and distribution of the new draperies in England', in N.B. Harte (ed.), *The New Draperies in the Low Countries and England*, Oxford: Oxford University Press, 1997, pp. 217–44.

Hudson, P., *The Genesis of Industrial Capital: A Study of the West Riding Wool Textile Industry c.1750–1850*, Cambridge: Cambridge University Press, 1986.

Hughes, R., *The Fatal Shore*, London: Vintage Press, 1987.

Hunter, L.C., *Steamboats on the Western Rivers: An Economic and Technological History*, Cambridge, MA: Harvard University Press, 1949.

King, M., *The Penguin History of New Zealand,* Auckland: Penguin, 2003.

Klein, H.S., *A Population History of the United States,* Cambridge: Cambridge University Press, 2004.

Kossman, E.H., *The Low Countries 1780–1940,* Oxford: Clarendon Press, 1978.

Landes, D.S., *The Unbound Prometheus: Technological Change and Industrial Development in Western Europe from 1750 to the Present,* Cambridge: Cambridge University Press, 2003.

Lanning, G. and Mueller, M., *Africa Undermined: A History of the Mining Companies and the Underdevelopment of Africa,* London: Pelican, 1979.

Larkin, D., *Mill: The History and Future of Naturally Powered Buildings,* New York: Universe Publishing, 2000.

Laslett, P., *The World We Have Lost,* London: Methuen, 1965.

Lavoisier, A. *Oeuvres,* 6 vols, Paris: Imprimerie Impériale, 1862–95.

Lewis, M.J.T., *Early Wooden Railways,* London: Routledge & Kegan Paul, 1970.

Martin, L., 'The rise of the new draperies in Norwich, 1550–1622', in N.B. Harte (ed.), *The New Draperies in the Low Countries and England,* Oxford: Oxford University Press, 1997, pp. 245–74.

MacLeod, C., *Heroes of Invention: Technology, Liberalism and British Identity 1750–1914,* Cambridge: Cambridge University Press, 2007.

McLellan, D., Introduction to F. Engels, *The Condition of the Working Class in England,* Oxford: Oxford University Press, 1993, pp. ix–xx.

Mokyr, J., *The Lever of Riches: Technological Creativity and Economic Progress,* Oxford: Oxford University Press, 1990.

Mokyr, J. (ed.), *The British Industrial Revolution: An Economic Perspective,* Boulder, CO: Westview Press, 1993.

Morris, J., *Pax Britannica: The Climax of an Empire*, London: Penguin, 1968.

Namier, L., *The Structure of Politics at the Accession of George III*, 2nd edn, London: Macmillan, 1957.

North, D., 'Industrialization in the United States', in M. Postan and H.J. Habakkuk (eds), *The Cambridge Economic History of Europe*, Vol. VI, Part II, pp. 673–705.

Oxford Companion to British History (ed. J. Canyon), Oxford: Oxford University Press, 1997.

Oxford Companion to Ships and the Sea (ed. I.C.B. Dear and P. Kemp), Oxford: Oxford University Press, 2006.

Pakenham, T., *The Scramble for Africa*, London: Weidenfeld and Nicolson, 1991.

Pearson, R., 'Thackeray and *Punch* at the Great Exhibition: authority and ambivalence in verbal and visual caricatures', in L. Purbrick (ed.), *The Great Exhibition of 1851: New interdisciplinary essays*, Manchester: Manchester University Press, 2001, pp. 179–205.

Penguin Dictionary of Quotations, London: Penguin Books, 1960.

Pincus, S., *1688: The First Modern Revolution*, New Haven: Yale University Press, 2009.

Poni, C. and Mori, G., 'Italy in the *long durée*: the return of an old first-comer', in M. Teich and R. Porter (eds), *The Industrial Revolution in National Context: Europe and the USA*, Cambridge: Cambridge University Press, 1996, pp. 149–83.

Prebisch, Raúl, 'Latin America's Keynes', *The Economist*, 5 March 2009.

Priestley, U., 'Norwich stuffs, 1600–1700', in N.B. Harte (ed.), *The New Draperies in the Low Countries and England*, Oxford: Oxford University Press, 1997, pp. 275–88.

Quinault, R., 'The Industrial Revolution and parliamentary reform', in P. O'Brien and R. Quinault (eds), *The Industrial*

Revolution and British Society, Cambridge: Cambridge University Press, 1993, pp. 229–53.

Randall, A., *Before the Luddites; Custom, community and machinery in the English woolen industry 1776–1809*, Cambridge: Cambridge University Press, 1991.

Reynolds, T.S., *Stronger than a Hundred Men: A History of the Vertical Water Wheel*, Baltimore: Johns Hopkins University Press, 1983.

Richards, E., 'Margins of the Industrial Revolution', in P. O'Brien and R. Quinault (eds), *The Industrial Revolution and British Society*, Cambridge: Cambridge University Press, 1993, pp. 203–228.

Robb, G., *The Discovery of France: A Historical Geography from the Revolution to the First World War*, New York: W.W. Norton & Company, 2007.

Rolt, L.T.C., *George and Robert Stephenson: The Railway Revolution*, London: Longmans, 1960.

Rolt, L.T.C., *Thomas Newcomen: The Prehistory of the Steam Engine*, London: Macdonald, 1963.

Rostow, W.W., *The Stages of Economic Growth*, Cambridge: Cambridge University Press, 1960.

Saville, J., *1848: The British State and the Chartist Movement*, Cambridge: Cambridge University Press, 1987.

Simmons, J., 'The Continent and the Explorers', in M. Perham and J. Simmons (eds), *African Discovery: An Anthology of Exploration*, London: Faber and Faber, 1952, pp. 23–33.

Slicher van Bath, B.H., *The Agrarian History of Western Europe, A.D. 500–1850*, London: Edward Arnold, 1963.

Stowe, H.B., *Uncle Tom's Cabin or Life among the Lowly*, New York: Limited Editions Club, 1938.

Symons, D., 'Matthew Boulton and the Royal Mint', in M. Dick, (ed.), *Matthew Boulton: a Revolutionary Player*, Studley: Brewin Books, 2009, pp. 170–84.

Tann, J., 'Matthew Boulton', *Oxford Dictionary of National Biography*, online edition, Oxford University Press, 2009.

Taylor, A., *American Colonies: The Settling of North America 1700–80*, New York: Penguin, 2001.

Teich, M. and R. Porter (eds), *The Industrial Revolution in National Context: Europe and the USA*, Cambridge: Cambridge University Press, 1996.

Teulings, A., *Philips: Geschiedenis en praktijk van een wereldconcern*, Amsterdam: van Gennep, 1976.

Thompson, F.M.L., *Gentrification and the Enterprise Culture: Britain 1780–1980*, Oxford: Oxford University Press, 2001.

Tilly, R., 'German Industrialization', in M. Teich and R. Porter (eds), *The Industrial Revolution in National Context: Europe and the USA*, Cambridge: Cambridge University Press, 1996, pp. 95–125.

Trinder, B., 'Abraham Darby II', *Oxford Dictionary of National Biography*, online edition, Oxford University Press, 2009.

Uglow, J. *The Lunar Men: The Friends who made the Future, 1730–1810*, London: Faber and Faber, 2003.

van der Wee, H., 'The Industrial Revolution in Belgium', in M. Teich and R. Porter (eds), *The Industrial Revolution in National Context: Europe and the USA*, Cambridge: Cambridge University Press, 1996, pp. 64–77.

van Zanden, J.L., 'Industrialization in the Netherlands', in M. Teich and R. Porter (eds), *The Industrial Revolution in National Context: Europe and the USA*, Cambridge: Cambridge University Press, 1996, pp. 78–94.

Vance, J.E., *Capturing the Horizon: The Historical Geography of Transportation*, New York: Harper & Row, 1986.

Walter, R.C. and D.J. Merritts, 'Natural Streams and the Legacy of Water-powered Mills', *Science*, vol. 319, pp. 299–304.

Walvin, J., *Making the Black Atlantic: Britain and the African Diaspora*, London: Cassell, 2000.

Wilson, R.G., 'Benjamin Gott', *Oxford Dictionary of National Biography*, online edition, Oxford University Press, 2009.

Winchester, A.J.L., 'William Cookworthy', *Oxford Dictionary of National Biography*, online edition, Oxford University Press, 2009.

Wrigley, E.A., 'A Simple Model of London's Importance in a Changing English Society and Economy 1650–1750', in P. Abrams and E.A. Wrigley (eds), *Towns in Societies: Essays in Economic History and Historical Sociology*, Cambridge: Cambridge University Press, 1978, pp. 215–44.

Zola, E., *Germinal*, Paris: G. Charpentier, 1885.

INDEX